First published in 1995 by

Two Heads Publishing
9 Whitehall Park
London
N19 3TS

ISBN 1 897850-36-0

Acknowledgements
Achieved with thanks to the following individuals and organisations: –
Elizabeth Barrett, Pat and Tony Booth, Phil Dade, Simon Hooton,
Priscilla Houstoun, Stuart Morris, Ken Pyne, David Short, Terry and
Terry and Jacqui from Thetford, Mr Wilkie from Dorset County Council,
The Forestry Commission, Defence Land Agents, Icknield Way Assoc.,
Peddars Way Assoc., East Anglia Trails.

Lettering and illustrations by BRICK
Photographs by the Author and Sandy Bywater
Cover design by Lance Bellers
Maps by Julie Sinclair
Printed & bound by Caldra House Ltd.

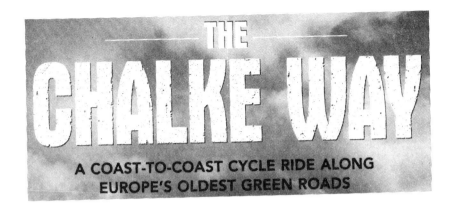

THE CHALKE WAY

A COAST-TO-COAST CYCLE RIDE ALONG
EUROPE'S OLDEST GREEN ROADS

JOHN STUART CLARK

Research and Resource by
Sandy Bywater

TWO WHEELS

The Chalke Way Coast to Coast

Showing the watersheds of southern England and the ridgeways R. Hippisley Cox mapped. Linking prehistoric earthworks.

DISTANCE – 403 m
648 k

NORTH SEA

Castle Rising
Castle Acre
Thetford C.
Arbury Banks
Wilbury Camp
Ravensbury C.
Maiden Bower
Totternhoe C.

Wendover C.
Cymbeline Mount
Pulpit Hill
Beacon Hill

R. Trent

R. Severn

AVEBURY

R. Avon

Uffington C.
Liddington C.
Barbury C.

Bradbury Banks
Old Sarum
Castle Rings
Hambledon Hill
Dogbury C.
Pilsden Pen.
Coney's C.
Musbury C.
Hawkesdown C.
Maiden C.
Chalbury C.
Hod Hill
Sidbury Hill
Segsbury C.
Parborough C.

ENGLISH CHANNEL

KEY

- - - Chalke Way
· Earthworks
‿ Rivers
━ Ridgeways
▒ Chalk edge

Contents

Maps, Directions and Resource

Map Key

	Bed & Breakfast		Wet weather route
	Campsite		Water
	Camping shop		Youth Hostel
	Stores		Trig point
	Garage		Tourist Information
	Bike shop		Earthwork/Monument
	Public House		View
	Something to see		Sentry Post
	Woods		Hills
	Plantations		Railway
	Places to eat		Disused railway
	Railway Station		Churches
	Danger Area		

Directions

Directions to ride:
- **R** – turn right
- **L** – turn left
- **SO** – straight on

Features:
- **RA** – roundabout
- **CR** – crossroads
- **TJ** – T-junction
- **BW** – bridleway

Signposts:– names and symbols on signposts in capitals i.e. WEYMOUTH

Resource

The order of entries in the Resource section is as follows:–
Tourist Information
Bed & Breakfast
Campsite
Camping shop
Bike shop
Places of interest
Railway information
For stores, pubs and places to eat please refer to the map

Introduction

Not to put to fine a point on it, the Chalke Way is probably the best coast-to-coast cycle ride in Europe. It is certainly the oldest, possibly the most extraordinary, maybe the wildest and definitely the most complete. It is a ride that carries us passed remarkable World Heritage Sites, enigmatic ancient monuments, mysterious crop circles and rampant hill carvings of giants and dragons. It trundles us across Roman battlefields where armies still do battle, reclaimed deserts that remain a wilderness, rolling countryside that inspired poetry, and royal estates thick with paparazzi stalking through the conifers.

It wends us under ancient beeches, through quaint thatched villages, beside burbling torrents, over vast prairies and along windy ridges to arrive at a lonely beach where squawking flocks peck amongst the blackened stumps of a petrified forest. It takes us to meet visionaries and ogres, gods and queens, stallions and deer, and invisible hounds on a mission from hell. Mostly it spirits us into another world, away from the roar of traffic and the hustle of the blacktop, on an adventure through the green holes in civilisation.

That all this lies hidden beneath the bushel of the heavily populated south eastern corner of England might be surprising. That it is linked by a single turnpike which has never been mapped for cyclists before is certainly so. There has never been any secret that some form of ancient byway sliced across Britain, linking the North Sea with the English Channel. Ramblers' literature frequently refers to a long distance footpath without mapping its' full course. They concentrate on sections like the Icknield Way and Ridgeway, and involve themselves in speculation about where the coast-to-coast begins and ends. In the north, Wells and Holme-next-the-Sea are most favoured for its Norfolk beginnings, while Lyme Regis and Seaton in Devon are prime contenders for the Channel end, though few publications reason why. They argue about the age of the route, whether the Icknield is older than the Ridge, and talk about a grass track cutting a swathe across the country like some prehistoric motorway, in parts lost under tarmac and the plough, elsewhere still there, unimpressive drove roads churned to porridge by farm traffic.

Trying to map the route from a mention here and a cross reference there was proving a nightmare until one steaming hot day entombed in my Central Library I noticed a peculiar entry in the computer index under the listings for 'Green Roads'. The book was a bit of a mess and in store the librarian explained, but I could certainly have a look at what turned out to be a 1914 edition of *The Green Roads of England* by the splendidly named R. Hippisley Cox. It was the key that unlocked the Pandora's Box and the oldest published record I had found of a complete coast-to-coast. Where 16th and 18th Century charts had revealed nothing significant, this tatty volume mapped an extensive network of ancient routeways radiating out across southern England. It had the advantage of being published a decade before tar was first spread onto John McAdam's hardcore turnpikes and our green roads began to turn black, but to this day I have no idea who or what Mr Hippisley Cox was.

By plotting the prehistoric causewayed camps of England, south of a line drawn between the Rivers Severn and Trent, then studying the topography of the region, Hippisley Cox showed how these large tribal communities of Ancient Britain were linked by a spiders web of grass tracks that hugged the main watersheds and focused in on an area trapped between the two Rivers Avon, flowing through Bristol and Salisbury, and the River Thames. Even now, most of us take for granted that our ancestors were unlikely to have travelled much further abroad than one, maybe two communities down the line. Eighty years ago Hippisley Cox questioned this, suggesting the very nature of the great roundabout where all roads converged indicated travel was no less a part of Neolithic life that it was in the Middle Ages.

The hub of the network was Avebury in Wiltshire. Despite centuries of abuse and a concerned effort by god-fearing Christians to obliterate what they believed was a pagan temple, Avebury henge remains a haunting reminder of Neolithic society and its elusive culture. Close by stands Sidbury Hill, the largest artificial and unexplained mound in Europe, and the West Kennet Long-Barrow, the oldest burial site in Britain, and Windmill Hill, where the earliest pottery of the Beaker people was unearthed. Clearly Avebury was at the centre of no ordinary gyratory. Something more was going on here than just a few travellers stopping off for a wolfburger and coffee *en route* to haggle over flint.

At this point it is necessary to mention that the earliest recorded history of Britain dates from only 550 BC. While the written word has never been any evidence of truth, it is important corroborative evidence. All history prior to that date is called `prehistory' and is unsubstantiated, limited to informed guesswork based on archeological clues. So when Hippisley Cox claims that Avebury was the seat of political and spiritual power for a great commonwealth of Neolithic tribes linked by super highways radiating out from Central Headquarters, he is as likely to be correct in his speculation as he is to be certifiable. It is certainly within the realms of possibility that edicts emanating from a Council of Tribes at Avebury could be on the table of a local chief in the far north of Norfolk within ten days, but whether the clans were that united and centralised is another matter.

Of more interest to us is the unbroken line of earthworks he maps, still to be seen on the ground, that runs from Hawkesdown Castle in the south to Castle Rising in the north. Given that Hawkesdown stands high, overlooking what was the Lyme Bay port of Axmouth, and that The Wash once sloshed against the defences of Castle Rising, could these be the two definitive ends of the fabled coast-to-coast?

The water shed this particular string of camps perch upon is formed by a great wave of chalk that crashed diagonally across the south of the country, gradually petering down to a gentle lapping as it travels north east. To the north of the crest stretch the clay beaches of the great vales, a sudden flatness extending from the Blackdown Hills near Taunton through to merge with the Lincolnshire Fens. To the south of the watershed, the land slips away in folds of smaller waves building up a head of water on the back of the breaker. In places the crests are cut by deep downs rushing away from the chalk edge, as if a rock has interrupted the ebbing tide and exposed a dry gulley within the backwash. If ever there was a topographical feature that was a natural for strategic settlement and a line to travel along it is this chalk escarpment that then must have stood boldly against the skyscape, high above the vast forests of southern England.

A hundred million years ago, when dinosaurs ruled, much of Britain lay under a shallow warm sea, rich in plant life, plankton and algae. This was the Cretaceous period, spanning a mere 70 million years during which South America tore away from Africa and drifted west, North America split from Western Europe and Eurasia began to form. On dry land, Europe might have been a desert, even a swamp, but on the sea-floor calcerous deposits were building up, layer upon layer of dead coccoliths, ammonites, rudistids and echinoids, accumulating at the breakneck rate of one foot (0.3 m.) every 30,000 years.

In effect the south of England was a coral sea-bed, fed by a geological period when all sorts of invertebrates and molluscs were dropping like flies and becoming extinct. As the continents stretched, compressed and tilted, and the waters receded, the coral cemented together, emerging as the calcium carbonate wedge that separates London and the south east from the rest of the country. In places the chalk deposits are over 1,500 ft (457 m.) thick. Multiplied by 30,000, this gives you some idea of how long it took the surface of the Chalke Way to form. Take care of it.

Fast forward a whole lot of millions of years to a mere 10,000 BC, and we find a landscape scarred and rubbled by a melting Ice Age that waters the saplings of a burgeoning north European forest. Already mature areas have flourished on the rich alluvium, blossoming into a tangled temperate jungle, dark and inaccessible, prowled by wild beasts, fowl and ravenous *homo sapiens*. On the crest of the chalk, where deposits of clay are thin and vulnerable to erosion, fewer trees have taken root. A way through is easier to see. Like a col or a ridge in a mountain range, the chalk edge reveals itself as a natural line for movement.

First there would have been the packs and herds of animals migrating across country in search of fresh water and pastures, warmer climes and salt. Then there would have been the nomadic hunter-gatherers, chasing dinner back and forth, but also exploiting the same watering holes and salt deposits. Then around 6,000 BC, our relationship with the beasts of the earth changed. We burnt and hacked down clearings in the forests encouraging the wild herds not to move on but graze a little longer near our camp, where the benders were filling up with the clutter of a site that has been around a while. When they did move on, we still followed, but this time left behind members of our family and maybe others, for the species now realised the limitations of the lone hunter and had developed the social skills to operate as a group, herding and stalking with the other families to ensure a constant supply of food. We were also learning the skill of sowing a few seeds and nurturing edibles, of capturing wild fowl and penning them, and shaping simple tools. By the time the hunters returned we has knocked up a crude extension to the bender.

If this is the prehistory of the chalk ridgeway Mr Hippisley Cox identifies, and the line of causewayed camps that evolved along its back, then three important observations can be made. Firstly, herds of animals do not travel in a long line, nose to tail. They spread out, particularly in lowland. Even at a river crossing or through a narrow valley they present a broad front, creating any number of trails for predators to follow. Along a ridge on a particularly windy day, they might opt for a lower route than usual, sheltered in the lee of the hill, or take a wide detour around an area that has turned to swamp since last they passed. Thus, far from being a single track, the earliest routeways would have been broad 'zones of communication' or 'of movement' anything up to five miles (8 km.) wide, scarred by numerous tracks heading in the same direction. Like tributaries flowing into a river, the major routes would have also been fed by minor trails, worn down by herds joining the migration from north or south along, for example, the Chalke Way.

Secondly the idea that human beings cleared the forest, creating moorland and heath for grazing, contradicts the commonly held belief that primeval people were exposed to the whims of nature and prey to the elemental vicissitudes of their harsh environment. We now know that by the Neolithic period the human species was beginning to take control of their hinterland and dominate the environment, and that the weather conditions were not that different from todays. Thirdly, as you will see when you read about the Isle of Portland, we have evidence that far from being a stay-at-home bunch, the Neolithics were quite happy to trudge hundreds of miles along well-defined animal tracks to exchange their surplus for items unavailable in their neck of the woods.

But there is two thousand years between the semi-permanent benders of the Mesolithics and the earliest causewayed camps of the Neolithics. 4,000 BC is a ballpark date you will frequently come across exploring the Chalke Way. It marks the next quantum leap the species took into the New Stone or Neolithic Age, a period of remarkable social development notable for its pottery, extensive farming, intensive industry and the organised communities of causewayed camps. These were small settlements of round thatched huts enclosed within an earth mound (more to contain animals than for defence), with one track in and one out. While the portage of clay and access to fields obviously created regular if localised routeways, the distribution of flint tools from the Neolithic 'axe factories' of England and Wales indicates the concept of long distance tracks over 6,000 years old is not so far fetched. In his book *Roads and Tracks of England* the archaeologist Christopher Taylor plots nearly eighty locations in East Anglia where stone tools produced at Great Langdale in the Lake District have been discovered. Similarly, while the bulk of the pots dug up at Windmill Hill near Avebury were made from local clay, some contained minerals unique to Cornwall, suggesting either the raw materials were brought in or, more likely, the pots were made in the West Country then carted up to Wiltshire.

The arrival of the metal ages a thousand years on adds a further layer to our considerations of the earliest trackways. The technological revolutions of the Copper, Bronze, and Iron Ages barely alter the story so far, but for the fact that the population was now firmly rooted, building substantial farmsteads and villages, and interning the skeletons of their dead in various shapes and sizes of barrow or tumuli. Aerial photography has enabled us to log prehistoric sites that are indistinguishable on the ground, revealing that, despite textbook depictions of a tangled wilderness dotted with the occasional primitive settlement, prehistoric Britain was actually well populated and exploited, and necessarily serviced by an extensive network of interlinking tracks. Remembering that the Fens were still emerging from the sea, our map of the eastern leg of the Icknield Way, much of which we follow as the Chalke Way, indicates just how densely occupied the area was, and by comparison with the South Dorset Downs, Cranbourne Chase and Salisbury Plain, this region was relatively under populated.

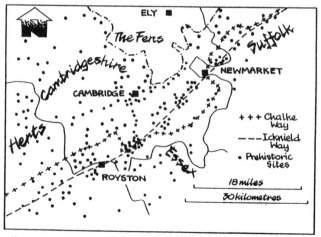

Known prehistoric sites along the eastern section of Icknield Way

As we trundle towards the Roman invasion and move from prehistory into history set fast on the page, we learn from the classical author Strabo that Britain was in contact with the expanding Roman Empire long before legionaires set foot on our island. He catalogues corn, cattle, gold, hides, slaves and hunting dogs as our principal exports. While French axes and Mediterranean wine jars dating from the Bronze Age have been found in this country, they could have been gifts. It is not until Strabo puts quill to parchment that we have hard evidence of trans-continental trade in goods that could only reach English ports via pack-horses or, by now quite common, carts pulled by oxen, horses or humans.

So if the British Isles were criss-crossed by a complex lattice of ancient routeways centuries before Rome surveyed the first cobbled straight, where are they now? The easy answer is we still use them, only now they lie under a hardcore of stone and an icing of tarmac. Certainly many will have disappeared, like the curves of flaking tarmac we often see deserted beside a newly rationalised clearway clinging to the side of a Pennine valley. In time they too will succumb to nature or give way to farming.

Others will have changed course or classification. What was a broad drove road might now be a popular footpath, so narrow ramblers have to give way to oncoming backpackers. And there will be new thoroughfares, shaped by the land enclosures of the 18th Century or forged across an Area of Outstanding Beauty by a mindless Ministry of Transport. Our road infrastructure is never static and it never has been. Following the line of the Chalke Way we avoid motorways and dual-carriage ways, pedal grit-sprayed lanes and broad green roads, charge along firm farm tracks, struggle up glorified bridleways and clatter down narrow paths all of which can lay claim to have felt the leather of Neolithic sandals on their back.

Within an acceptable zone of movement, we have tried to follow R. Hippisley Cox as closely as possible, even though his route is clearly wrong in at least one respect. In Norfolk, the chalk seam swings up to meet the sea at Hunstanton, not Castle Rising, but there is no evidence of a prehistoric settlement at Hunstanton. Rather than opt for one or the other, we have decided to cover all three, throwing in Holme-next-the-Sea for good measure. But when it comes to the fine detail, a number of 20th Century impediments have dictated the final course of our Chalke Way, most particularly the black holes in the British Rail network. Although a heritage track runs into Seaton on the English Channel, the link with Axminster and the national network has been severed. For reasons made clear in the guide, we therefore start you at Weymouth station more than 30 miles (48 km.) east of Hawkesdown Castle, a shift that allows us to take you passed Maiden Castle and the Cerne Giant, two of the most extraordinary ancient sites in Europe.

Other impediments include conurbation you wouldn't want to be seen dead in, expressways that give you a fright just watching the whapping and whappy commuters, off-road routes that are too damaged to entertain extra traffic and others where the sensitivity of endangered species has encouraged us to map detours. Finally, having ridden the lot several times, I have tried to pace it, aware that many cyclists find bridleway riding too rattling to be enjoyable. Fortunately the roughest terrain is crossed in the first few days of our ride, when enthusiasm is high and the knowledge that it all gets a lot easier keeps us chipper.

The title of the route has no basis in anybody's history, unlike the Icknield Way. It simply refers to the geological base underwheel. Since the only place name along its length alluding to the earth beneath is 'Chalke Valley,' a local title for what is mapped as the Ebble Valley, we added the 'e'. But this really is a chalk way, exceptional in following a single geological feature for its full length, unique in providing us with an extraordinary insight into the intimate relationship between what's below and what's above *terra firma*. For 380 miles (611 km.) the chalk we ride dictates the flora and fauna, the topography and water sources, the position of settlements, nature of industries, type of building materials, the very colour of the land we traverse. It even affects the weather (to our benefit).

But this is not a repetitive landscape, the same from beginning to end. While it takes an informed eye to detect the subtle changes in the fine detail of, for example, the use of flint in building from one side of the country to the other, the topography itself undergoes dramatic transformations. In the south we honk up and down the distinctive whalebacks of the high chalk downs. In the north the chalk has been sanded, rasped down to a gentle rollercoaster of rippling peaks and troughs. Between the two lie the wide open flatlands and extensive prairies of the corn belt. And within each section there are wonderfully discordant passages that surprise and delight, the more exhilarating for being totally out of context.

Largely a rural landscape, what we cross has been heavily altered by wind, rain, ice and water, but mostly by human intervention. Rivers have been diverted to feed flax mills, land has been laid waste to feed stomachs, hills have been hacked down to fuel lime kilns and contours have been supplemented to create strongholds. Well away from the sprawling townscapes, human claws have left their talon prints. In Britain you can forget the romantic notion that escaping into the hills is like stepping through a looking-glass into the unadulterated world of nature in the raw, but this doesn't detract from the sheer beauty of much of what you will encounter.

As Christopher Taylor writes `roads in themselves are not very interesting . . . their real significance lies in what they enable human beings to do to their environment and to themselves.' Either side of us, the route is lined with clues, but each should be viewed with a good deal of suspicion. Each is a historical document frozen at a particular point in time, heavily disguising layers of intrigue where humans have tinkered with the evidence. Take Stonhenge for example. While the building blocks might tell us something about their Neolithic designers, the actual circle tells us more about our grandparents in the 1950's, when it was restored, and the unsympathetic enclosure stands as a sorry indictment of our parents generation. It cowers on Salisbury Plain, after all these millions of years still recognisable as a Cretaceous seabed, but in places pock marked by Iron Age pimples and the scars of the 18th Century furse-cutters. The sumptuous wilderness, however, owes more to 20th Century military conservationists, if that's not a contradiction in terms.

I use the word 'wilderness' advisedly. There are long sections of the Chalke Way that cross thrillingly empty tracts of land where, though crops and pasture might extend to the horizon, the chances of encountering another human soul are slim. If not in physical size, in feel these areas possess all the unsettling qualities of a wilderness. In a land as densely populated as the UK, civilisation and wilderness sit cheek by jowl, and in the course of a morning we can cycle from a bustling city centre to a bleak moor where a buckled wheel means a full days tramp to the nearest phone.

Cruising in and out of these extremes affords us plenty of time for reflection. Between bouts of concentration dodging traffic, there is the boundless space to let your mind wander, to succumb to the rhythm of cycling, freeing the imagination to take off. And on a journey spanning 6,000 years, there is every opportunity to weave a web of conjecture between the few facts we have at our finger tips. Each of us can become an amateur historian, anthropologist or sociologist along the Chalke Way, expounding a pet theory that has every right to be taken seriously, regardless of how outrageous it might appear at first glance.

Take for example the entertaining case of Alfred Watkins. A magistrate, inventor and pioneer photographer, Alfred was also an amateur antiquarian, prone to breaking car journeys so he could compare features on the landscape with signs and symbols on his crumpled map. On one such occasion in the summer of 1921, Alfred noticed that a number of hill tops and ancient monuments appeared to lie in a straight line drawn across his chart. According to his son, Allen, 'Then without warning it all happened suddenly. His mind was flooded with a rush of images forming one coherent plan. The scales fell from his eyes and he saw that over many long years of prehistory, all the track ways were in straight lines marked out by experts on a sighting system'.

If Alfred was shattered by this revelation, the archeological establishment was outraged. It ran totally counter to the contemporary view that Neolithic man was still dragging his knuckles along the ground and that Neolithic woman was wooed by wacking her about the head with a club. To accept Alfred's thesis meant acknowledging the ancients were skilled surveyors and astronomers, which was plainly ridiculous. Dismissed as a crackpot, Alfred spent the remaining fourteen years of his life consolidating his theory and covering maps with ruled lines.

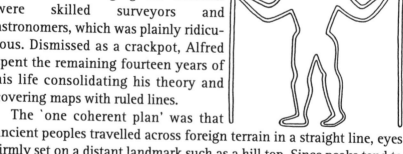

The 'one coherent plan' was that ancient peoples travelled across foreign terrain in a straight line, eyes firmly set on a distant landmark such as a hill top. Since peaks tend to disappear from sight the closer one gets to them, Alfred believed Neolithic surveyors employed a pair of tall staves spaced maybe 'a dozen yards apart' to align between the two poles and the hill in front or behind. Once satisfied the line was true, the surveyor would build a cairn on the spot and move on to continue the process. Alfred argued that the chalk figure cut in the turf at Wilmington, Sussex was a depiction of one such surveyor, holding a shoulder high pole in each hand.

Over the years, the cairns were replaced by more prominent features such as trees, buried mounds, hill settlements or beacons. Ponds and moats also featured in the alignment process, water reflecting the sun, moon or a beacon to help travellers navigate. In time these landmarks were further superseded by churches, village crosses and castle mounds.

In plotting his old straight tracks, Alfred noticed how time and again they ran through villages, hamlets or farms bearing the element 'ley' ' within their name. He surmised the tracks were therefore called 'leys'. In Celtic (possibly the language of our prehistoric tribes) the word 'dodi' means 'to lay' or 'to place'. This gelled with a number of points on the tracks that had names like Dodford, Dodlee and Dodman's Point. Further research revealed that 'dod' could also mean a small rounded hill, a staff or a club. Alfred concluded the first surveyor had to be called 'the dodman' and what he surveyed were called 'leylines'.

Two books of his theories fired the imagination of the chattering classes and spawned the Straight Track Club. Then, in 1927, Alfred published his DIY guide *The Ley Hunter's Manual.* Suddenly anybody who could read a map could stroll into the countryside, plot four or five markers aligned within ten miles and declare they had found themselves a prehistoric highway. The fledgling Rambler's Association promoted the activity as a wholesome way to spend a day out with the family.

Though Alfred's theories were firmly entrenched in the tangible he did allude to a mystical dimension. In *The Old Straight Track* he wrote, 'I feel that ley-man, astronomer-priest, druid, bard, wizard, witch, palmer and hermit were all more or less linked by one thread of ancient knowledge and power . . .' It was this dimension that predictably gave the study its second wind in the 1960's, fuelling what was to become the dropout, back-to-nature, plug-into-the-vibes culture of the Hippy movement

In 1961, in *Skyways and Landmarks*, Tony Wedd suggested there was a link between Watkin's discovery and those of the French ufologist Aime Michel. Michel had observed that sightings of unidentified flying objects (UFO's) over a specific period could be plotted along a straight line. He surmised the extraterrestrials travelled along navigational paths called 'orthotenies' a bit like modern flight corridors. Wedd suggested these were in fact leylines, followed either because the ancient landmarks were prehistoric signposts or because both leys and UFO's followed primeval lines of a magnetic current. Eight years later *The View Over Atlantis* by John Mitchell refuted Wedd's theory but developed the idea that the current was a mysterious form of earth energy which the Neolithics could tap into but which either was no more or was inaccessible to insensitive post-industrial folks like you and me.

Archaeologists were not amused. Just when they were coming to terms with the possibility that prehistoric people were not the dumb savages they had supposed, and might even have possessed basic navigational skills, up pops some whacko claiming they were actually tuned into mystical forces no modern technology could measure. There was further chagrin when one of their own, Alexander Thom, an Emeritus Professor from Oxford University, dared to suggest the neanderthals were also pretty good at geometry, mathematics and engineering, not to mention a snazzy line in astro-calenders. His surveys of megalithic monuments in Britain and northern France indicated they were laid out using a constant unit of measurement Thom called the 'megalithic yard' (2.72 ft. - 0.8 m.). Believing sites like Stonehenge were orientated towards where the sun rose on winter and summer solstice (an idea first proposed in 1771 by Dr. John Smith), Thom further calculated the Neolithic year was divided into 16 nearly equal months. By observing the moon on a different alignment, he thought they might well have been able to predict eclipses.

The ley hunters were delighted. Not only did the venerable Professor give credibility to the notion of the sophisticated primitive, but his use of alignments implied if not stated that the old straight track was indeed a fact, whatever its function or powers. The flood gates opened. Spaced-out ley hunters dropped another tab and conjured up groovy little scenarios of energy highways, karma filling stations and Neolithic dudes levitating their way home after a hard day erecting sarsen stones by the same will power. Through the purple haze, the distant past suddenly became a futuristic world of Taxislabs hovering down multi-carriageway leylines, Energy Revitalising Docks for run-down UFO's and Community Clinics plugged in to the healing power of the Force. Far out, man!

It is easy to go off on a tangent on this ride, without ever going off the route. There is the open space to let your mind go walkabout and there are the ancient enigmas to sign post its way, for if ever there was a journey into mystery and imagination, it is this one. More than a coast-to-coast, more than a heritage trail, more than a pleasant potter through glorious countryside, the Chalke Way is a concept ride. It is a narrative with reoccuring themes and an underlying thread, at the same time entertaining, challenging and educational, but always damn good fun. Most of all, it's a real adventure.

Enjoy.

Isle of Portland Circuit

DISTANCE – 20m 32K

OS 194

English Channel

WEYMOUTH

WYKE REGIS

PORTLAND HARBOUR

English Channel

ISLE OF PORTLAND

ISLE OF PORTLAND

BILL OF PORTLAND

English Channel

Pedestrian Underpass

Disused Railway

Ferry Bridge

Chesil Beach

Portland Castle

R.N. Docks

FORTUNESWELL

The Verne

The Grove

EASTON

Museum

Rufus Castle

WESTON

Southwell

Pulpit Rock

BILL OF PORTLAND

Pulpit Rock

Directions

1 R out of rail station opposite Queens Hotel.

2 L at RA TOWN CENTRE.

3 R at Bethany Hall and over Westham Bridge. At end, dismount and walk under pedestrian subway on right. Follow HEALTH CLINIC.

4 Up ramp, R and remount. Pedal past Catholic Church and continue up Abbotsbury Road.

5 L at The Rock Hotel along Newstead Road, Just before railway embankment, FOOTPATH on right. Cross road carefully and take track up to disused railway. Follow to end and the sea.

6 Dismount, down bank on right onto short FOOTPATH. Cross A354 onto pavement cycleway across causeway to Isle of Portland.

7 At end of cycleway, cross RA on to one way system. Follow A354 all the way to PORTLAND BILL

RETURN LEG

8 L at TJ WESTON

9 L at mock Italian Church, St. George Portland. FORTUNESWELL

10 L to retrace route to Weymouth rail station.

Resource

ISLE OF PORTLAND
Tourist Information
St. Georges Centre
Reforne
01305 861333
If closed contact
Portland Museum
217 Wakeham
01305 821804
Fee (entry to museum)

Mandy and Phil Jones
12 Coastguard Cottages
Portland Bill
DT5 2JT
01305 861044

Alessandria Hotel and
Restaurant
71 Wakeham
Easton
DT5 1HW
01305 822270

No campsites on the
island as yet.

Portland Castle
Castletown
01305 820539
Open April to Oct.

Portland Bill Lighthouse
Open all year round,
11am till sunset.

Prologue: Isle of Portland

Sat on the English Channel like a wedge of cake on a plate, this disconcerting slab of limestone is not strictly part of our coast-to-coast odyssey, but having come this far it seems a shame not to pay a visit. Treat it as a pre-tour crit. The Tour de France begins before it starts with a warm up criterium, so the Tour de Chalke begins with limestone, a massive battered angled chunk of the stuff, supporting a strange and harsh landscape.

The Isle of Portland has had its knocks and its people are true islanders. They call outsiders 'kimberlins' and grow nervous at the mention of the word 'rabbit' in the same way actors do about 'Macbeth', superstitions to be respected. Many pursue a kind of crofting existence, holding down a number of small island jobs to make ends meet, and their grey terraces, broad streets and dry stone walls give the villages an air of the Outer Hebrides or Anglesey in Wales. The causeway has tied them to the mainland for less than two hundred years, but like a umbilical rudely plugged onto a forty year old, it hasn't done a lot for bonding. Their beliefs, customs and turns of phrase are still more akin to the Channel Islands than to Dorset.

Like many off-shore islands, the place has been abused. It is pitted and pocked with gun emplacements, quarries and fortifications. Its skyline is dominated by a Victorian prison built by convicts. Its' cliffs are ripped and torn by ferocious Neptune, and on top there is hardly a tree in sight. For all that, 'The Rock' has its' character, because Portland has always been a strategic outpost, a source of building materials and wide open to the forces of nature. Crude Mesolithic tools made of the silicaceous rock, chert, thought to be over 8,000 years old, have been discovered at Land's End and as far afield as Surrey, Hampshire and Gloucestershire. In southern England, the only source for this rock is the Isle of Portland. Over the millennia, the exploitation of rich seams of minerals has been the driving force that has shaped the island and its people into such a curious identity. On the surface it is grim-faced, but lurking under the skin there is a raw beauty that deserves recognition.

For riders who arrive late in Weymouth and choose to start the Chalke Way on a new dawn, the pedal to Portland Bill is short and surprisingly pleasant. A disused railway presents the cyclist with just over three miles (5 km.) of gentle off-road through the sprawl of the conurbation. At times leafy but always busy with cycle commuters, dog-walkers and pram-pushers, this permissive way is a great asset to Weymouth, cutting out the need to fight hills and tourist traffic along the A354. At Ferrybridge, where the old Portland ferry used to dock, we pick up a pavement cycle path across the causeway, a further bout of relaxed pedalling and a chance to get a good look at the ugly slice of limestone looming up before you. This is certainly no Mont St Michel.

In the foreground colourful windsurfers zip and flip within Portland's sheltered harbour, their living-wagons and bar-b-ques parked and smoking in the lee of the West Bay breakwater to your right. Behind them the battleship grey and menacing superstructure of NATO defence vessels glide discreetly in and out of the Royal Navy Base. A helicopter takes off from the Naval Air Base and your eyes rise and refocus to take in the detail of **Fortuneswell**, the island's northern-most village, until now just a backdrop. 'The towering rock, the houses above houses, one man's doorstep rising behind his neighbour's chimney, the gardens hung up by one edge to the sky, the vegetables growing on apparently almost vertical planes . . .' The village hasn't changed much since Thomas Hardy described it in *The Well Beloved*. (Hardy gets a lot of airplay in the Wessex sections of this book, principally because his descriptions of fictional places and landmarks are so opaquely of real places and landmarks, some of which we pass, and let's face it, he's a lot better writer than what I am.)

Looming over Fortuneswell is the **Verne Citadel**, a Palmerston fort built in the 19th century to protect Portland Harbour from the threat of a Napoleonic invasion. At nearly five hundred feet (152m) above sea level, the cyclists' first impression of the vantage point is 'Damn, I've got to climb that!' but the reward for a few minutes of lung-bursting effort is more than just. From the top, the view across South Dorset is spectacular. Looking due north through binoculars, the course of the River Cerne slicing through the chalk escarpment on the horizon marks your route forward for the next couple of days. Sweeping round to the north west, the graded shingle of **Chesil Beach**, Dorset's Great Barrier Reef, carries the eye 16 miles (26 km.) along a whiter than white tide mark to Bridport. Daniel Defoe called this natural and unique phenomena 'a prodigious riffle of beach', riffling that grades the stones from the size of peas at Bridport to that of oranges at

Weymouth. It is said of local people that, presented with a pebble from Chesil Beach, they can tell you precisely where it came from. I tried. They said, 'Chesil Beach.'

Chesil is a beachcombers paradise. All manner of flotsam and jetsam ends its oceanic voyage beached on the shingle banks, including, in 1757, a mermaid. Reports have it, she was 'no beauty.' Smugglers have exploited its wilderness, and maybe still do, sinking their contraband in the freshwater lagoons behind the beach for leisurely distribution later. And once upon a time, the eastern end of the reef was a munitions store, supplying perfectly weighted sling stones to the Celtic defenders of Maiden Castle. A photograph in the Dorchester Museum shows an impressive mound of 20,000 slingstones that never got the chance to make their mark on the Roman invaders.

The good news is the ride to the **Bill of Portland** (and the island is the shape of a bird's head) is virtually down hill all the way. Yes it is a busy main road, but drivers seem to sense they are somewhere quite unusual and knock their speed back. The tourist catering at the Bill is nicely restricted to couple of wooden cafes, an ice cream stand and a shambles of creosoted beach huts, but this is not the place to bring junior swimming. Your bikes will be quite secure locked around the railing of the attended car park while you scramble over the limestone slabs at the cliff edge and explore the layered stack of Pulpit Rock. Here the sea whips itself into a lather as it unstintingly battles against the scarred defences of the island's ramparts. Weathered information boards provide details about the stone, the Roman quarries and Portland's contribution of materials and masons to St Paul's Cathedral in London. There is the famous lighthouse to bust a gut climbing and the Bird Observatory, but mostly Portland Bill is about buying an ice cream, finding a sheltered cranny and parking your bum for a quiet contemplation of swooping sea birds, rolling waves and distant horizons.

Chill out and get work out of your system. You are about to launch into an extraordinary adventure. Aside from everything else, this journey is about rhythm and pace, and right now you are hyper, still running at the pace of the rat race. I estimate you won't find your natural pulse until Salisbury, but a damn good siesta in a cosy suntrap on Portland Bill will go a long way towards preparing yourself for having some fun.

The return leg takes you via **Weston** and the opposite side of the island generally ignored by day-trippers. Throughout the ride you will be dogged by the monstrous carbuncle of H. M. Borstal, Grove, standing solid on your right. It is a dark headstone, an eerie reminder of the uses and abuses governments and businessmen have for poor old Portland. As I write, islanders are contemplating a bleak future, and what they will do when its main employer, the Ministry of Defence, closes the Naval dockyards.

But here in the west the similarity to parts of Scotland's Outer Hebrides is most striking, if slightly confused by the dusty roads and mock-Italian facade of the Georgian church of **St George Portland, Reforne**. Built by Portland stonemason Thomas Gilbert, this quirky landmark is surrounded by the stony desolation of quarries that once rang with mallets and chisels chipping out the lintels of that long abandoned church. Just north of it, Tout Quarry Sculpture Park presents an opportunity to literally go into the islands' industrial heritage. While the remains of commercial quarrying are much in evidence, the old West Weares works is now a modern sculpture park with one or two pieces guaranteed to inspire you to don the French beret and fisherman's smock and play the Rodin. Summer schools are held here, but we have a journey to make.

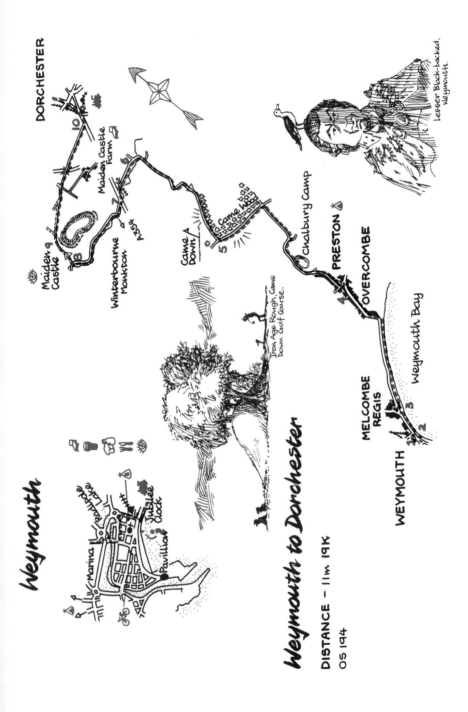

Weymouth

Marina
Radipole Lake
Jubilee Clock
Pavilion

Weymouth to Dorchester

DISTANCE – 11m 19k
OS 194

DORCHESTER

10

Maiden Castle Farm

Maiden Castle

9

8

7

6

A354

Winterbourne Monkton

Came Wood

Came Down

5

Chalbury Camp

PRESTON

OVERCOMBE

4

Iron Age Rough, Came Down Golf Course.

A353

MELCOMBE REGIS

WEYMOUTH

3

2

Weymouth Bay

Lesser Black-backed. Weymouth.

Directions

1 L out of rail station opposite Queens Hotel.

2 L at Clock Tower.

3 Follow A353 WAREHAM round church, along sea barrier and inland.

4 L at **RA** DORCHESTER then **1st R** up Combe Valley Road. Follow DORCHESTER until you reach Came Down Golf Course after Came Wood.

5 **R** CAME DOWN GOLF COURSE.

6 L after Lorry Prohibition sign along South Winterborne valley and lime tree avenue.

7 L then **1st R** over A354 WINTERBORNE MONKTON. (Fast main road. Get off and walk across if unhappy).

8 **R** at corner, through farmgate hidden by rowan tree, onto **BW.** Blue arrow.

9 If you prefer to take your bike with you up to Maiden Castle, **R** just after brow of hill, through gate onto track leading to sturdy fence at its western end where bike can be secured. The car park is unattended, but very public, with sturdy fences for your machine's security.

10 L opposite cemetery and **SO** into TOWN CENTRE. Entrance to Maumbury Rings through gate on right after traffic lights. Turn to town map.

Resource

WEYMOUTH

Tourist Information
The Pavilion Complex
The Esplanade
01305 785747

St. Helens Hotel
3 Westerhall Rd
DT4 7SZ
01305 786584

Pebble Bank Camping Park
90 Camp Rd
Wyke Regis
01305 774844
Open April to mid October.

Port Information
01305 206423

Railway Information
01202 292474

Seaview Holiday Camping Park
Preston
01305 833037

Millets Camp Shop
St. Mary Street,
01305 786002

Westham Cycles
128 Abbotsbury Rd
01305 776977

Nothe Fort & Gardens
01305 787243
Open May to Sept otherwise Suns and Bank holidays. Fee.

The Deep Sea Adventure and Old Harbour Heritage Centre
9 Custom House Quay
Old Harbour
01305 760690
Fee.

Weymouth – Dorchester

A S ENGLISH SEASIDE TOWNS GO, WEYMOUTH SUFFERS LESS THAN MANY FROM the annual invasion of candy-floss and 'Kiss Me Quick' holiday-makers, the type who will make it a holiday if it kills them. Even the obligatory Top Rank Touring Park manages to show remarkable restraint. Its very description is a gross understatement for 700 'statics', 90 'hook-ups' , 30 'free-standing' and 80 'canvas', campers jargon for a gargantuan caravan holiday camp, complete with pool, takeaway and 'New Spatz Nite Spot'.

Rows of catalogue-furnished caravan homes smother the Lanehouse hills like troops amassed for battle. But just when you're beginning to get annoyed at the regimentation and the half-hearted attempts to stamp a little character onto the ranks, the lines of tin boxes break off to reveal a broad clearing at the epicentre of the park. A unimpressive stream has soaked its banks and created a damp patch wet enough to pour cold water on Top Ranks' plans to obliterate the land. With your back to the wail of cabaret artiste Mad Michael desperately singing it his way, you look across the clearing to a rippling lagoon where four swans perform synchronized swimming and the sort of regimentation you could die for.

So it is with the town of **Weymouth**. Nature has got in the way of the sort of coastal sprawl that would destroy the place. If its' not sodden earth, its' the sea cliffs, or the constricting shape of the little knuckle of peninsula the whole lot sits on. In place of acres of stomach-churning fun fares, the town proffers nature reserves, a sea-life park and a swannery. Everything is rather charming and under-scored in Weymouth, which is probably its' attraction for the thronging hordes. The beach is a glorious arc of unbroken sand, but the sea and Way estuary has lured more than burning flesh and see-through lilos. The 17th Century harbour is an island haven for fisherman, 'yotties' and the odd millionaire aboard his fibreglass gin palace. Beyond the Pavilion Complex you may be up early enough to see Condor 10 depart for the Channel Islands, the sleekest ferry on three hulls.

And there's more. The original port of Melcombe Regis attracted the Black Death in 1349, although 'imported' would be a better word, and a second epidemic of plague proportions in 1381. Between them they wiped out a third of the county's population. Then there is George III who was attracted to the town for medical reasons in 1789 and made an annual pilgrimage for the next 20 years. And finally the lady at the Tourist Information will gleefully inform you, Weymouth imported the very first Labrador dog into this country. She ends, "Not a lot of people know that."

In high season Weymouth isn't the best of places to cycle. The pavements are overflowing, the tail-backs hot and bothered, and around the port, when the crowd decides to part, rail lines suddenly open up in the tarmac. Unless you are making a bee line out of town, you are better to walk and take in the spectacle, particularly along the esplanade where you will catch sight of the first of several chalk figures to be encountered on the Chalke Way. Look to the north east and you will see the grey silhouette of mad King George riding away from Weymouth, some say because, while loving the air, he loathed the parochialism of the Dorset town. Others say because the locals were pleased to see the back of the obstinate old goat.

Either way the figure was cut in 1808 to commemorate the man who put Weymouth on the map as a beach resort, attracting investment and the bourgeoisie who transformed a sleepy fishing harbour into a boom town. Here gents in high collars took the air with their greyhounds and fully clothed ladies tipped a toe in the water from a bathing machine pushed up to its axles in the sea. Look above awning height and there is some splendid Georgian architecture to be studied along the sea front, while round the corner, on Gloucester Street, the Old Royal Stables house the towns' cinema, prevented from expanding into a multiplex by its' deserved status as a listed building.

Climbing Greenhill out of Preston, up a leafy avenue fronting chintzy bungalows, with a stream gurgling away to your right, the relief at being free of the hullabaloo of trippers is tangible. Within minutes you have honked up to the seclusion of the southern edge of the chalk escarpment and emerged on your first ridgeway. Already the rolling reaches of open downland will have made their mark, if only in pearls of sweat on your brow. The fields are stony and stippled with lumps of chalk like a pointalist painting gone wild with the white. The coomb valleys are broad and sweeping in their views south over bay and Rock. To the north the tangle of Came Wood hides concrete standings where World War II hardware was mustered and camouflaged prior to shipping through Weymouth for D-Day. Then, on the corner of **Came Down** Golf Course, you happen across the first clear example of literally thousands of ancient monuments littering your way through to Norfolk. A carefully mown round barrow flanked by a cluster of tress and a huddle of golfers waiting to tee off from the sixth. The mound is the ancient monument.

Take a break on the grass verge of the club car park after the brow of the hill. You have turned north and before you the vast panorama of the Frome valley opens out to reveal a gentle horizon that looks like the edge of the world. This is the northern chalk ridge along which our ancestors bisected the country, the goal of the first two legs of the Chalke Way. To the west, the phallus is Hardy's, as in the 'Kiss me, Hardy' of nautical fame, a memorial to Admiral Nelsons' Flag Captain. In the valley nestles the Roman town of Dorchester, maybe smaller than you imagined, and totally overwhelmed by the quiet magnificence of **Maiden Castle** on its doorstep.

This is the best view you will get of the hillfort, particularly on an evening when the low sun casts long shadows that throw into relief the full depth of its impressive ramparts. The ride along South Winterborne valley serves to emphasise the full scale of the earthworks and your first stretch of off-road up between Hog Hill and the Castle gives you some idea of how Vespasians's Roman legionaires might have felt, faced with such formidable defences. As we shall see, they weren't intimidated for long.

In the height of summer, it is quite possible the South Winterborne stream will be a dry, cracked river bed. This is a regular feature of the chalk downs, where the stone soaks up moisture like a sponge, then releases it grudgingly as a haze under a hot sun. The word 'Winterborne' alludes to the seasonal appearance of surface water and is one of many place names along the route that provide a clue to an area's geology, farming or bygone crafts. At night the atmosphere over the downs is thick and humid. Campers will find their flysheet wringing wet until a morning breeze quickly blows it dry. Between the arid land and seasonal streams, residents on the upland have always had a problem collecting and storing water. Historically the answer was to dig a shallow basin, line it with straw or rushes sealed with a layer of boulder clay, then wait for nature to do its' bit. Heat radiating from the chalk warms the evening air and makes it heavy with moisture, but over the basin, where the radiation is checked, the air chills, releasing dew onto non-conductors like flysheets and straw.

This is the principle behind **dew ponds** and you will find a good example of one near the indentation in the southern flank of Maiden Castle.

There are over 3,000 hill forts in Great Britain of which 'Mai Dun' or Maiden Castle, has to be the most remarkable. There is certainly nothing to touch it on the European mainland. Covering 18 hectares and measuring 1.5 miles (2.5km.) around the inner ramparts the site probably started out 5,000 years ago as a small causewayed camp housing the Neolithic ancestors of the Durotriges tribe of Celts. By 400 BC it had expanded to encompass six hectares and a hundred years later to its current internal size, but still the 'castle' would have been a safe community more than a true hillfort. From 100 BC, strengthening defences began in earnest and accelerated when the Belgic tribes of Gaul, forced off the continent by the advancing legions of Julius Caesar, began invading the British Isles. The ramparts were built higher, topped with a stockade, and two more lines of earthworks dug. The two causeways, east and west, were further elaborated into a maze of peaks and troughs designed to snarl and confuse a full frontal attack.

In AD 43 Claudius landed on British soil with a mission to conquer. A year later **Vespasian** invaded the south west of the country and set in motion a pincer action, planned to trap the British tribes between the two Imperial phalanxes. By the year 44 his Legio II Augusta had fought their way along a line of Durotrige hillforts and were camped in the Frome valley, hyping up for the push on Maiden Castle. According to Mortimer Wheeler, director of excavations at the hill fort in the 1930's, inside the stockade a town of some four to five thousand souls awaited their fate with trepidation. They were farmers, crafts and trade people, men, women and children whose only weapons were the tools of hunting, tilling, forging and building. Yes there would have been warriors as well, but their sling stones were clearly no match against the sophisticated catapults and siege machines of a highly disciplined colonialist's army. Within days Mai Dun had fallen.

History skips the details of the assault, but excavations of war graves at the east end of the hillfort suggest little quarter was spared. **Dorchester's County Museum** displays a grizzly couple of skeletons, one with his skull caved in, the other with a Roman arrow head lodged next to his spine. By AD 70, survivors from the hillfort had settled in the Roman garrison town of Durnovaria, later called Dorchester, and a small farming community had returned to reside on the mound. In the 400's, a Roman-Celtic temple 40 foot (12m) square was erected in the western quarter of Maiden Castle where archaeologists have unearthed an unholy alliance of pagan deities. That a three–horned Celtic Bull was worshiped cheek by jowl with idols of Diana and Minerva indicates how the two formally antagonistic cultures merged and went forward as something quite new, cunning called Romano-British by the boffins.

But all the dates, developments and speculation are as nothing once you are stood on the battlements of this spectacular earthwork. Now owned by the Duchy of Cornwall (another of Prince Charles' trinkets) and cared for by English Heritage (central government) the site oozes a tranquillity that belies its torrid past. On an evening it is criss-crossed by Dorchester's dog-walkers and courting couples. During the day, tourists clamber between the enormous mounds marvelling at the human endeavour or just sit on the top and soak up the commanding prospect. Fair weather or foul, Maiden Castle is an experience as humbling as the Taj Mahal, and on a hillfort that was once home to thousands of people it is hard to feel crowded when a coach party arrives.

Of particular to us is the escarpment to the south east of the castle. Looking back, pick out your route down the edge of Came Down Golf Course, then cast your eyes westwards along the horizon. You should be able to count at least a dozen tumuli or barrows, little nipples standing erect and stretching in a broad arc round to where the River Frome cleaves the chalk. There are actually hundreds in the area, but this striking row on the South Dorset Ridge gives you an idea of just how busy it must have been around here in the Bronze Age. After Salisbury Plain it seems Cranbourne Chase and South Dorset were the main centres of tribal population in the British Isles of our prehistory. Either that or folk travelled a mighty long way to bury the relatives somewhere nice.

Dorchester – Cerne Abbas

OKAY, SO YOU DIDN'T COME OUT FOR A BIKE RIDE TO SPEND YOUR TIME INDOORS peering into glass cabinets full of dusty exhibits. But if you visit no other museum along the course of the Chalke Way, I recommend at least checking out the archeological section of Dorchesters'. Like most County Museums it is small enough not to be wearing and laid out with sufficient aplomb not to be confusing. On a voyage of discovery like this where you will encounter ancient monuments that call for great leaps of the imagination, it helps if you can take this opportunity to pull up a stool to the fireside of the prehistoric people who shaped so much of what you will ride on, through and passed. Amongst the sophisticated ceramics of the Beaker people and the humble tools that achieved so much, you will find quirky curios like the eccentric Ernest Channon, who launched his prototype plane off Maiden Castle in 1909. The rest of the museum is also very enjoyable, but I understand if you want to get back out into the fresh air.

And the air is not bad in Dorchester. Traffic and Planning have managed to steer sufficient gas-guzzlers round the houses to leave the centre smelling leafy and clean. It is a pleasant county town for pleasant county people, and appears to have successfully wedded the old and the new. Strong traditions are suggested by little book shoppes, Barbours and green wellies, saddleries and chunky tweeds draped on shapeless mannequins. You could be forgiven for half expecting a straw sucking yokel in a smock-frock and gaiters to come lurching round the corner clutching his flaggon of 'scrumpy' cider. The modest pedestrian precinct reflects the new, with chain-store shop fronts that look the same wherever you are in Britain, but in summer, street stalls and performers brighten the blandness and give a nod to Hardy's bustling fictional market town of Castlebridge. **Dorchester** feels relaxed and comfortable. It's a survivor.

Durnovaria owed much to its location beside the River Frome and astride the Via Iceniana, the main Roman artery between Essex and London, now a grass track extending to the north east. Rapidly expanding into an important trading post and garrison fort, the old streets are still laid out in the linear pattern originally plotted by Roman town planners. The fortifications have all but gone, replaced by the lime and chestnut lined Walks that delineate the old town. Here

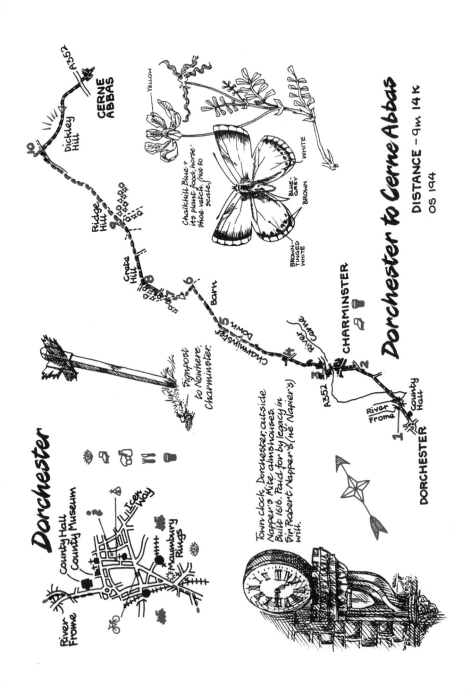

Directions

1. **R** at petrol station SHERBOURNE (ALTERNATIVE ROUTE)

2. **L** at broken sign post.
Follow road through Charminster.

3. **R** onto A352 GODMANSTONE then **L** CHARMINSTER DEPOT.

4. **SO** through farmgate. Follow blue arrows **SO** up track then over grass field.

5. **R** through farmgate in far right corner of field. Blue arrow. **SO** along **BW** past barn keeping hedge on right.

6. **L** where hedge turns sharp right and field opens out. Up **BW** curving round side of combe.

7. **R** at woods through farmgate to right. **SO** onto track and ridge. Blue arrows.

8. Through farmgate then **R** through another. **SO** along ridge. Keep hedge on right. Ignore blue arrows pointing left and right.

9. **SO** where arable field juts up to woods, across field to gate in hedge opposite. Blue arrows. Hedge now on left for a short distance, then **SO** through gate. Keep hedge on right along ridge to road.

10. **R** up then down hill to Cerne Abbas.
Cross A352 into VILLAGE.

Resource

DORCHESTER
Tourist Information
1 Ackland Road
01305 267992

Maiden Castle Farm BB
DT2 9PR
01305 262356

Mountain Ash BB
30 Mountain Ash Rd
DT1 2PB
01305 264811

Mrs M Lee
Timsgarry
32 Culliford Rd
DT1 2AT
01305 262717

Great Western Camping Shop
Great Western Rd
01305 268787

Dorchester Cycles
31 Great Western Rd
01305 262735

Dorchester County Museum
High West St
01305 262735
Opens Mon to Sat.
Suns in Jul/Aug.
Fee.

Dinosaur Museum
Icen Way
01305 269880
Fee.

Tutankamun Exhhibition
High West St,
01305 269571
Fee.

Railway Information
01202 292474

CHARMINSTER
Riverhill House BB
7 East Hill, DT2 9QL
01305 265614

Three Compasses Inn
DT2 9QL
01305 263618

you will find a trio of figures by sculptor Elizabeth Frink that commemorate 16th century religious martyrs. Like so many of the places along the Chalke Way, behind Dorchesters' quiet facade lies a blood and thunder history. Further to the south, but still in town, **Maumbury Rings** has been a Neolithic henge, a Roman sports arena, a Civil War gun emplacement and a public gallows in its time. Today people soak up rays on banks that more than once soaked up blood.

And the gore doesn't end there. As Dunovaria gave way to the Saxon name Dorwaraceaster, and ensuing Dark Ages reduced much of the country to near ruin, Dorchester managed to hang in there, emerging at the end of the Middle Ages as the regional centre of local government and law. In the 17th century, it is the meeting out of justice that puts the town on the popular history map. Here the infamous '**Hanging Judge' Jeffries** sentenced 74 doubtful rebels to be strung up by henchman Jack Ketch, and deported a couple of hundred others. Heads were impaled on the railings of St. Peters' church and delightful packages of severed members were dispatched around the county as dire warning to anybody not rooting for the Monarchy, so be careful what you say about Charles and Di.

To join the cross-country ridgeroad, our ancestors had a choice of three pack routes north from the ford over the Frome - either up the Cerve valley or along one of the two edges that shepherd the river. Two of these are now lost to the motor vehicle, but the western rim is still exclusive to animal powered transport, to walkers and riders of horse flesh and alloy. The journey is on bridleways, much of it cushioned by meadow or on firm farm tracks that take you beside the eastern then the western edge of the hill chain. In places it gets sticky in the wet, but these sections are mostly where a bit of pushing allows time to take in the serenity of the inter-locking patch work of combs that slip away from the ridge. Depending on the season, it is here, on the climb up Charminster Down, you will first encounter the crazy antics of the phenomena known as '**mad cow stampede.**'

This begins with a curtain raiser where these barmy critters jog across from the four corners of the field and take up a position, broad-side on, right in front of your path. Their blank expressions and motionless jaws clearly suggest you are a creature from another planet, benign but not to be trusted. The signal to bolt comes a cows length before you collide, at which point they scare the hell out of cyclists by suddenly lurching onto their hind legs, charging towards you, then veering round either side like bow waves, to bring up the rear in a swell. Five seconds later they canter passed you, again on both sides, and assume the original barrage formation of dumb animals transfixed by curiosity.

This performance will be repeated the full length of the field and when you finally close the gate behind you, there is the look of disappointment that you couldn't stay and play longer. Should you then ride along the edge of the field next to theirs, the lasses will thunder after you in a clumsy charge, udders shaking milk like a barman shakes a cocktail. This also can be a sight disturbing and inclines one to think any minute now the trainer will be called on to attend to a groin injury. Cows just aren't built for running, despite leaving Linford Christies lunchbox in the starting blocks. To see them exercise much more that their jaws is wonderful, but don't go out of your way to bring them the message of aerobics.

By the time you reach the woods between Crete and Ridge Hills you will be engulfed in what can only be described as an area of outstanding natural beauty made noticeable by the total absence of buildings and roads. In fact almost 40% of Dorset is officially an AOND (**Area of Outstanding Natural Beauty**), safeguarded, by unique laws and policies that control the management and development of the land. From the Bill of Portland to leaving Cranbourne Chase you will be riding through an AOND, and it shows. Initially city slickers might feel frustrated they can't identify this yellow breasted bird, that maple-leafed tree or the other vibrant purple flower. But the profusion of darting fauna and dazzling flora quickly reassures you that it is more important to know *that* they are, rather than *what* they are.

There are 38 AONBs in England and Wales, including five traversed by the Chalke Way - Dorset, the West Wiltshire and North Wessex Downs, the Chilterns and the Norfolk coast. Launched in 1949 by the same Act of Parliament that created our National Parks, AONBs are entrusted to the Countryside Commission to preserve as an irreplaceable part of our natural heritage. This hasn't prevented central government driving the odd motor or dual-carriageway through a few of them. On the other hand it has encouraged groups like the Council for the Protection of Rural England to recommend banning off-road cycling. The expression 'Might is Right' springs to mind.

After six and bit miles (10 km.) negotiating hoof prints and tractor ruts you are rewarded with tarmac and the best view going of the Man with the Big Willy, aka the **Cerne Giant**. This bloke really puts Linford to shame. As you reach the brow of the hill, look slightly to your left and across at the opposite hillside. Of the horses, kiwis, lions, Dodmen and regimental badges that remain etched in chalk, this horny monster is the wildest, though a good view of his credentials is often obscured by long grass.

Nobody knows for certain the origin or purpose of the figure. Nobody seems to have given it much heed in the past. No mention of it is made in writing until the 18th century. The current hot theory is that the giant was cut on the orders of Emperor Commodus around 2 AD to compliment the Romans modest conviction that he was Hercules reincarnate (and rampant!). The figure does bear a striking resemblance to Gallo-Roman statuettes of the club wielding superhero except, slung over his left arm, Hercules is usually portrayed carrying a lion's skin. If the left arm (right as you look at it) of the Cerne Giant looks a little adrift, computer analysis of resistivity-meter readings reveal it is also missing a looping wavy line that used to hang below it, possibly representing the lions skin. Local chronicler Rodney Legg claims he has also discovered the outline of a dog identical in shape to Roman bronze terriers found at Wroxeter lurking beneath the turf 150 feet (46 m.) from the giant's right leg. Since Hercules final ordeal was to bring the hound from hell, Cerebeus, out of the underworld, this would seem to clinch the matter.

Hill carvings are vulnerable works of art that tend to change shape as bits are grassed over and not scraped back, or as new outlines are cut next to the old and unrepairable. Many will have disappeared forever, neglected by the local community responsible for their upkeep. At Cerne, the scouring took place every seven or eight years under the direction of the lord of the manor, and was a ritual attended by festivities, a holiday and probably wagon loads of whatever was the equivalent then to 'crusties.' The left side (right as you look at it) of the Giant has shifted over the years and he has lost a nose that dangled between his eyes like a limp penis. His erect penis has grown to 30 feet (9 m.), incorporating what used to be his belly button, and points east to where the sun rises. Like mortal men, it appears Hercules also wakes up in the morning with a stiffy.

Traditional explanations of the cartoon range from the ridiculous to the mildly interesting. He bears a similarity to engravings of Cernunnos, the horned Celtic god who, Thor-like, wielded the invincible mallet. He could have been a piss-take of the local abbot, known to be a randy devil, cut by the monks of Cerne Abbas after a particularly riotous evensong. There again the figure might be the first scene-of-crime outline of a murder victim, in this case a real giant slain by local folk after he had munched his way through several flocks of sheep and laid down to nap. Whatever his rhyme and reason, the Cerne colossus is one of the oldest chalk images still extant and definitely the most fertile. The story goes that barren wives of the parish used to spend the night on him, so to speak, chaperoned by hopeful husbands. To the right of his club, on the crest of the hill, is a terraced earthwork knowns as **The Trendle** or Frying Pan. While its' origins remain as elusive as the Giant's, a maypole was permanently erected here in the Middle Ages, and various fertility rites and spring festivities indulged in. Puritan party-poopers removed the maypole in the 17th century and chopped it up to make a village ladder, an act of emasculation that must have brought tears to some villagers eyes.

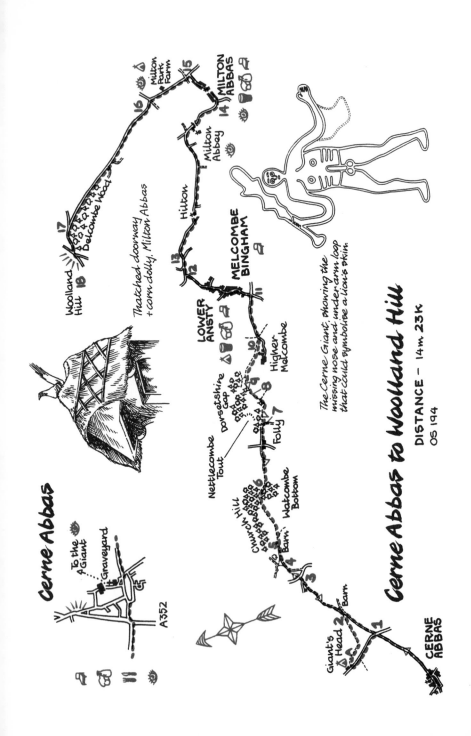

Cerne Abbas

To the Giant
Graveyard
A352

Cerne Abbas to Woolland Hill

DISTANCE – 14m 23k

OS 194

Milton Park Farm

15

MILTON ABBAS

16

14

Milton Abbey

Hilton

13

12

Woolland Hill 18

Belcombe Wood

17

Thatched doorway + corn dolly, Milton Abbas

MELCOMBE BINGHAM

LOWER ANSTY

11

10

Higher Melcombe

Dorsetshire Gap

9

8

Folly 7

Nettlecombe Tout

6

5

Church Hill

Barn

Watcombe Bottom

4

3

Barn

1

Giant's Head 2

CERNE ABBAS

The Cerne Giant, showing the missing nose and under-arm loop that could symbolise a lion's skin.

Directions

Via Giants Head Campsite

1 L BUCKLAND NEWTON. Campsite .5m (1km) on right.

A Through gate in far right corner then follow **BW** keeping hedge on left. At end of field, follow blue arrows **L** through two farm gates. Keep hedge on right down hill to join track at **2**.

1 SO across field to join down hilltrack. No blue arrows but OK.

2 L at barn, through farmgate then **R** along track.

3 L onto B3143. Immediate **R** onto **BW** up hill between blue arrows.

4 Branch **R** onto uphill track (if you miss it, **R** at trees NOT through gate). Keep hedge on left & follow blue arrows all the way to Folly.

5 SO through farmgate at brow of hill. Turn **L** keep hedge on left. After earthwork on right, bear right through farmgate.

6 L through farm gate.

7 L off track onto **BW**. Follow blue arrows up through farm gate and avenue of trees, then **L** across open field.

8 SO over brow of hill, following blue arrows through gate and round field to farm gate into woods opposite.

9 SO through farm gate, down green lane through Dorsetshire Gap to open fields (steep descent). Follow blue arrows **SO** through farm gates to Higher Melcombe. Keep to right edge of fields.

10 L onto road.

11 L MELCOMBE BINGHAM.

12 R after chapel (private house) HILTON.

13 L HILTON.

14 L W. STICKLAND into Milton Abbas.

15 L STICKLAND.

16 L BULBARROW.

17 L BULBARROW.

18 R OKEFORD FITZPAINE (left of signpost is entrance to picnic site).

Resource

CERNE ABBAS

The Singing Kettle Tea Rooms
7 Long St
DT2 7JG
01300 341349
BB and food.

Mrs M. English
47 Long St
DT2 7JG
01300 341377

The New Inn
The Old Market House
25 Long St
01300 341274

Giants Head Camping Park
Old Sherbourne Rd
DT2 7TR
01300 341242
Open Easter to Oct.

MELCOMBE BINGHAM

Mrs L. Dowsett,
Badger Sett,
Cross Lanes,
DT2 7NY
01258 880697

LOWER ANSTY

The Fox Inn
DT2 7PN
01258 880328
BB and camping.
Also contains village store and PO.

MILTON ABBAS

Sharon & Barry Dunn,
Damer Cottage,
DT11 0BP
01258 880508

Wyvern House BB
DT11 0BL
01258 880089

Milton Abbey
Open daily during daylight hours.
July to Aug parts of the house
are open. Contact Mrs Illingworth
01258 880489

Milton Park Farm Museum
01258 880704
Open from Apr to Sept.
Campers welcome. First night
includes admission price.

Cerne Abbas – Wolland Hill

IMAGINE SOMEBODY HACKING THE NAKED OUTLINE OF SLY STALLONE, TOM Cruise, or some other present day demi-god out of a hillside over-looking your back yard. You would be outraged, and might be incensed to do everything in your power to have the blot on the landscape removed. That the Benedictine monks of Cerne Abbey made no attempt to prevent villagers from regularly scraping the pagan fertility symbol that lurked over their shoulders is, to say the least, strange. For over 1,800 years the clerics of **Cerne Abbas** put up with a 200 foot (70m) pictogram that was basically a flagrant insult to their Christian beliefs.

Today the abbey is a few lumps in the ground you walk across to visit the Giant close up, just beyond the graveyard wall. It was flattened during the reign of Henry VIII, and Thomas Corton, the last Abbot, was accused of being a red hot lover with a passion for enter-taining the ladies at his cellarers house. He ran a disorderly order known to indulge in a little pre-mass gambling and post-coital boozing. Whether he attributed his fall from grace to the unholy influ-ence of the Man with the Big Willy or just a mission from God to initiate women in to the ways of the church isn't recorded.

An earlier attempt by St Augustine and his monks to bring the word to the 'demoniac inhabitants of a heathen village' was met by tying fish to the tails of their robes and hounding them out of the valley. When he returned St Augustine struck his staff against the ground and a fountain issued forth, still sloshing around in the centre of the graveyard. In fact the well is likely to be much older, possibly blessed by the Celts as a fertility well where folk would make offerings for a bountiful harvest, family or flock. As we have seen, tribal inhabitants of the arid chalklands were somewhat concerned about water and the lack of it. It took on mystical significance. Different wells had different powers. They were the dwellings of gods and goddesses, guarded by nymphs and supernatural creatures, where the occasional offering of an enemy's severed head was thought to boost the sponsor's strength and potency. You might try dropping a coin in. The climb out of Cerne is a stiff one.

By the 19th century, Cerne was a village that aspired to being a market town. A walk around the back streets confirms it must have been a hive of industry, at one time boasting a tannery, malthouse, brewery, mill and foundry. With the advent of railways that bypassed the village, the regular stage service was put out to grass and Cerne became a ghost town, 'silent and well-nigh deserted' by 1906. It was the internal combustion engine that revived its fortunes and is today clogging the narrow streets with coaches, dormobiles and bumper to bumper BMWs. Why the whole place hasn't been white lined and restricted to residents only parking defies explanation, since the attraction of the village lies in its' picture-postcard Tudor houses and thatched cottages, often obscured by the superstructure of some ghastly Spacecruiser.

Some will find the six miles (9.5 km.) of cross country to Melcombe Bingham challenging. There are a couple of steep lumpy-bumpy descents where a lapse of concentration could find you over the handlebars, a couple of stiff overgrown climbs Miguel Indurain would baulk at and stretches of deep tractor ruts guaranteed to catch your pedals. Mostly, however, it is a dawdle along well posted farm tracks with excellent all-weather surfaces that carry you up and down an unexpectedly exciting and varied landscape. Despite starting the leg on an unmarked bridleway, Dorset rates as one of the best way-marked counties in the country. The Downs also rate as something of an undiscovered playground for country walks and riders, with over 3,000 miles (4800 km.) of challenging routes to explore. At times the little blue arrows reach Spaghetti Junction proportions and you have to search for the one pointing your way, often lurking a little deeper in the woods. Red arrows signify RUPPs (Roads Used as Public Paths), which are also a right of way for cyclists in this area. Yellow arrows are for footpaths.

The dragon like symbol enhancing the Ridgeway disc is a wyvern, a two legged monster different to the quadruped Welsh dragon. The wyvern was the rallying emblem of the kingdom of Saxony and King Harold's banner, as depicted in the Bayeux Tapestry, sports a magnificent creature, 'full rampant'. It was adopted by Dorset County Council to waymark the Wessex Ridgeway devised by Ms. Priscilla Houston, a wonderful free spirit approaching her eighties, who set out to map a ramblers' link along the chalk edge, from Avebury down to the south coast. Though she can barely walk three miles at a stretch, Ms. Houston is currently surveying a long distance footpath linking all the hillforts and causewayed camps of Dorset.

You are now travelling east along the green road identified by R. Hippisley Cox. On crossing the B3143 you will be midway between the prehistoric settlements of Dogbury Castle, 2.5 miles (4 km.) due north of Cerne, and Nettlecombe Tout, the hillfort on your left up the track from Folly. To call it a ridgeway misrepresents the terrain. Here the chalk is lacerated with combs and the edge poorly defined. Avenues of beeches and indigenous woods obscure the northern aspect. Occasional glimpses of broad sweeps to the south hint at the majesty to come, but this leg is uncharacteristic in feeling cosy. Nature wraps you in a warm embrace of valleys and foliage, then opens out to let you breathe awhile before drawing you into its bosom again. Just once, crossing the highest peak in the area, before the Dorsetshire Gap, might you feel exposed and vulnerable.

As soon as you enter the meadows on the brow of **Church Hill** the awareness of being somewhere quite special sneaks up with the breeze from Lyscombe Bottom and nudges you. As the notice explains, the hill is now under Countryside Stewardship, an excellent scheme spearheaded by the Countryside Commission to conserve, enhance and rehabilitate selected areas of the English landscape. In the chalklands the emphasis is on management of the thin top soil that precariously supports a range of grasses and flowering plants like cowslips, wild thyme and different orchids. These are important for sustaining the butterfly population, particularly the chalk hill blues that feed on horseshoe vetch. Farmers and landowners who fit the criteria and enter into a ten year agreement receive cash incentives to open access, restore hedgerows, protect earthworks, rebuild drystone walls and so forth. While a percentage of agreements are to repair the damage of previous farming trends, only a cynic would dismiss the slow but vital improvements stewardship is making to the countryside and our enjoyment of it. Sadly it is severely limited, inevitably, by the clammy hands of central government tightening the purse strings. Our lords and masters clearly don't agree with Sir Roy Strong, art historian, gardener and Royal buddy-buddy, when he recommended the whole of rural England be designated a National Park, or at minimum receive the investment necessary to bring the entire land under Stewardship.

The throbbing metropolis of **Folly** is worth a mention, both of its houses, if only as the hamlet with the most appropriate name. The house called 'The Old Fox' used to be the Old Fox Inn. Its nearest competitor was a full 1.5 miles (2.5 km.) away in the village of Plush.

Between the two lived a lot of teetotal hares, hedgehogs and frogs. Presumably No 1 Folly relied on the residents of No 2 for its regular takings, not what one would call a sound customer base for a publicans business, unless of course No 2 was occupied by a distant relative of Oliver Reed. In ye olde days, public houses were places where you drank and collapsed outside in the street. Inns were places where you ate, drank and collapsed upstairs in bed. Today the distinction is blurred. There are pubs along the Chalke Way that do home cooking you would marry for, and invite you and the one you're stuck with to pitch a tent at the bottom of their private garden, "Breakfast's at eight". There are inns that haven't made up a guest room since the stage coach capsized into a pot hole drowning two horses, "But we can offer you a watercress sandwich".

The main distinction between watering holes is whether they are plastic or genuine, and most of the country pubs lining our route are blissfully unspoilt by the onslaught of kitsch. There are pubs where dogs out-number drinkers, where the bar is a rude plank on a couple of up-ended whiskey casks, where the bric-a-brac is the envy of the county museum and where they still brew their own wicked potion, often legally. They are a subculture you happen upon when overtaken by thirst or lousy weather, still an important focus for the community but struggling with the new efficiency ethic demanded by conglomerate breweries. The Fox at Little Ansty, once the home of Ansty Ales, is now poshed up and has a residents' pool. It also has a magnificent collection of Toby Jugs, mucky customers who arrive by tractor and the village post office under its roof.

The ride to Wolland Hill is through dinky villages where houses, garages, walls and wells are thatched. If a cat stood still long enough, they would probably thatch that. Many of the reed crowned walls you see along the Chalke Way are vulnerable erections made of chalk ashlar (blocks) or cob, a cheap-jack conglomerate of flint, chalk, straw rubble and anything else lying around, mixed with lime plaster and poured between temporary shuttering. That they have survived the centuries is a measure of the water resistance of the reed or straw cap. While it might appear extravagant to thatch everything that doesn't move, it is actually sound building sense and it is said the reason so few Roman villas have survived the British climate is principally because they rejected organic roofs in favour of Mediteranean tiles.

These are thoroughfare villages that line the road with no

discernible centre, one community merging into another strung out along a country lane cut deep into the earth by the traffic of an age before macadam halted wheel erosion. In spring the thick hedgerows are a riot of purples, pinks and yellows, and appear to rise as high as an elephants eye over your head. Half of this is the depth of the bank, refuge to squirrels and stoats who whip out, freeze at the sight of you, then whip back to have a minor heart attack. One of the great tragedies of the English countryside during the post-war years has been the up-rooting of our **hedgerows**. At a peak rate, over 5000 miles (8000 k) a year was destroyed during the 1960's. When you reach the Cambridgeshire plains and think back to Dorset you will appreciate the full horror of the devastation there.

Today less than 2,000 miles are annually ripped out for the convenience of mechanical harvesting, still far too much, but reinstatement projects balance the figures. Some of our hedges are 1,000 years old, planted by the Saxons as estate boundaries. During the Middle Ages the practice developed slowly until the surges of the 15th and 18th Century enclosure movements, when hawthorn hedges provided cheap fencing to pen sheep and delineate arable fields. We can date our hedges by the number of plant species sheltering under their thorns. Along a 30 yard (27.5 m.) stretch, each plant species represents 100 years of the hedge's life, enabling botanists to calculate that a few with over 500 species flowering beneath the thicket were growing at the edge of the forest some 5,000 years ago.

It is not only the loss of the plant life that gives cause of concern. Hedgerows are lines of movement for animals, insects and small mammals, organic highways where they can safely truck across open country from one wood or pond to the next. They are sanctuaries for wildlife, particularly for birds. Of the 91 land species that breed in lowland Britain, 65 of them do so in hedges. They are in themselves a rich variety of woody plant species, including ash, elm, field maple, hazel, holly, oak, privet, rose, sycamore and of course hawthorn. And finally, they bind the earth and act as windbrakes. Remove sufficient hedgerows and, in exposed places, the land will become a dust-bowl, whipped up by fierce winds into sandstorms that can drown farmsteads and destroy livelihoods, as you will discover when we cross the East Anglian Brecklands. As you ride through the bushy lanes of Dorset enjoy their profundity. You will see less and less of them.

The North Dorset Downs is the sort of lush, well kept area where farmers display their old machinery like museum pieces at the entrance to their spreads, and its the sort of area where it is no surprise to find an exclusive public school. Rounding the hill out of Hinton, the valley opens into the precision trimmed grounds of **Milton Abbey**, all cricket greens, running track and headmasters tea lawn. The scene oozes privilege. The mansion is the house that Jo built and the abbey came with the land. Thrown in with the deeds were four inns, a brewery, school, shops and 100 houses comprising the medieval village of Milton that once stretched south from the abbey to the tip of the present lake.

Jo was Joseph Damer M.P. aka Lord Milton, aka the Earl of Dorchester. In 1752 Jo bought the estate. A decade later he commissioned Sir William Chambers to design a new house and Capability Brown to landscape new grounds. This was the era when an enlightened establishment was expressing concern for the lot of the poor. Philanthropic as the next member of the ruling class, Jo extended Chambers' and Browns' contract to include the creation of a modern village for his labourers, just round the corner from the old in a narrow combe leading up to Hoggen Down. It was to feature two rows of dainty cottages lining a single street where all the original community facilities would be rehoused or removed stone by stone from Milton and rebuilt in Milton Abbas.

But Joseph Damer was a nasty piece of work who was never likely to do anybody any favours. The local grammar school backed on to his mansion and, boys being boys, he was subjected to a number of pranks. They stole eggs that were ear-marked to become fighting cocks, lobbed stones down his chimney and nicked his cucumbers. Damer replied by devoting 25 years of his parliamentary career to trying to introduce a bill banishing the school to Dorchester, Blandford, anywhere but his backyard. Milton village was too close for comfort and his philanthropic plans were more about creating splendid isolation than somewhere decent for people to live. There was virulent opposition which Dammer drowned by opening the sluice gate in the Abbott's pond above the old village, flooding several residences. By fair means or foul, he bought up as many leases as he could, evicted the tenants and demolished the buildings. One day he heard the church bells ring out as he left for London. Believing they celebrated a recent victory for the village in one of the many Damer v.

The People court cases, he ordered the bells be immediately removed and sold. They were actually celebrating Guy Fawkes Day.

Milton Abbas is a weird anachronism. It makes Milton Keynes look 200 years behind the times. Turning left into the street you are immediately impressed by the brilliant white of the cottages, the breadth of the street and the open sky that for miles has been hemmed by bushes and branches over your head. Your second impression might be that this place was designed by computer and is the final twist in the tale of prisoner No. 6. Mini-mokes with little stripy awnings driven by chaps in boaters and blazers wouldn't be out of place here.

But behind the toy-town facade, the meanness of Joseph Damer continued. What appear to be spacious dwellings ,in fact houses two families living either side of a common front door and porch. Where there are two doorways, four families lived in apartments, the one building home to at least 20 people. The walls are of cob finished off with a skim of lime plaster. In their day the cottages looked grey and the grass verge a mess, but then they peeked from beneath massive chestnut trees that happily upset the uniformity. Today a lick of paint, the Fly-mo and chain-saw have transformed Milton Abbas into a living museum that is spacious and surreal, where the living still deserve our sympathy. The pressure to keep up appearances and not stick a satellite disc or giant butterfly on their property must be awesome. The final irony that snotty little boys now scamper quite freely through Joseph's former chambers will not be lost. Neither is the sense that Milton Abbas is the 18th century rural equivalent to the 1960's inner city tower blocks.

This is by far the toughest leg of the Chalke Way in terms of what's under wheel. The fields and bridleways of Dorset are well pitted and there are short sharp sections where even someone with the skills of a cyclo-cross rider will find themselves pushing. Don't panic and start thinking you have bitten of more than you can chew. That's it. With the exception of one bit of rough I know she would hate (because she loathes pigs) the rest of the Chalke Way my granny could ride. And if that sounds boring for you frog-legged lycra hunks, you will find all the excitement you need if you take every bit of rough at the break-neck speed I know your adrenaline can generate. Trouble is, you won't see anything.

Wolland Hill – Win Green

WELCOME TO THE EDGE. AFTER 29 MILES (47 KM.) FLOGGING UP HILL AND down dale through the South Dorset Downs, you have arrived at the Northern Edge where the Chalke Way finally opens into a discernible ridgeway. At a height of 853 feet (260 m.), Wolland Hill is hardly a Munro mountain but the panorama it affords across the Vale of Blackmoor is no less inspiring. On a clear day locals claim you can see across seven counties, over to the Mendips, Wales and probably Reykjavik if you squint.

This is the 'Valley of Little Dairies' 'Thomas Hardy described in *Tess of the D'Urbervilles.* 'After plodding northwards over calcerous downs and cornlands, (the traveller) suddenly reaches the verge of one of these escarpments, (and) is surprised and delighted to behold, extended like a map beneath him, a country different absolutely from that he has passed through . . . There, in the valley, the world seems to be constructed upon a smaller and more delicate scale; the fields are mere paddocks so reduced from this height their hedgerows appear a network of dark green threads overspreading the pale green of the grass. The atmosphere beneath is languorous and is so tinged with azure that what artists call the middle distance partakes also of that hue, while the horizon beyond is of the deepest ultramarine. Arable lands are few and limited; with but slight exceptions the prospect is a broad, rich mass of grass and trees, mantling minor hills and dales within the major.'

The colour of the Vale has changed since Hardy's day, redecorated in the brilliant primaries of the modern cash crops of oil seed rape and linseed. In full bloom, the contrast to the muted tones of the chalkland is quite startling. To your right the stub nose of Bell Hill leads the eye back up onto the open escarpment, virtually stripped of vegetation, and to fields so large and arching, the far side is out of sight. Everything is tinged with white, bushes and tree trunks splattered by the same relaxed brushstroke that slapped the line of the track across its back. Hardy called the hills 'colourless', but what they lack in pigment is richly compensated by their spatial dynamism.

The sweep round Iberton Hill is on tarmac, soon replaced by crushed chalk where the road drives over the edge and we take to the rough. From here until Eastcombe Wood the route exhibits all the character-

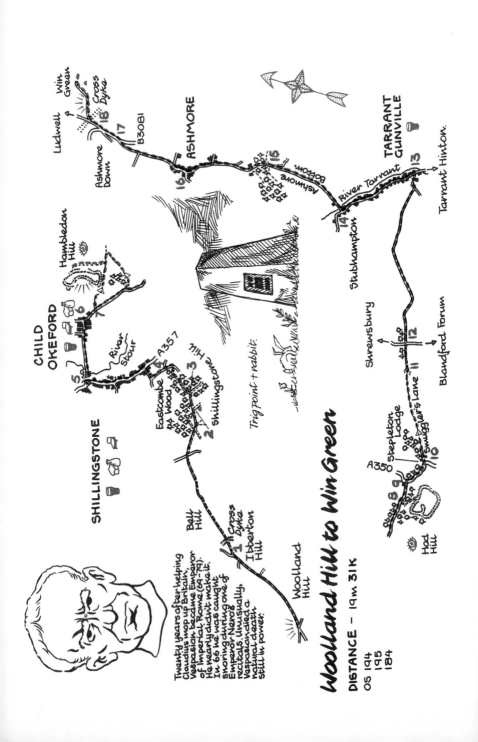

Directions

1 On corner after turn off to Ibberton, **R** onto left track through **BW** gate.
   Follow blue arrows **SO** along ridge into Eastcombe Woods.

2 **SO** where blue arrows branch right near trig point. Keep trees on left.

3 **L** at opening in woods before track sweeps right.
   Follow blue arrows downhill to road then **L**.

4 **L** at TJ. Follow road into Shillingstone then **L** onto A357 (busy road).

5 2nd **R** CHILD OKEFORD (dangerous corner turn-off).

6 **R** HANFORD **SO** to A350, unless visiting Hambledon and/or Hod Hill.

7 To Hambledon Hill, up drive to **BW**. Sign hidden by wood footpath, sign to Gold
   Hill. Follow blue arrows to hill fort and back down to Hanford.

8 To Hod Hill. **R** through farmgate then follow track. Return same route.

9 **R** BLANDFORD (busy road).

10 **L** at corner to layby next to Stepleton Lodge. **SO** up track then **BW** – Smugglers Lane.

11 **L** onto track then curve **R** onto **BW**. Keep hedge on left.

12 **SO** over road to TARRANT GUNVILLE. Follow signs into village.

13 **L** IWERNE MINSTER.

14 **R** before sharp bend and up track. ASHMORE BARN FARM. Past modern farmhouse,
   SO through two farm gates, then **SO** off track up grass valley to woods.

15 **SO** through farm gate following track up tarmac road at Well Bottom.
   SO up hill into Ashmore.

16 **R** after village pond (beware of kamikaze ducklings in spring).

17 **L** SHAFTESBURY then **R** DONHEADS.

18 **R** before descent, to broad track. WIN GREEN take highest track to viewing plate. **SO**.

Resource

SHILLINGSTONE
Pam Gowlett
Wishing Well Cottage
Main Rd
DT11 0SF
01258 860985

Bere Marsh House
DT11 9BT
01258 861133

Seymour Arms
Cookswell
DT11 0QZ
01258 860486

CHILD OKEFORD
Mrs J Langley
Bartley House
Upper St
DT11 8EF
01258 860420

Saxon Inn
Gold Hill
01258 860310

istics of the classic ridgeways. Between you and the gods there is nothing save the incessant twittering of a skylarks soliloquy and the rolling convolutions of the cloudscape. Should the sky turn angry and decide to dump on you, there is nowhere to hide. Scrabby hawthorns and immature rowans straggle beside the way in weak clumps that barely break the breeze drifting up from Blackmoor Vale or the valleys. Farm buildings are few and very far between. Either side the hill slips away in a broad arc., unblemished but for the occasional cattle path or furrowing of a wheat field. Under wheel the track has been squeezed from a tube of zinc white and left to dry. In part it is rock hard with shards of flint and chunks of chalk embedded in a setting of cracked clay and coarse grass. Elsewhere working vehicles and wet weather have combined to churn it into a mess of ruts that slip in and out of each other like the rails of a shunting yard. Here the cyclist is on his or her own. Now and again the silhouettes of a lone buzzard or handful of crows passes over head, but mostly you are left to your inner most thoughts. Fantasies of the saddle tramp, Clint, Gary or the Duke, riding the range under the big sky. Day dreams of Thelma or Louise, on the run from boredom and the law of diminishing returns. The ridgeway has the space to become whatever you want to make it, wherever you want it to be.

Joining the A357 at **Shillingstone** is a rude awakening, requiring a rapid readjustment from the carefree experience of wilderness riding to the eyes-in-the-back-of-your-head approach to survival on the blacktop. Originally called 'Shilling Ockford', the village grew up around the site of the original ford across the River Stour, then set in the heart of the oak forests of the Vale of Blackmoor. Once the centre of a profitable lime industry (the quarry is behind you cut into Shillingstone Hill) and a regular supplier of moss to Covent Garden, the village is now being shaken to its foundations by a steady stream of trucks carrying other peoples products to market.

We bring you off the chalk edge not to admire the boarded up pubs of luckless Shillingstone, but to take in the two hill forts of Hambledon and Hod Hill. After the majesty of Maiden Castle, all the other causewayed camps are bound to be a little disappointing, but if it is time for a pit stop, one of the two is certainly worth the climb. **Hambledon Hill** is rated second only to Mai Dun encompassing 10 hectares of a natural spur overlooking the Stour Valley and the strategically important ford. Originally the camp was a Neolithic settlement focused around a long barrow that still survives on the brow of the hill. During the Iron Ages it was modified and enlarged to the fort's present size, its outer defences contouring for three miles (5 km.) round the sides of the spur. Archaeologists have estimated over 30,000 timber posts were needed to build the stockade that surmounted the earthworks, which goes some way to explaining what happened to the oaks in Okeford. Further felling accounts for the 200 or so hollows pitting the site, probably the location of post holes supporting hut platforms and the Durotriges' idea of a des res.

Hambledon is certainly in a commanding position, with brilliant sight-lines for a sentinel monitoring the flow of traffic off the Downs. From the foot of the spur, the fort is considerably more intimidating than Maiden Castle, perched above the Stour like a predator poised to pounce. In the 18th century its steep ramparts encouraged General Wolfe to station his troops near Child Okeford and to use the hill as a training ground for Britain's planned assault on the Heights of Abraham and the French garrison of Quebec. A hundred years earlier it was the chosen battleground for the last stand of the **Clubmans Rising**, one of those eccentric little rebellions that give character to British history. Sick of the internicene struggle between the Cavaliers and Roundheads, the Rector of Compton Abbas (just up the road) inspired an army of what Oliver Cromwell called 'despairing yokels' to take up rakes and hoes against the two sides tearing the country apart. In 1645, 5,000 of them took then lost Castlehill near Shaftesbury. They retreated to Hambledon Hill where a depleted rabble of 2,000 yokels faced 50 of Cromwell's crack dragoons. Twelve Dorset farmers were killed in the final showdown, and 300 were imprisoned in the church at Iwerne Courtney, peeking out of the trees to the east. The rest fled. After a suitable cooling off period, Cromwell ordered the release of 'these poor silly creatures.' He had bigger heads to chop.

That two hill forts were built so close together indicates this nick in the chalk was a busy economic and social centre for the Durotriges, possibly a capital but definitely a strategic lynchpin. Hod Hill is considerably smaller than its neighbour and is situated like a cork in the neck of a broad valley cut into the chalk by the River Stour, which is still an important trade route to the south east. It was always a fort more than a settlement. Its south-east corner has never been ploughed, leaving undisturbed traces of a tightly packed warrior community and their storage pits. Farming disturbance has revealed amongst other

Celtic finds, a bronze skillet handle depicting an aggressive naked deity similar to the Cerne Giant.

Hod Hill has the unique distinction of being the only Durotrige settlement to merit further development by the conquering armies of Rome. Our old friend Vespasian was having a busy year. He arrived at Shillingstone barely days after taking Maiden Castle and duly ransacked the two hill forts. In the north-west corner of Hod Hill he set the natives to work building a fortified garrison for 600 troops . They occupied the site for twenty years, an emphatic statement to the tribes of Devon that Rome had arrived, or as Julius Caesar put it in that immortal sound-bite, 'Veni, vidi, vici.'

At Shillingstone you entered the historic hunting grounds of **Cranbourne Chase**. Again writing in *Tess,* Hardy describes the Chase as '. . . one of the few remaining woodlands of England of undoubtedly primeval date, wherein Druidical mistletoe is found on aged oaks, and where enormous yew trees, not planted by the hand of man, grew as they had grewn when they were pollarded for bows.' It must have been lovely. In 1830 an Act of Parliament opened up the Chase to forestry and most of the ancient woodland is now cleared and farmed. The long ride up Smugglers' Lane gives you a taste of what it might have been like galloping through the sun-speckled forest clutching your long bow, hot on the heels of a deer, but most of our ride is under wide open skies.

A `Chase' becomes a `Forest' when the hunting rights pass to the monarch, and Cranbourne has a history of slipping in and out of royal control. William the Conqueror gave it to his queen, who passed it on to their son Rufus who passed it to his cousin. Henry I and King John both had their hands on it for short periods, but the lordship of the Chase mainly rested with lesser earls and viscounts who bowed deep at the Royal Court. Like Sherwood Forest, Cranbourne also has a history of harbouring brigands, outlaws and smugglers. The link between Chesil Beach, the route we have taken and the Chase suggests we might well be following clandestine footsteps, heavy with the weight of booty but light enough to tip-toe passed the excisemen. In 1779 a party of Royal Dragoons were ignominiously routed by fifty smugglers travelling through the forest with a convoy of twenty laden pack horses. No doubt the local peasants were delighted. They were locked in a bloody war of attrition with the game keepers who were frantically trying to police the 101,175 hectares to prevent poaching and the enclosure of land. Adding insult to fatalities, unique laws empowered the owner of the hunting rights to levy a toll on all packhorses and waggons entering the Chase during the rutting season. Presumably the `cheminage' was to recompense his lordship for any preying eyes that might cramp his stags' style.

Today the hunting fraternity aim their sights at foxes and the herds of fallow and roe deer are studied and regulated by keepers and the Forestry Commission. The place to keep an eye out for them is **Ashmore Bottom**, north east of where the River Tarrant bubbles to the surface near Stubhampton. Before then lies **Tarrant Gunville**, one of eight villages lining the valley that pay tribute to the river by calling themselves Tarrant This, Tarrant That or Tarran T'other. These days the demand of thirsty towns has lowered the watertable and reduced the Tarrant to a trickle, but a hundred years ago the river was a torrent controlled by hatches that, when closed, flooded the lower reaches of the valley. Houses and roads were not spared the drowning, a practice designed to create water-meadows by saturating the land to bring on an early carpet of lush grazing for cattle eager to get their teeth into something more substantial than hay, the winter ration.

As you ride north back up to the ridge, you can almost feel the land getting drier, and the difference of a distance of five miles (8k.) is the difference between thick calf-high meadows and dusty stubbled pasture. These are the highlands of Cranbourne Chase, the inner sanctum of the deer, the headquarters of keepers and foresters, and the dry zone where, within living memory, water had to be carted in when underground wells failed. That said, when you emerge into **Ashmore**, Dorstes' highest village at 700ft (213m.), the first thing you clap eyes on us a village pond, white and murky from the chalk, but unaccountably full. Even in the drought of 1976, the pond managed to retain a sizeable puddle. Maybe once every twenty years it dries up, and while nobody can account for its' existence, the symbolic significance of this swallow-hole, dewpond or whatever it is has not gone unmarked by the residents of Ashmore. Traditionally they held a bun-fight when the pond disappeared, all stood around and in the hollow munching specially baked cakes. Given that twenty years is a long time between parties, they more recently celebrated their good fortune with an annual Midsummer `Filly Loo', where country dancers jigged to the strains of a fiddle band playing on a cart pushed out into the water. Presumably this was to ensure the band stayed sober.

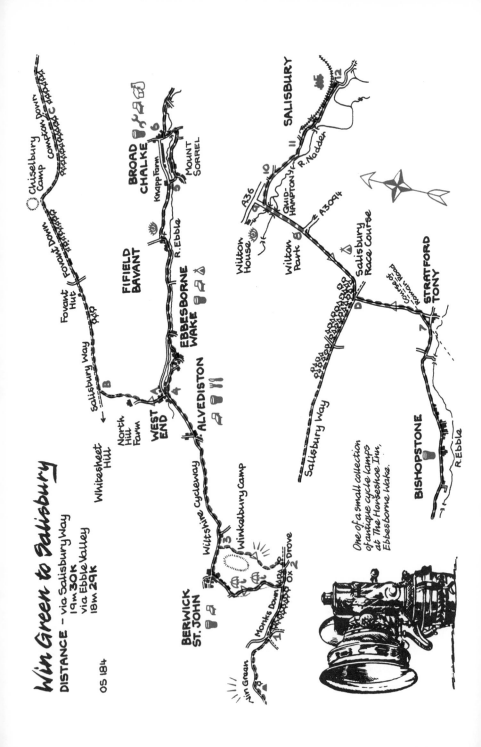

Win Green to Salisbury

DISTANCE – via Salisbury Way 19m 30k
via Ebble Valley 18m 29k

OS 184

Chiselbury Camp

Compton Down

Fovant Down

Fovant Hut

Salisbury Way

Whitesheet Hill

North Hill Farm

B

BROAD CHALKE

Knapp Farm

MOUNT SORREL

FIFIELD BAVANT

R. Ebble

EBBESBORNE WAKE

A

WEST END

ALVEDISTON

4

Wiltshire Cycleway

Winkelbury Camp

3

Monks Down

Ox Drove

2

BERWICK ST. JOHN

Win Green

1

SALISBURY

12

11

R. Nadder

10

A36

QWID-HAMPTON

Wilton House

Wilton Park

A3094

Salisbury Race Course

6

Salisbury Way

D

Rotmton Road

Bake Road

STRATFORD TONY

7

BISHOPSTONE

R. Ebble

One of a small collection of antique cycle lamps at The Horseshoe Inn, Ebbesborne Wake.

Directions

1 Branch **L** at stone car park and 5 ways junction, onto road left of trees.

2 **SO** onto Ox Drove track, then **1st L** onto **BW** through left farmgate. Follow **BW SO** down hill onto track.

3 **R** onto Wiltshire Cyclway (WCW).

Via the Ebble Valley

4 **R** before the bridge & up the hill.
L between the lorry access limitation signs into Ebbesborne Wake, then **L** again down hill to rejoin WCW.

5 **R** opposite Knapp Farm down to Mount Sorrell. Keep turning **L** through village.

6 **R** opposite Queens Head pub to rejoin WCW.

7 **L** WILTON uphill to join A to C.

Via Salisbury Way

A Over bridge & **L** at corner NORTH HILL FARM. On corner before PRIVATE ROAD, **SO** up track to ridge.

B **R** onto Salisbury Way. **SO** for 9m (14k.) crossing all roads until SALISBURY RACES.

C **SO** do not swing left where sign says BRIDLE PATH ONLY.

D **L** at SALISBURY RACES to join WCW.

8 **SO** along A3094 WILTON. Follow WCW into Salisbury.

9 **R** QUIDHAMPTON.

10 **R** LOWER BEMERTON.

11 **R** at Chapel.

12 **R** at **RA** into Salisbury. Turn to city map.

Resource

BERWICK ST. JOHN
Mrs Follett
Easton Farm
Water St
SP7 0HS
01747 828148

ALVEDISTON
The Crown Inn
SP5 5JV
01722 780335

EBBESBOURNE WAKE
The Horse Shoe Inn
BB & camping
01722 780474

BROADCHALKE
The Queens Head Inn
SP5 5EV
01722 780344

NETHERHAMPTON
Coombe Nurseries
Caravan Park
Race Plain
SP2 8PN
01722 328451
Site behind Salisbury race course. Open all year.

WILTON
Wilton House & Grounds
Open daily from Apr to Oct.
01722 743115

Win Green – Salisbury

And So, back up to the northern edge and Win Green, out of Dorset in to Wiltshire but still within Cranbourne Chase. At 909 ft (277 m.), Win Green is the highest point along the Chalke Way, and a magnet for those who like to grapple with the wind. Arrive early evening and the chances are the hill will be buzzing with kite-fliers and pilots of radio-controlled gliders. Tarry awhile because some of these guys and gals are wicked with a stunt kite and lay on a hypnotic display of aerobatics that make 'dog-fights' look like scheduled flights. Dogs do fight up here and their owners do walk, but the post-modernist approach to exercise seems to be to release the mutt from the Range Rover at the start of the track, then drive up and down until the fleabag is exhausted with the chase and ready for the pub. Henry Ford has a lot to answer for.

Look to your right as you swing onto the ridge track and you will see a clearly defined trench the Ordnance Survey marks as a **Cross Dyke**. The Chalke Way has already passed several of these ancient earthworks, but this one, cut between Quarry Bottom and the plunge in to the Nadder Valley, is the clearest example so far of the strategic siting of tribal borders across a narrow col. It is also where ancient meets modern and gets jumbled up; where a Roman road running north from Badbury Rings , here sealed in 20th century tarmac, bisects the ridgeway, a prehistoric track adopted by 18th century coach operators as one of the two routes east to Salisbury. Standing with your back to the spinney, looking east across the humps of the hills, it requires little effort of the imagination to picture a stage-coach lurching round the bend, driver gripping reins for grim life, hooves and wheels sparking on the flint, the whole caboodle trailing a cloud of billowing chalk dust.

This is the Ox Drove. The other route east is the Old Salisbury Way starting from Whitesheet Hill, the western tip of the ridge you can see running parallel and to the north of the Ox Drove. Both are extraordinary green roads. Between the two, the **Ebble Valley** cuts into the chalk and confuses those looking from on high by falling west to east, the River Ebble joining the Avon at Bodenham, south of Salisbury. Maybe this accounts for the discreet, almost private atmosphere the valley exudes. Along its length there is one road in and one road out, of no use to anybody but the residents. From off the two ridges however there are over fifty accesses into 'Chalke Valley', as parishioners call it, only a handful of which are suitable for motor vehicles. Utilising the old stage routes and the valley road, this abundance of bridleways present rough riders with a mind boggling number of variations on a theme of circuits and figure-of-eights. You could spend a week riding the big dipper of Chalke Valley and not run across your own tyre tracks. If you fancy a break from travelling, and a day or two riding *sans baggage*, this is the area to explore.

The Chalke Valley is private, as in 'tucked away' rather than 'Gerroff my land!', and while Wiltshire's sign-posting leaves a lot to be desired, the people welcome cyclists who know what they are doing. Part of the Wiltshire Cycleway runs down its length and there is even a valley fun ride, drawing historic clunkers dug out of the cowshed and hosed down for the occasion. It runs nine miles (14 km.) and calls at ten pubs (or is it the other way round?), the winner wobbling of to a free weekend at the Betty Ford Clinic (I jest!). After talking to organiser Phil Dade, we've decided not to map the off-road paradise of his neighbourhood. "Discover it for yourselves" is his message, but we do give you a choice of routes through to Salisbury Race Course. Neither is any better than the other, both are beautiful, each is very different.

If you want ruff-stuff, perfect isolation and miles of languorous pedalling under gently rustling leaves take the high road, the Old Salisbury Way. End to end it runs for 14 miles (22.5 km.) and we ride most of them. The surface is fine, in places gravelled and the views through gaps in the tunnel of trees, north to Salisbury Plain and south across Chalke Valley and the Ox Drove, are all we have come to expect. Once upon a time every mile was counted by a wayside marker for the benefit of coach passengers, and Fovant Hut, the only house still occupied on the ridge, was a staging post. In the 1500s the Earl of Pembroke, denizen of Wilton House, instigated a horse race along its length, one of the first point-to-points in the country.

The low road is equally charming and relaxed, quietly rolling down the Ebble flood plain, meandering between sweeping hills puckered with the tell-tale signs of early settlements, packtrails and medieval field systems. Our valley route differs for the Wiltshire Cycleway by wending you through Ebbesborne Wake and Mount Sorrel, two of the most delightful villages along the course of the river. The chocolate boxtop hasn't been produced that can do justice to some of these houses, with their freshly painted wattle and daub, wonderfully groomed thatches and of course, the *de rigeur* stone mushrooms set in immaculate pebble drive-ways you would dare drive on. Okay these are the domicile of commuters and home-workers, and a peek through leaded windows is like opening a spread in *'Homes and Gardens'* but there remains a sizable community who earn a crust from the surrounding land, gardens through to gallops. At Mount Sorrel water-cress is still grown in pans irrigated by the river and the amount of mud on the road suggests not too many farmers spend their day in a deck-chair getting fat off set-aside.

Thatching is the oldest building technique still practiced in Britain, certainly dating back to the Bronze Age, probably to the beginning of human time. The term applies to any roof made of vegetable matter, so the simplest of shelters covered with branches, bracken or turf (a bender) was technically thatched. With the advent of fire, living under an organic roof was like living in a tinder-box, even after the occupants had progressed from a hole in the thatch to a chimney. Tall stacks protruding well above the roof didn't appear in this country until the 13th century, by when it was forbidden to build any new thatched property in many of our big cities. As a token towards fire proofing, a lime based plaster was often applied to the roof, and in remote regions of Scotland and Wales examples can still be seen.

Each area had their own style of thatch, usually dictated by the type of material employed which in turn was dictated by what was grown locally. Aside from materials already mentioned, brushwood, water reeds, heather, wood chips and corn straw were all called into service. Today the materials are trucked, even shipped in and tend to be either water reed or corn straw. Traditionally the reed came from the Norfolk wetlands but pollution and acid rain have taken their toll to the benefit of French, Polish, Turkish and Dutch suppliers. I know for a fact the first cottage on your left as you enter Milton Abbas (the blacksmiths), is adorned with Moroccan reed. I nicked some to try and make a corn dolly in June '94 when it was laid.

Corn straw encompasses the long stems of either wheat, barley, oats or rye and is now specially grown and then harvested by damn clever combines that somehow turn the stems to all point the same way, then nips the heads off the cut crop without damaging the stalks. Of the two, Norfolk reed is more resilient, almost twice as expensive and will last a good thirty years. The stalk has a round cross-section whereas corn straw (known as Devon reed) is slightly oval and more likely to break or fracture. The ridge of the roof is often covered in sedge to increase water resistance, and the whole caboodle is usually placed under a hairnet of wire mesh to protect against birds. Unfortunately this encourages rot and a better method might be the one devised by the inscrutable Irish in the 1800's. Every two paces along the roof they placed a small clump of reed that had been soaked in whiskey. Within minutes they were walking round the house picking up legless Tweetie Pies.

In the course of our journey the general shape of thatched roofs will change, from the chunky rounded cap of the Wessex thatch to the steep pitch and sharp edges of those in East Anglia. The small county of Dorset is home to over 4,000 thatched buildings and there are nearly 50,000 in the country, most of them adorning pretty ancient properties. To pay £20,000 to have a large house re-thatched is not excessive these days, but often unaffordable, particularly if the house is a barn and comes in at twice the price. The fact that so many historic buildings survive is a tribute to the properties of organic roofs, and a boon to our national heritage. Subsidies and grants are therefore available to preserve the stock and insure them though, as always, the demand outstrips the supply. But I digress.

As you pootle down Chalke Valley, count the pubs and churches along the way. The battle between God and the Devil must have been quite a tussle in the Middle Ages, with Old Nick possibly having the upper hand. That could account for the need to erect so many splendid churches so close together, but the number of both houses is certainly a measure of how prosperous and populated this modest valley must have been. The House of God to visit is **St Martins'** at Fifield Bavant, though 'hut' would be a better description. Ten paces from the front door and you are sprawled on the alter. A mere 35 feet (10.5 m.) long, this spartan 13th century flint and stone chapel claims to be the smallest church in England. On stooping through the doorway, your retina is suddenly attacked by a kaleidoscope of psychedelic colours rushing up from the floor. Forget the architecture, this place is a gallery of exquisite country needle-point, each kneeler a little gem of the traditional country craft, each with a story more interesting than the sermon. You get the impression Peggy and Shula Archer have been stitching their hearts out.

On the way into the city, foreign visitors in particular might like to stop off at **Wilton House** and take in the opulent splendour of a very English stately home. Wilton used to be the capital of the Saxon kingdom of Wessex. On the site of Wilton Park, Alfred the Great founded a Benedictine abbey which by 1544 was dissolved and the land granted by Henry VIII to the first Earl of Pembroke. The estate has remained in the Pembroke family ever since. The original house went up in flames in 1647 but was partially saved and most of what you see is a product of Inigo Jones and John Webb trying to out French the 17th century French. The *coup de grace* are the semi-baroque state rooms. Heavy gold wall embosses drip down white walls from classically bold plaster work that frames ceiling murals rampant with swirls and twirls, organic stuff and optical illusions. As was demanded of the period the whole place is totally over the top, the mystery being how anybody was expected to live amongst such decadence without going totally bananas. Of course, this might explain a good deal about the English aristocracy.

But the Earls of Pembroke were not totally self indulgent, and in the 18th century invested heavily in the town's weaving industry. While far from being a major industry, things had been happily ticking over for at least 200 years when the then Earl brought in a French master craftsman to modernise local weavers and impart his knowledge of tufted carpet weaving. By the end of the century , the fame of Wilton carpets had extended into Europe, and the industry was looking to expand. In 1835, when the Axminster carpet factory in the Devon town of the same name went bust, Wilton bought up the redundant hand looms, carted them and a few skilled workers back to Wiltshire, and kept the name alive right up to modern times. Hand tufting was replaced by the power loom in 1958 but the quality of Wiltons and Axminsters remains the envy of Western carpet manufacturers, deserving of the Royal Warranty bestowed on the Wilton Royal Carpet Factory by the last four British monarchs.

There is an exhibition centre housed in the picturesque 17th century works and factory tours can be booked, though during the off-peak seasons you can usually gate-crash one unannounced. Hopefully it will still be there to gate-crash. As we go to publication, a battle royal is being waged between the new American owners, who want to close the works and centralise operations in Yorkshire, and the workforce haggling for a buy-out to save the factory, their jobs and 400 years of weaving at Wilton.

Salisbury – Larkhill

IN 1927, H. V. MORTON WROTE, "SALISBURY IS . . . THE ONLY EXAMPLE IN England of a town established on a hill which suddenly packed up, lock, stock, and barrel, and marched into the plain to begin again . . . It is surely the most peaceful cathedral city in England. It seems that all its tragedy was packed into the history of Old Sarum and with its removal into the valley came a delicious uneventfulness." Mr Morton couldn't have predicted the impact of the motor car.

Salisbury lies at the hub of nine major roads and though the by-pass rumbles day and night with the persistent stream of through traffic, the city itself has not been spared. Its medieval streets groan under the weight of too many cars and coaches searching for too few parking spaces in a one-way system that only serves to frustrate. Following the Wiltshire Cycleway, riders fare better than other visitors to the city, but the tragedy of questionable progress has turned a charming medieval new town into a noisey, grimey and unsavoury chaos. Or so it seems after the Chalke Valley.

The hill the town was originally established upon is **Old Sarum**, to the north of the city, which we visit out of historical sequence as we head off for Salisbury Plain. Its origin is as uncertain as that of all the other hillforts, though by the Iron Age the Celtic settlement was a fortified stronghold commanding excellent sight-lines over the valley confluence of the rivers Nadder, Wylye, Avon and Bourne. Possibly it was an inland port, before the Avon silted up. The Romans developed 'Sorviodunum' into a major trading post, with straight roads radiating out across the Downs much like wiggly ones now do from New Sarum. Then the Saxons came, then the Danes and then the Normans, each adding their bit to the 12 hectare site. Finally we have to picture a massive stone wall with regularly spaced turrets and two portcullised entrances surmounting the outer earthworks. Within, a cathedral occupies the north-east corner, the rest of the area dotted with servants quarters, kitchen gardens and pastures. An inner circle behind higher earthworks and walls contains a mighty Norman keep, the Bishop's palace and no doubt work-out areas for Knights at Arms. In totality 'Sarisberie' must have felt thoroughly secure and impregnable in the 12th century, before the clergy started to kick up a fuss.

Except for the rampant nepotism, the niggle between the royal

Salisbury to Larkhill

DISTANCE – 11m 18K
OS 184

LARKHILL

The Cursus

Stonehenge

A344

A303

Norroton Down

Springbottom Farm

Stonehenge before the stones?

MIDDLE WOODFORD

UPPER WOODFORD

LOWER WOODFORD

NERTON

LITTLE DURNFOLD

LAKE

R. AVON

R. AVON

R. AVON

Old Sarum

SALISBURY

A345

Wiltshire Cycleway

Wiltshire Cycleway

Playing Fields

School

R. AVON

Ringroad

Ringroad

Ringroad

The Chequers

Car Park

YHA

R. Avon

R. Avon

Cathedral Close

A little bit of Old Sarum in the wall of New Sarum.

Salisbury City Centre

Directions

To leave Salisbury follow Wiltshire Cycleway along bank of River Avon through estate and **L** at TJ.

1 **R** at thatched cottage on corner and across recreation ground to OLD SARUM.

2 On leaving Old Sarum, **L** before farm buildings then through gates between two farm gates. SO following track.

3 **L** before thatched cottage onto road.

4 **R** at TJ.

5 **L** before corner, down lane and onto path (dismount across bridges).

6 **R** at road.

7 **L** at telephone box, along track then follow curve of gallops SO.

8 Curve **L**, then **R** past barn then **SO** to Stonehenge.

9 **L** at A303 (fast main road). 1st **R** onto BYWAY.

10 Car Park for Stonehenge on **R**, otherwise **SO** along BYWAY.

11 Descision time – via Central Range Road or via Old Marlborough Road.

Resource

SALISBURY
Tourist Information
Fish Row
01722 334956

Mrs C Coppack
Castle Avon
15 Wyndham Rd, SP1 3AA
01722 339087

Holmhirst Guest House
Downton Rd, SP2 8AR
01722 410407

Milford Hill House YHA
Milford Hill, SP1 2QW
01722 327572

The Caravan and Camping Club
Hudsons Field
Castle Rd, SP1 3RR
01722 320713 no calls after 8pm
Close to Old Sarum.

Hayball & Co. Cycles
26-30 Winchester St
01722 331290

Outdoor Gear Ltd
17 Cross Keys
Winchester St
01722 411378

Old Sarum
Open daily
Fee to visit inner bailey, walk around outside for free.

Salisbury Cathedral
Open daily, fee optional.

Railway Information
01703 229393

LOWER WOODFORD
Mrs E Randall
Manor Farm Cottages
01722 73393

MIDDLE WOODFORD
Mrs S Cates
Great Croft
01722 73357

Stonehenge
Open 1 Apr–31 Oct, 10–6.
1 Nov–31 Mar, 10–4. Fee.

garrison and the different bishops isn't well documented. One can imagine loyalties being challenged in times of dynastic strife, while the peace was probably punctuated by arguments over water supplies, rights of access when the gates were locked and the whole question of whose was the higher authority. At the end of his tether, **Bishop Richard Poore** eventually got permission from both king and pope to move cathedral and clergy into the marshlands between the rivers south of the Norman town. A year later, in 1220, he laid the foundation stone of what has become the most painted, photographed and cooed over cathedral in the land. In the same year Bishop Poore mapped out the ground plan for the future town, arranged on a Roman style cross-grid that defined the rectangular builing areas known as `chequers'. Successive bishops drained the marshes, bridged the tributaries and built earthern defences around the embrionic town. By the end of the century, New Sarum was attracting trade off the great western route and had grown into a busy civic centre that needed a mayor. Old Sarum meanwhile was quietly being deserted.

If the lead was taken by religion, commerce quickly took over the baton in the 15th century and ran with it all the way to the bank. The chequers are studded with splendid Elizabethan houses, now shops or pubs, built for the wealthy wool-merchants and clothiers who traded at one of the four medieval market crosses in the city. The craft workers' cottages lining Castle Street are futher evidence of the large wool industry that powered Salibury for over 400 years, but even then the focus of attention rarely shifted from the cathedral and its Close. This is what makes Salisbury a city. Whatever you feel about the Church, its architecture and the blood that was shed to defend the faith, do go out of your way to sit on the grass and gaze up at the glittering spire.

'The spire of **Salisbury Cathedral** has that power to challenge and to comfort which only the very greatest works possess. Whether you see it from miles away in the open country or from across the Avon (the view Constable immortalised), in sunshine or storm, at dusk or daybreak, you will be strangely insensitive if you are not moved every time. To give orders of great merit to buildings is to risk the wrath of man, but this spire is, for me, the most perfect single feature possessed by any of them.' Patrick Cormack is less enthusiastic about the rest of the building but it is easy to see why so many artists have tried to capture the cathedral on canvas or film.

Built from start to finish to Bishop Poore's blueprint, the stonemasons were unencumberd by previous buildings or earlier ground plans. They were starting from scratch, with none of the left over bits and bobs other cathedral developers had to work around. A model inside gives you some idea of what a monumental and inspiring task it must have been. Although the complex of cloisters, chapter-house and the spire took nearly a hundred years to complete, there is an integrity and balance in the Gothic design that makes this the wedding cake of all English cathedrals, intricate and pretty, if a bit rich.

Inside it is a grave disappointment. For a start, while maintaining that 'No payment is required or expected', the entrance way is designed to prise the recommended fee from the tightest wallets, but don't let that prevent you from striding passed with a token payment. Many of the original internal features have been destroyed by 'improvers' like James Wyatt who, in the 1790's, removed the screen, rearranged fixtures and fittings and gave the vaulting a once over with a coat of lime wash. During the Reformation the stained glass windows were smashed, later replaced by plain glass that makes the interior unexpectedly light and breezy. Whilst killing the broody, slightly threatening atmosphere associated with such palaces of worship, the lack of vibrant glazing helps to emphasize the sheer brilliance of the **Prisoner of Conscience Window** in the Trinity Chapel. Brilliant in its design and execution, dark and contemplative in its colours, this gem of a stained glass window is the work of French master craftsman Gabrile Loire. It was dedicated in 1980 and is a symbol of the important work the diocese does in the field of international human rights. Where else but at Salisbury would one find the first all-girl choir?

In its own way equally wonderful, particularly to those in love with cogs and chains, is the timepiece dated 1386. Almost certainly the oldest working mechanical clock in the world, it takes a cyclists' understanding of design simplicity and the power of rhythm to really get off on this exhibit. Equally compelling in this vast emptiness are the pigeons fluttering around the transepts. A jolly verger once informed me they regularly laid poisoned bait, but since it was Easter and the time of the Ascension, they thought they'd leave them to fly around for a few days, just in case.

The beautiful settting in which the cathedral sits was an integral part of Bishop Poore's original master plan. though in the Middle Ages the lawn was a graveyard and the whole **Close** chopped into little bits of wet bogland by a stinking lattice of open ditches that frequently overflowed into the cathedral. The wall was built in 1327 to protect the hierachy of the Church from the thronging massses, thronging with intent to throttle corruption out of the institution . Their Worships still lock the gates at night. It was built of stone recycled from the evacuated cathedral up on the hill at Old Sarum, and in places incongruous Roman or Saxon carvings are cemented out of context where they once would have been the fine detail of a fine edifice. The ground plan and a few walls of the old cathedral can still be seen at the hill fort, as can a reconstructed 'ruin' of the Keep and Bishop's Palace.

When you finally get there what is most striking about **Old Sarum** is its size. After Hambledon Hill and Maiden Castle this is a baby. Particularly during the Norman tenancy, one imagines there was little room for the plebs, who probably lived in a sprawling shambles stretching down to the river and ran like hell up from the river when the alarm rang out. By 1540 the site was a ruin but as late as the 19th century Old Sarum still retained two M.P.s to the Houses of Parliament, one of whom was its owner. It was the 'rotten borough' that returned William Pitt, Earl of Chatham and P.M. in the 18th century, but as democracy goes, you couldn't quibble with this exceptional example of proportional representation. At the time, the only residents were two shepherds. There are now no residents except stray sheep and the wheel has turned full circle. The peace and quiet and 'delicious uneventfulness' that H. V. Morton found in Salisbury has shipped out and moved back to Old Sarum where it is only occasionally upset by underwhelmed foreign toursits who can't make head nor tail of the site.

Our direction now is north, along the **Upper Avon Valley** where the river flows in middle age, broader than the flighty young thing issuing from the Vale of Pewsey, but not as rambling as the senior citizen that meanders south of Salisbury through the Dorset heathlands. According to Ron Curtis of the National Rivers Authority, 'the River Avon and associated ditch system is one of the most important in Britain for the diversity of plants and animals which it supports.' Its upper catchment area is home to over 200,000 people, many of whom play an active role in making this the most conservation-rich river system in the country, with a budget of nearly £15 million in 1994-95 for protection programmes. Here the Avon is thick with reeds, rushes and the pink bouquets of waterside weeds. Voles stroll across water lillys like reluctant office workers returning from lunch. Swans swan around pretending they don't know they're the sexiest thing in webbed feet. An hour spent dossing on the bank will exhaust your powers of anthropomorphism. This could be the Wind in the Willows country, but it isn't, for this is 'General Country'.

We are on the gravelpath leading to the army's playground up on Salisbury Plain. As you will discover, we are not talking a handful of tanks and a couple of Nissen huts here. Even in these days of military cut backs the turnover of personnel passing through to service the garrisons and training schools must be quite staggering. Inevitably, some fall in love with the area and stay, or return after they have been demobbed someplace else. Thus South Wiltshire is full of retired Majors, Colonels, Brigadiers and old Generals. Check out the gardens, those that aren't walled. Regiments of smart foxgloves, battalions of lupins and squads of delphiniums along the well patrolled herbacious borders. It's hard to break the discipline of a lifetime.

Of course the valley isn't simply a place where old warhorses are put out to graze. Above the water meadows the hillside is thick with wheat and barley during the season, and as you climb up to the plain, gangly thoroughbreds pace up and down spacious paddocks searching for fresh shoots to tear off and chomp. In 1826, the famous traveller William Cobbett rode through and recorded that he felt ,'deep shame, as an Englishman, at beholding the general extreme poverty of those who cause this vale to produce such a quantity of food and rainment. I verily believe it to have the worst-used labouring people on the face of the earth.' One wonders what he would make of the gentrification of labourers' cottages, the Mercs parked half on half off the manicured verge and the diversifications into the equine leisure industry?

From one side of Salisbury to the other and the detail of thatched roofs has already changed. Here they are more ornate than in Dorset of the Chalke Valley, frequently sporting scallops and points at the foot of the ridge and decorated with a cross-hatch or trim of hazel twigs. This is very much a quirk of the thatcher's, as are the straw pheasants, peacocks, foxes and rooks that adorn the apex. These corn dollies were traditionally a good luck charm for a full harvest and were made from the last sheaf of corn loaded onto the final waggon of the previous summers harvest. They are a pig to make, as my efforts with the

Morrocan reed proved, and have become a show piece of the skill of the thatcher. When you cross the Vale of Pewsey, look out for the family of ducks strutting along the ridge of Manor Farm in Broad Street.

As you climb the sweeping gallops up to **Normanton Down**, you have to be emotionally retarded (or totally knackered) not to get a little excited by the knowledge that the greatest megalithic monument in the world, Stonhenge, lies just over the brow of the hill. As a prelude, the horizon is lined with a string of barrows - bell, bowl, pond and disc-barrows, silhoueted against the sky like samples in some Bronze Age funeral directors' catalogue. To judge from the relics uncovered, these are individual tombs for the master class of Celt, dating back some 4,000 years. Lesser beings were disposed of in communal barrows (like the West Kennet long barrow we visit later), though within 500 years the fashion had changed and everybody who was anybody was being cremated. Two more turns of the crank and suddenly there it is, framed between the edges of the green road leading straight to it. **Stonehenge**, the jewel in the crown of English Heritage, or as a dear friend of mine put it, "Is that it!?".

For anybody who has only seen paintings or photographs of the henge, the real McCoy is bound to be something of a let down. This is simply because those images rarely include human beings walking amongst the stones and are frequently captured with a telephoto lens or placed under a vast sky (like our front cover). Without the benefit of a comparative scale, the imagination picures a veritable monster of a monument with lintels the height of a four storey building. Rising from a plain apparently the size of the Sahara, they also cunningly omit the two horrendous roads that whap either side of the tightly fenced triangle the poor thing is caged in. The helicopters, police cars and security guards that fend off hippies, Druids and others who have nothing but respect for the place are also omitted, and while we all apppreciate the need to cater for and contain the erosive impact of rampaging day-trippers, it is not until you see the facilities that you realise how tacky the complex is. In brief the site is a little sad, the monument cute rather than impressive, and the whole experience rather bitter-sweet.

But those who have been before will tell you the way to approach the debacle is to contain your disappointment, buy a ticket and plant yourself within the compound some way from the tarmac path. There you can take your time over the megaliths, let them seep in, and get to grips with the surrounding landscape as your mind slowly comes to terms with the shock of finding yourself in the middle of Piccadilly Circus. Stonehenge is a remarkable edifice, fully deserving its status as a World Heritage site, on a par with the Pyramids. It would be a shame to be put off by things that won't survive a fraction of the lifetime of the henge.

'Henge' is a saxon word, meaning 'hanging', a term that was applied to all stone circles in the 1920's despite few of them having lintel formations. It is thought Stonehenge started out as 'Earthwork' some 3,500 years ago. The circular bank and ditch were higher and deeper than the present remains and probably encompassed a large wooden building, some say covering the whole site. A single causeway fed into a straight track shooting off to the north east, now known as **The Avenue**. A thousand years later two concentric circles of Welsh bluestone were planned for the centre of the earthwork, but only two semi-circles were erected, along with the **Heel Stone** at the mouth of the causeway (the stone next to the fence). Phase Three was held up a mere 500 years at the Planning Office before the sarsen stones were rolled in and planted in a large circle supporting a continuous ring of lintels. Within that, five trilithons (the big jobs) were raised to form a horseshoe, open side pointing to the entrance. A bit later the old bluestones were recut and arranged in an oval within the henge, but that didn't work, so a few hundred years after that they were rearranged into a circle within the sarsen circle and a horseshoe within the trilithon horseshoe.

How do we know this? Well, obviously there is no way we can be certain the ancients planned a full bluestone circle but ran out of steam, materials or sub-contracters and had to make do with a couple of semi-circles. Similarly the classic story of Neolithic hairies rowing and dragging the stones almost 200 miles (321 km.) from the Preseli mountains of Wales is a bit of informed speculation, as valid as the other theory that they were glacial deposits found locally, like the sarsen stones. What we do know is this was no ordinary stone henge. As the tallest, uncapped trilithon clearly showns, these stones were 'dresssed', shaped and smoothed by chipping away with hammer-stones or antler picks. The lintels were linked end to end by tongue-and-groove joints and fitted snuggly onto the uprights by means of mortice-and-tenon joints. From bottom to top the uprights get thinner and the lintels thicker. Then there's the alignment, with the entrance and Avenue pointing to where the sun rises on Midsummer's Day (well roughly). And the setting. Look around and wherever the eye falls there is a lump or a line or a ditch that suggests this down was more than a dot on the Neolithic map. Whatever was going on here was pretty spectacular.

The final stage of building was in 1957 when Prof. Richard Parkinson and his crew restored the ruin to match its 18th century appearance, possibly accounting for why the present monument does not match Turner and Constable's paintings of the same. Aside from a stray reference by the contempory Greek writer Hecateus to the henge as a temple dedicated to Apollo, we have to warp-drive forward to the 16th century before there is any documentation of what this mysterious work originally looked like. We know stones were broken up and used to fill potholes or build walls, and that Avebury henge was pillaged to the benefit of Stonehenge. It follows that some of what you are looking at is fiction though by no means as fanciful as the theories expounded for the circle's purpose.

The **Druid** connection propounded three hundred years ago by antiquarian John Aubrey has stuck and is nutured by present day week-end pagans. Unfortunately the henge had been around at least a thousand years before this order of Celtic priests came into existence. They might have adopted Stonhenge, in the same way the Romano-British did later, but even that is unlikely. Their polydemonous belief in elves, gnomes and the power of sacred animals like hares and cocks is better suited to ceremonies in a natural setting such as Cranbourne Chase. At any rate there are no obvious indications Stonehenge had anything to do with religious worship, though there are plenty of hidden signs that it lies at the heart of a powerful energy grid. Dowsers have mapped no less than 27 lines of hidden energy running to or from the centre of the circle. Make of that what you will. Similarly dear old Alfred Watkins had a field day with the site, plotting ley-lines left, right and always through the centre.

The idea that Stonehenge was a Neolithic astronomical observatory is equally debunked by archeological records and alignments that simply don't and probably never did. But the fact of not knowing is half the excitement of the place. It encourages the imagination to go walkabout and allows for possibilities the modern corporate mind just can't get it's head round. From a distance, with the guards, the choppers, the fencing it looks like a scene from *The Day the Earth Stood Still*. Presume it's hostile until proven otherwise.

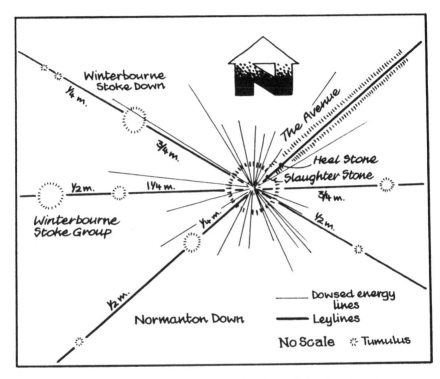

Plan of leylines and energy lines located by dowsing radiating from Stonehenge

For my part, the local Wiltshire explanation of how and why is the most satisfying. One night, up to his old tricks again, the Devil threw down the henge to confuse us mortals. As he flew of sniggering that nobody would know how it appeared, up popped a priest and said `Ahha, that's more than thee canst tell!'. In a fit of rage Lucifer turned and hurled one last stone. The priest dodged but it clipped him on the back of his foot. That was and is the Heel Stone. Full stop. End of explanation.

A couple of small points before we head off to Salisbury Plain. For all the information boards and notices, English Heritage neglects to mention Stonehenge closes at 6 pm, so don't wait till you are moved off the circle if you want to buy postcards. The shop will be shut. And if you hope to camp wild around here, forget it. The police will have you down the cop-shop and blood tested before you can say,"I'm a traveller, not a Traveller!" Finally ,at the time of writing, central government has pledged the two roads sandwiching the henge will be ripped up and grassed over (no mention of the ruddy great scar in the hill to the east). There are three options for alternative routes. A detour south is extremely unpopular with the Tory voters in the Upper Avon Valley. A £250 million tunnel is abhorrent to the Treasury, Chancellor and all who try to put a price on the priceless. That leaves a northern route, through Fargo Wood and across the track you take up to Larkhill. Amongst other ancient earthworks, the new road could destroy **The Cursus**, another exraordinary Neolithic mystery. 2,625 feet long (800 m) and the shape of a cheroot, The Cursus is thought to have been either the religious centre before Stonehenge or a ceremonial race course. This monument is quite unremarkable on the ground, but is that any excuse? Start painting your placards now.

Larkhill – Vale of Pewsey

CENTRAL GOVERNMENT BEGAN BUYING UP SALISBURY PLAIN FOR WAR GAMES straight after the Boer War. In 1897 they took possession of the area east of the River Avon and by 1987 the Ministry of Defence had charge of ten percent of the County of Wiltshire, about the size of the Isle of Wight. End to end the training area is 25 miles (40k.) long and 10 miles (6 km.) deep and is the principle training ground in the country, used by air and land units from the U.K., Europe and the USA. Of the six in the country, **Salisbury Plain** is the only one suitable for use by armoured divisions. Live firing by heavy artillery takes place roughly 340 days of the year, and by 1990 it was estimated over nine million large-calibre rounds had whizz-banged across the land. Surrounding the plain there are five garrison towns, along with two of the largest training schools in NATO for artillery and infantry, and a couple of 'trials organisations' who presumably use the area to find out if the latest method of killing one's fellow man or woman actually works. Between them, at the last count, they employ about 14,000 soldiers. Then there's the civil servants who work with them, and the civilians who work for them, and the farmers who rent off them, and . . . this operation is big!

For your average pacifist Salisbury Plain is probably one stop away from Purgatory and you might wonder why in the name of Gandhi we bring you this way. Firstly, almost certainly the Neolithics lugged the sarsen stones for Stonehenge across the plain from Overton Down, east of Avebury, which we will soon visit. Secondly, our route has followed Vespasian's march of conquest from hillfort to hillfort, and while it is easy to dismiss this bloody episode as ancient history, the actions of Rome are not a million miles from the recent actions of Serbia. Every era has its little fascists and every country the need for conventional defence or peace-keeping forces, which might be a sad indictment of the human condition but what's new? This opportunity for a peek behind the lines puts a human face on the military machine. It is hard to pedal passed the married quarters at Larkhilll and not feel sorry for the families of squaddies who could be asked to sacrifice their lives to preserve the status quo. Frankly, they are living in slums. That is the status quo.

But the main reason for trucking you across Salisbury Plain is

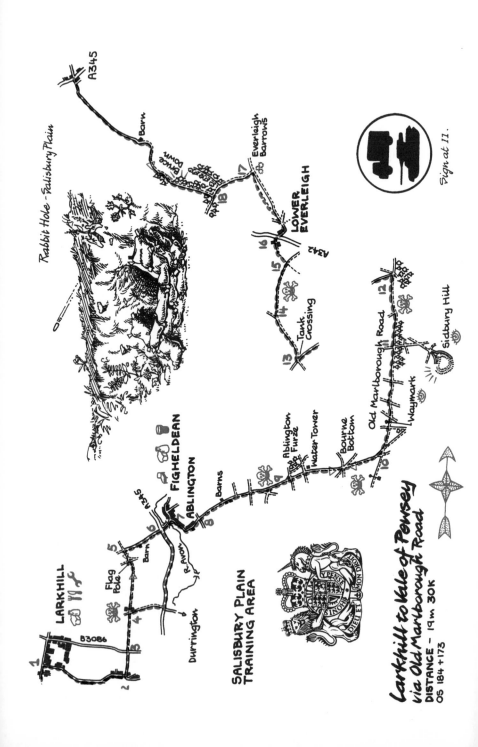

Rabbit Hole - Salisbury Plain

A345

Barn

DOWN
DOWN

Everleigh
Barrows

18

17

LOWER
EVERLEIGH

16

A342

15

14

Tank
Crossing

13

12

Sidbury Hill

Old Marlborough Road

Waymark

Ablington
Furze

Water Tower

Bourne
Bottom

10

9

FIGHELDEAN

ABLINGTON

Barns

8

7

A345

6

Barn

R. AVON

5

Flag
Pole

4

LARKHILL

B3086

1

2

3

Durrington

SALISBURY PLAIN
TRAINING AREA

DIEU ET MON DROIT
HONI SOIT QUI MAL Y PENSE

Sign at 11.

Larkhill to Vale of Pewsey
via Old Marlborough Road
DISTANCE - 19m 30k
OS 184 + 173

Directions

1 **R** opposite army married quarters.
2 **L** at phone box TOMBS ROAD.
3 **SO** DURRINGTON SPORTS GROUND.
4 If red flag flying, **R** then **L** at A345. Otherwise **SO** (Danger Area).
5 After flag pole and CROSSING C, **R** in valley onto **BW**.
  Pass barn. (Danger Area).
6 **R** if on A345, otherwise **SO** FIGHELDEAN.
7 **R** ABLINGTON.
8 **SO** STOP.
9 **SO** heading for water tower, across stone road and onto TRACK.
10 **L** onto broad dusty tank track. This is the **1st L** after Bourne Bottom.
  Look right for distant sentry post, put back to it and **SO** up Old Marlborough Road.
11 To Sidbury Hill – **R** between plantations at truck 'n' tank sign.
  Head for gap in trees around Sidbury Hill and return same way.
12 **L** onto road.
13 **R** at tank crossing between yellow and black posts. THROUGH TRACK.
14 Keep right of two hawthorn trees then **SO** up combe.
15 **L** onto tractor track with hawthorns lining right edge. **SO** to A342.
16 **R** then **L**, then **SO** past houses onto track.
  At brow of hill, head for barrows across open field.
17 Join track at barrows then **L**.
18 **R** through gate before track enters wood. **L** at field and along track through trees.
  Keeping hedge on left, **SO** to A345.

Resource

FIGHELDEAN
Vale House
SP4 8JJ
01980 70713

because it is a magnificent wilderness and, ironically, the largest nature reserve in the country. There are 13 sites of Special Scientific Interest within the 37,637 hectares as well as 1,700 Neolithic, Roman and Medieval remains. These are protected by the Defence Land Agent and by three of the military's own Conservation Groups, voluntary groups of mixed service and civilian membership. They keep exact records of the flora and fauna, and were proud to inform us a new variety of wild iris had recently been discovered in the Training Area. In fact the presence of the army has effectively kept this chunk of sweeping chalkland wild, out of the clutches of the developers and motorway builders who would otherwise scar the landscape for at least the rest of our lifetime.

You have two choices. The route up the Central Range Road from the Bustard Hotel can only be travelled certain evenings and some weekends. Even then an unexpected brushfire or military breakdown could keep it closed. You must contact the Defence Land Agent at Durrington for the lowdown (see Resource). They are very helpful but this does make planning your journey a little tricky, so we include an alternative route, open at all times, across the eastern portion of the Training Area. Dipping and diving over Figheldean Down, this choice picks up the **Old Marlborough Road** outside the Danger Zone and the live firing, but if you picture something like the Old Salisbury Way, think again.

Out here there is nothing save the gently undulating scrub, criss-crossed by enough dusty tank roads to get really lost. Follow the directions closely. A barrier, flag and sentry post blocks the entrance to the Danger Zone, so there is little chance of straying into a rogue bullet, but that still leaves a dangerous expanse of no-go area in which to flounder. Shelter is sparse, though the army is proud of reinstating several hectares of indigenous broad leaf trees, principally to assist military training. We use them to assist route finding, but once you are on the Old Marlborough Road, the excitement starts. Whatever else the boys do on the plain, they put a lot of energy into maintaining public rights of way, and like as not you will come across a gaggle of engineers with earth movers and bulldozers repairing damage to a wonderful stretch off-road the Tour of Britain could happily pound down.

Then, behind the crest of the hill, a dust storm suddenly wells up. The racket of skylarks ominously stills and a rapido klack-klack-klack reaches a crescendo as a small convoy of missile carriers looms up over the brow. In the sky above a whirly-bird swings into sight and behind you there is an echoing boom that sounds like thunder, but you know isn't. In a plantation to your right there's a movement as a camouflaged radio operator makes a run for a better vantage point. Slowly your eyes adjust and the wood is littered with tanks and squaddies. "Hell! What is this?"

Just keep on trucking. Unless you are way off course, the lads will ignore you, and carry on playing Kelly's Heroes, but drink in the scene. This is the closest most of us will get to the military in action and quite honestly, given we know there is no enemy, it looks damn good fun. And the context couldn't be more fitting. To your right the giant hump-back striped with chalk tracks is yet another hillfort, Sidbury Hill, now a tangled mass of almost impenetrable undergrowth and ancient beeches whose grandparents were probably pissed on by Roman legionaires. It is an easy climb on excellent dirt tracks to the top where you can see for miles and miles and kilometres (if you are metric). Salisbury Plain is unique and, weather allowing, this ten minute detour is not to be missed.

But for the elements in the raw, take the **Central Range Road**, which actually starts on tarmac and only gradually merges into packed stone. This charges across the Larkhill Artillery Range where you will see only scant remains of military action - the odd hulk of a Churchill tank, a patch of charred land, maybe a formation of personnel carriers lined up on Rushall Down like pawns on a chess board awaiting the big guns. Either side large notices shout "Do not do this or that!". Read and inwardly digest. These guys don't shoot paint-balls and whatever the temptation, stick to the straight and narrow. There should be no temptation because, by virtue of the hours it is open to the public, there is nothing going on out here. The occasional traumatised rabbit or shell-shocked deer might lurch along in front of you for a while, but outside of that the thrill of the range road is it's tingling isolation.

You might imagine a landscape like Beirut without the ruins, but this part of the Plain is more like a Pennine moor without the peat bogs. It might have been several thousand millennia ago, but you can still picture the plain as a sea bed. The colours are all wrong but the contours are definitely maritime, current forms rather than river. Coarse grasses have overwhelmed the dainty primroses and clematis that add colour to Figheldean Down. Regular clumps of scruffy

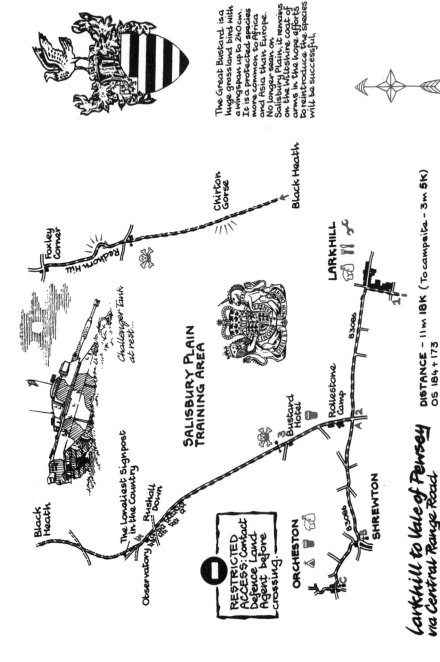

The Great Bustard is a huge grassland bird with a wingspan up to 240cm. It is a protected species more common to Africa and Asia than Europe. No longer seen on Salisbury Plain, it remains on the Wiltshire coat of arms in the hope efforts to reintroduce the species will be successful.

Foxley Corner

Redhorn Hill

Chirton Gorse

Black Heath

SALISBURY PLAIN TRAINING AREA

Challenger Tank at rest...

The Loneliest Signpost in the Country

Rushall Down

Observatory

Black Heath

RESTRICTED ACCESS: Contact Defence Land Agent before crossing.

ORCHESTON

Bustard Hotel

Rollestone Camp

LARKHILL

B3086

SHREWTON

B3086

Larkhill to Vale of Pewsey
via Central Range Road

DISTANCE – 11m 18K (To campsite – 3m 5K)

OS 184 + 173

Directions

1 SO then **L** at TJ after MEDICAL CENTRE.

2 **R** BUSTARD.

3 After Bustard Hotel, SO through sentry post onto BUSTARD VEDETE (Danger Area).

4 Curve **R** DEVIZES, through sentry post then SO all the way to road at foot of Redhorn Hill (Danger Area).

Via Stonehenge Touring Park

A SO to Shrewton.

B **R** then **R** again ORCHESTON.

C **R** at church ORCHESTON ONLY. Campsite on right after pub.

Resource

ORCHESTON
Stonehenge Touring Park
Near Shrewton
SP3 4SH
01980 620304
Open all year.

DURRINGTON
Ministry of Defence
Land Agent
Estate Office
SP4 8AF
01980 65269
If planning the Central Range Road route, it's important to contact the above. They will be able to give times when the army are not using the area and when it is safe to cross. Remember do not stray from the road. There are unexploded shells out there!

hawthorn spot the area, the odd iris gasps for air and as far as the eye can see, ours is the only road.

The real drama is overhead in an expanse of open sky so big you can see the earth's curvature. Of course the best of times is the worst of times, when a storm is brewing. In the distance a grey sheet angling down from a wodge of angry black clouds marks the approaching deluge. Immediately above, the setting sun fights a rear guard action, streaming through billowing clusters frantically trying to close the gaps and muster stragglers. Between the two a solid mass of shades of grey is sliding towards you with constantly changing hues and contours. Now it's the face of a gargoyle, now Thor's hammer threatening to strike lightening. Being dumped on is nobody's idea of fun, but on the kind of hot sultry evening the chalklands specialise in, this is the place to get drenched in a T-shirt and shorts and thoroughly enjoy it.

The Plain is also the setting for the opening scene of Thomas Hardy's *Return of the Native*. In a wonderfully eerie description of what he named Egdon Heath, Hardy captures the strange relationship between the land and the firmament as night falls. Either side of the Upper Avon Valley you will experience this phenomena, and while I'm sure it must occur elsewhere in Britain, the sheer expanse of the heath and your insignificance within it adds a unique Hammer Horror dimension. What happens, put simply, is that long before night should fall, the land appears shrouded in darkness while the sky continues to enjoy the full flood of day. It's as if the heath has soaked up the early wash of sky-grey and continues to sponge it up as the evening progresses, until the Plain is pitch black and the heavens still brilliant white. 'Looking upwards, a furze-cutter would have been inclined to continue work; looking down he would have decided to finish his faggot and go home.' Ignore the rest of the book if you will, but tuck into the first few pages of *Return*. You might find it becomes your travel reading.

Whichever you choose (and you could do a circuit), arriving at the northern edge of the plain is a bit of a relief. Before you stretches what Cobbet called a' land of plenty', the **Vale of Pewsey**, a patchwork of fields and villages sewn together with hedgerows and lanes. A couple of loose threads, the Great Western Railway and the Kennet & Avon Canal, stray east to west and the back drop is the now familiar whaleback of a chalk escarpment and the Marlborough Downs. We are back in the land of the living, but your selection across Salisbury Plain predetermines your route across the Vale. The western leg is all road work but virtually traffic free, twisting and turning towards the somewhat unimaginative White Horse cut into the side of Walkers Hill in 1812. The eastern leg is on and off-road, featuring the more attractive and exciting plunge off the plain. If you want my opinion, just to be awkward, the Central Range Road is preferred for crossing the Training Area, and the Wilcot line for crossing the Vale.

Fat lot of help that is.

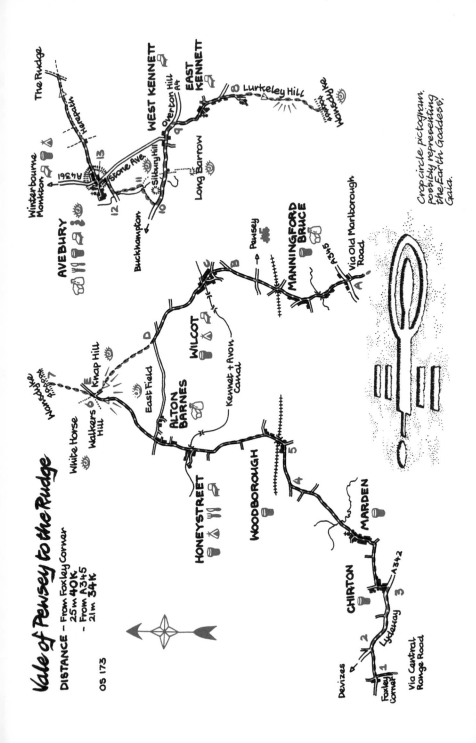

Vale of Pewsey to the Rudge

DISTANCE – From Foxley Corner
    25m 40K
    – From A345
    21m 34K

OS 173

The Rudge

WINTERBOURNE
MONKTON

AVEBURY

WEST KENNETT

EAST KENNETT

Herepath

A4361

Stone Ave.

Silbury Hill

Overton Hill

Long Barrow

Buckhampton

Lurkeley Hill

Wansdyke

White Horse

Walkers
Hill

Knap Hill

East Field

ALTON
BARNES

WILCOT

Kennet + Avon Canal

Pewsey

MANNINGFORD
BRUCE

A345

Via Old Marlborough
Road

HONEYSTREET

WOODBOROUGH

MARDEN

CHIRTON

Lydeway

A342

Devizes

Foxley
Corner

Via Central
Range Road

Crop circle pictogram, possibly representing the Earth Goddess, Gaia.

Directions

From Central Range Road

1 **R** at cottage.
2 **R** onto A342 UPAVON (busy road).
3 **L** CHIRTON then **R** MARDEN.
4 **R** WOODBOROUGH.
5 **L** WOODBOROUGH then **SO** up between Walkers and Knap Hills.
6 **L** through farm gate then **R** keeping fence on right. RIDGEWAY LINK PATH (RLP).

From Old Marlborough Road

A **R** then
B **L** MANNINGFORD BRUCE.
C **L** WILCOT.
D **L** ALTON.
D **SO** onto track at sharp left bend.
E **SO** across road, through farm gate then **R** keeping fence on right RLP.
7 **SO** across Wansdyke Path RLP.
8 Merge with road then **SO** through village to A4.
9 **L** at A4 CALNE (fast busy road).
10 **R** into Silbury Hill Car Park. **BW** in right corner.
11 Over bridge then **L**.
12 **R** follow A4361 round **L** into Avebury henge (busy road)
13 **SO** between cottages onto Herepath. NO THROUGH ROAD.

Resource

HONEYSTREET
Brenda & Fred Trowbridge
Well Cottage
Near Pewsey
01672 851577

June & Adrian Potts
The Barge Inn
SN9 SP5
01672 851705
Camping.

ALTON BARNES
Village store/PO.
Photos of crop circles in shop.

WILCOT
Oak Cottage
SN9 5NR
01672 63617

The Golden Swan
SN9 5NR
01672 62289
BB & camping

WEST KENNETT
Mrs Rendle
Silbury Hill Cottage, SN8 4EY
01672 539416

EAST KENNETT
Mrs A Rivett
Ridgeway House
01672 861520
BB & camping

AVEBURY
The Great Barn
01672 539425

Mrs J Fry
The Old Vicarage, SN8 1RF
01672 539362

The Red Lion
01672 539266
BB & Food

Alexander Keiller Museum.
Open daily, 10am – 6pm. Fee

WINTERBOURNE MONKTON
Mrs Mantock
Avenue Farm, SN4 9NW
01672 3338
BB & camping

Vale of Pewsey – The Rudge

IT WOULD BE LOGICAL TO THINK THE VALE OF PEWSEY IS A VALE CUT BY THE River Pewsey. In fact it is a very subtle hanging valley and there isn't a River Pewsey. All streams feed south into the River Avon. Once it was a chalk arch linking the downs of Marlborough and Salisbury Plain, but a few tens of millions of years after the sea receded, rain, frost and river erosion caused the arch to crack, splinter and collapse, leaving a broad fertile depression of gault clay covered with green-sand. The Vale has always had a reputation for good farming and high yields, and the bulk of the villages are still agricultural communities, often working in ancillary industries like the curing of ham. In the passed hundred years the area has been depopulated and many of the parishes are now served by the same minister 'gigging' from church to church. But there are no ghost villages like in the Pennines or South Wales. Each is an odd mish-mash of ancient and modern, with picturesque corners and garish eye-sores, thrown together and tied by ribbons of velvet grass verges and endlessly weeded borders. Window boxes are the rage around here and the Best Kept Village award is hotly contested.

We are back in an Area of Outstanding Natural Beauty, dotted with conservation zones like surrounds the village of Wilcot. We are also in the land of 'The Moonrakers', named after a folk tale located in the village of Bishops Cannings, a couple of miles off our route. One day, so the story goes, the excisemen were sniffing around when they came across a couple of yokels apparently trawling the village pond with their hay-rakes. They were actually trying to recover kegs of smuggled brandy hurriedly hidden underwater when the villagers first heard the excisemen cometh. The two lads thought the law had left. In reply to the officials' enquiry the rogues pointed at the moon reflected in the lake and quickly explained, "Zomebody 'ave lost thic thur cheese and we'm a-rakin' fo'un in thic thur pond." The excisemen guffawed and galloped off. They couldn't wait to tell their colleagues about the nutters in the Vale of Pewsey.

We come from Nottingham where exactly the same tale is told of the 'Wise Fools of Gotham', except ours is part of a village conspiracy to fend off King John's taxmen. In Germany and Poland there are similar yarns, but what they all have in common is an isolated rural community located in a broad valley lying between two administrative centres, in this case Devizes and Marlborough. Before the bicycle and increased personal mobility, the Vale of Pewsey must have been a world unto its own, ruled by the rhythms of nature and follies of those who tried to tame it. In the towns, the yokels probably had a reputation for being lawless and loopy, so in recent years, when news of the first **crop circles** hit the local press, you can imagine the reaction. "Bloomin' Moonrakers!"

The post-mistress in the village shop in Alton Barnes is no nutter. She has been monitoring crop circles in the Kennet district since they first appeared ten years ago, and on our last visit told us exactly which field on the climb up to Knap Hill they most regularly appear in. That evening I pedalled passed hopeful, but saw nothing. The following morning, early, we drove back and there in **East Field** was the most perfectly formed ellipse with what looked like bent tridents radiating from it at right angles. In the centre, the corn was flattened in a clockwise spiral but the outer two-thirds of the circle was quartered, the north-west and south-east segments pointing north, the north-east and south-west flattened pointing east. I told the postmistress. She smiled knowingly and said, "Ah, you willed it." I left quickly.

Once again, nobody knows anything conclusive about this recent and very strange phenomena, or why this corner of Wessex merits particular attention by who or whatever is causing them. Scotland, Surrey and as far afield as Australia has experienced some activity and we have seen them on the Chalke Way just south of Cambridge, but could there be a link with the concentration of ancient monuments in this area? Many of the more recent crop pictograms point towards Silbury Hill. Some of the earlier circles mimicked stone circles so closely they could have been ground plans for Avebury or Stonehenge. Very few are hoaxes. It is almost impossible to reproduce the sharp edges, swirling pattern and the fact that the stems of the flattened crop are not broken, allowing the corn to continue ripening. Whatever is going on, local farmers are very distressed, particularly by the further damage done by the curious. If you see a corn circle, admire it from a distance, from the road.

Over the last two decades, the designs of crop circles has developed from variations on a circle, a pattern of circles or concentric circles to large pictograms with all kinds of elements hanging off or closely associated with them. They do appear to be a recent phenomena, though in the 17th century there are traditional tales of a 'Mowing Devil' conjured up by aggrieved peasants to destroy the crops of tyrannical landlords. If corn circles did appear in the superstitious Middle Ages, it is unlikely farmers would have made it known for fear of being unable to sell their 'blighted' crop. But there is an undeniable similarity between the shapes we are seeing in rape, wheat and barley fields and circular motifs decorating Celtic and Romano-British stone, metal and ceramic ware. Even the complex pictograms match planetary and cosmic deity symbols. For a couple of years now the ancient symbol for the Earth Goddess, Gaia, has been appearing.

As to how they are reproduced, the popular theory was stationary summer whirlwinds, the frantic eddies we often see whipping across fields. That fell through when a circle with a pattern similar to the one described above appeared. Then it was thought an electro-magnetic plasma vortex, like a swirling aurora borealis, was the cause, but days after the book was published, up popped another crop circle whose shape totally defied the possibility. Any connection with UFO's was instantly dismissed by everybody except the press, but what is strange is that every time scientists think they have cracked the mystery the Mowing Devil mischievously goes to work and floors them. It's as if there is an intelligence at work, leading us somewhere, and there are many stories (including our own) of 'The Force' responding to human ideas. If that's not weird enough, many formations have been associated with high-frequency signals or light patterns that are by no means random. The general consensus amongst the boffins is that somebody or thing is trying to tell us something using an ancient language possibly last understood some two thousand years ago. Given the mess we have made of the planet since the Industrial Revolution, the appearance of Gaia in our fields does look a little ominous. Doomsday scenarios begin here, but one has to wonder, if this thing is so darn smart, why doesn't it simply spell it out in plain English right across the Vale? "You are heading up Shit Creek without a paddle!" Done.

Before leaving the Vale of Pewsey, a quick word about the Kennet and Avon Canal for those who elect to stay overnight or down a pint at The Barge Inn, Honeystreet. This hamlet used to be the hub of operations for anybody in the Vale making use of the waterways. A couple of commercial premises remain, but now the leisured classes moor their narrow boats, stretch their legs and sample the menu here.

Directly opposite the pub, people are surprised to see a 'pill box' so far inland from the coast. These World War II gun emplacements were built all along the canal after the 1940 retreat from Dunkirk, when the fear of invasion was heavy in the air. Should the Nazis get passed our coastal defences, the idea was for the civil and military population to beat a hasty retreat to the north bank of the canal where a second stand would be made at what was called The Blue Line.

Jump back a couple of thousand years and you would have found a similar line of defence running the length of Furze Hill. Today **Wansdyke** is just a muddy path destined never to dry out, thanks to the shelter of a tangle of trees that are downright creepy in the mist. It runs for 48 miles (77 km.) east to west over the Southern Avon Uplands, from Inkpen near Hungerford to the Bristol Channel, and averages 90 feet (27.5 m.) in width. It was, and in places still is, a deep ditch, dug as a border defence by the Saxons sometime in the early ADs, and it is possible the whole length was topped with a vicious stockade. We have come to accept the remarkable labouring feats of our ancestors, but the puzzle here is why did they build it? The Saxon style of warfare was all beating-your-chest-out-in-the-open stuff. None of this cissy hiding behind stockades or holding your ground in a hill fort, which is why there are so few large Saxon earthworks in the country. Could 'Woden's Dyke' have been the western limit of their domain, and on the side you've just pedalled up the Britons held fort? Was that King Arthur I just saw being swallowed up in the mist?

From war to peace once again, and the remarkable **Upper Kennet Valley** that now opens out before us. Resist the temptation to immediately bowl down Lurkely Hill. We are on the northern edge of a westwards bulge in the chalk. Before us the escarpment runs north from the opposite bank of the Kennet, before curving east to form the bulk of the Marlborough Downs. To the west Thorn Hill and Allington Down slip off the bulge and slide into the North Wiltshire Lowlands. It is comforting to be back in the hills, but there is something odd. Peeking out above the dying edge is a gigantic green creme caramel, perfectly formed, with a flat bit on top where the pot stands before it's turned out. And as you cycle through East Kennet, you notice one or two houses have their own little sarsen megaliths standing in the garden. Then as you honk up the hill of the busy main road, there it is again, the green caramel, rising with every turn of the pedal, until you reach the brow and finally see the base of this curious decapitated cone. Like an enormous cairn it guides us towards the valley, luring us into the most enigmatic triangle in the country, encompassing Avebury, West Kennet and Beckhampton. This is where R. Hippisley Cox believed all green ridge-roads led. This was the Piccadilly Circus of prehistory, the hub of a wheel and Avebury was its axle.

Taken as a group, the henge, the hill and the long barrow are far more impressive than poor old Stonehenge, and they aren't fenced in or chaperoned by a toll booth. In fact the tourist facilities are positively discreet, ranging from the man from the National Trust working out of a camper van in the car park, to a tucked away court-yard of thatched barn conversions where the museum, shop and tea rooms are housed. They must come but in all my visits to the area, I've never seen a coach party. Maybe because the site is so spread out, but the West Kennet triangle copes well with its perennial invasion of cars and camcorders, and has maintained its composure. I once stayed in the beautiful house of one of two elderly sisters who were born and have lived all their lives in the village of Avebury. The furthest either of them had moved was from one side of the Devizes road to the other. Inside her cottage the low walls were covered with old pictures and paintings of the stones and all kinds of local bric-a-brac hung from the wooden beams. People here don't live around the monuments, they live with them, and they have become stoic about the holiday hordes, even amused. With tongue firmly in cheek, the menu of the only hostelry in the world set within a stone circle offers 'Sizzling Sarsen Steaks', 'Solstice Salads' and 'A Crop Circle of Vegetarian Dishes'.

A layby on the left of the A4 is where you swing off and dismount to visit the West Kennet Long Barrow, worth the leggy if only to catch the New Age Travellers who occasionally feel this is a groovy place to learn to play the penny whistle. Take your torch. Not only is this one of the longest and oldest burial chambers in Britain it is also easily accessible. Behind the monstrous blocking stone, the chambers where the dead laid have been smoothed by centuries of hands exploring their edges. It is dank and eerie, but then you are in a tomb. Outside the Neolithics raised wooden platforms on which recently departed were stretched out beyond the reach of carnivores, much like the American Indian and Buddhist way of death. When the carrion crows finished their pecking, one bunch of bones was swept out of the chamber to make way for the new. It is thought this municipal grave was taking in customers for almost 1,000 years before it was packed to the ceiling and sealed with earth, stones and any old broken bits of pottery, tool or fibia. Inevitably grave robbers have had easy pickings down the decades, most notoriously one Dr Toope of Marlborough who in the 1860's used to nip up the hill to collect the ingredients for grinding into his 'noble medicine'. On a warm day it can be quite chilly up here on the ridge, the kind of chill that induces a quick shudder of the shoulders, as if a ghost has just walked through you.

No such encounters with the other side are experienced at **Silbury Hill**, only bafflement. What you see is what you get, a 130 foot high (39.5 m.) green caramel of a hill, the largest human-made prehistoric lump in Europe. Archeological digs have established its internal frame is a diminishing series of circular terraces constructed of blocks of chalk laid down using drystone walling techniques. Within that, who knows? Tradition has it the mystical King Sil is buried here, upright and sat on his horse, either encased in a gold coffin, or wearing gold armour, or simply accompanied by a life-size gold statue of themselves. Exploratory shafts driven into the side of the hill have revealed nothing telling, which in itself suggests Silbury was no bigwigs' mausoleum. Could it be an enormous representation of Gaia, the Great Earth Mother, squatting as if in the process of giving birth? Richard Daves who advanced this theory points to its location over a spring that periodically floods, suggesting menstruation. Or was it a shadow hill, a gigantic sundial with a pole stuck in the top, casting a shadow by which the true length of seasons and the year could be calculated? Judging from the graffiti in the area, this is actually 'Starship H. Q.' and Silbury Hill is the conning-tower, as feasible and explanation as any I suppose. We don't know if it was built to be climbed, but do so anyway for the most splendid view of the Avebury triangle. It is a lot bigger than you would imagine and the 100 ft (30.5 m.) diameter pitch has seen more than one cricket match played up there. Pity the poor sod who was fielding the boundary and had to retrieve the sixes.

For a society hacking away with antler bones, Silbury Hill is an extraordinary engineering achievement, maybe more incredible than our generation landing on the moon. Conservative estimates calculate the superstructure alone would have taken 500 people over a decade to erect, the whole edifice taking more than 18 million person-hours. That's the equivalent of every man, woman and child in the U. K. today dumping one bucket of earth per person at a predetermined spot. Meaningless figures for a meaningless folly, but all this mystery gets to you. 20th century man can't move a piece of paper from one side of a desk to the other without somebody's order note, and yet 4,000 years ago, a bunch of primitives could construct a magnificent skyscraper with out leaving so much as an internal memo behind. Some progress.

Pedal passed the short-cut into **Avebury**, passed the car park, and steel yourself for something special. As you approach the Avenue and turn the corner at the junction, the stones of Avebury henge emerge from behind the mound and welcome you. They are warm and friendly, open and accessible, unimpressed by the 20th century motoring through their midst. For all the trauma the henge must have suffered in it's long, long lifetime there is no resentment. It sits happily with a village in its lap, provides pasture for sheep and a distraction for people, but you can't help feeling it knows something we don't. Here we go again. Once more the cold facts tell you nothing except that a lot of scientists have done a lot of prodding and poking, measuring and scanning, and not a lot of standing and staring. Once again I encourage you to do just that, to soak it in, maybe sit on the edge of the south stone, first on the right as you swing into the site. Weird things happen here. Close your eyes, totally relax with your arms loose and don't wait for something to happen. It already is. Each person reacts differently (if at all) but I've watched arms and legs gently sway, heads gently roll, and always the subject reports a pleasurable ride.

Avesbury is a World Heritage Site but what you see is a pale shadow of what the Beaker people built. Informed opinion leans towards an original ground plan of circles within circles, possibly as many as eight, with a long avenue of stones tailing off to the south east. It is thought this was an umbilical to The Sanctuary at Overton Hill, another henge, since destroyed. Roughly 177 stones are known to have graced the enclosure, but what you touch and admire are random erections raised as recently as 1939. People died trying to destroy what they feared was a pagan temple and in the village there are houses built of recycled henge. Fires were lit, stones toppled and the tools of destruction applied. What did we fear? In 1990 hidden depths were discovered. Using electronic imaging, archaeologists found a circular structure, 130 feet (40 m.) in diameter, lying beneath the henge midway between the Herepath and the Swindon Road. Inevitably this has just compounded the confusion surrounding the site, but clearly what you see is not what you get at Avebury.

Like Stonehenge, it is thoughts this henge had a religious function, if not at its inception, then certainly 2,000 years later, though there is no reason to suppose our ancestors had to get a `change of use of premises' licence to convert Avebury in the latter years BC. 18th Century intellectuals believed the prehistoric religion practiced here was inspired by Middle Eastern theology long before Christianity found its way to these shores. They argued that the circle was built according to sacred mathematical formulae also utilised in ancient Egypt and classical Greece. This is supposedly the basis of Pythagoras' famous theory. Pythagoras was apparently a Druid, but like Christianity, it is believed the prehistoric religion was driven by divine revelation, and that Avebury henge was a symbol of God. The Avenue thus became a conduit down to the River Kennet, where His powers would fire the waters so crucial to life in the chalklands. I mention this as background to the totally unrelated fact that modern scientists monitoring the Wessex crop circles have found an alignment between the corridor where they most frequently occur and (wait for it!) the Giant Pyramid at Gaza. Curioser and curioser.

The other theory is that the henge was a pagan temple, the tall narrow stones representing penises and the shorter diamond stones vaginas. Possibly the henge was laid out as one enormous fertility symbol. Maybe the outer circle symbolised the womb containing the two inner circles, man and woman, Yin and Yang, plus and minus, positive and negative. Maybe the whole thing was just one gigantic Pirelli calendar for the year 4,246 BC. Wheels within wheels.

As we climb the **Herepath** out of Avebury it feels good to be grappling with the rough once again, negotiating the tangible. After the airy fairy notions we've been struggling with since first clapping eyes in Silbury Hill, the approaching ridgeway entices us to stretch out, get back into the rhythm and leave the world and her husband to their navel gazing.

Welcome to the Rudge.

Overton Down to Wanborough Plain

DISTANCE – 14m 23K
via Fyfield Down
16m 25K

OS 173 + 174

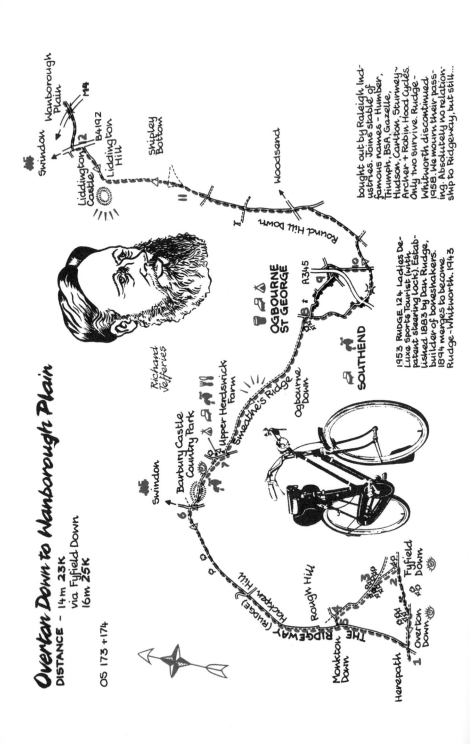

Swindon
Wanborough Plain
M4

Liddington Castle
2
B4192
Liddington Hill

Snipley Bottom

Woodsand

Round Hill Down

1953 RUDGE 124 Ladies De-Luxe Sports Tourist (with patent steering lock). Established 1883 by Dan Rudge, builder of boneshakers. 1894 merges to become Rudge-Whitworth. 1943

bought out by Raleigh Industries. Joins stable of famous names – Humber, Triumph, BSA, Gazelle, Hudson, Carlton, Sturmey-Archer + Robin Hood Cycles. Only two survive. Rudge-Whitworth discontinued 1958. We mourn their passing. Absolutely no relationship to Ridgeway, but still...

Richard Jefferies

OGBOURNE ST GEORGE
A345

SOUTHEND

Barbury Castle Country Park

Upper Herdswick Farm

Smeathe's Ridge

Ogbourne Down

Swindon

6
7

Hackpen Hill

Rough Hill

Fyfield Down

3
2

THE RIDGEWAY (RUDGE)

4
5

Overton Down
1

Monkton Down

Harepath

Directions

1 **L** to follow THE RIDGEWAY. Signposted all the way.

Via Overton Down

1 SO through farm gate to Overton Down, across gallops, down hill then swing **L** onto cinder track.
2 After farm gate, **L** through farm gate HACKPEN.
3 SO through farm gate and woods.
4 **L** onto stone track. Blue arrow.
5 **R** at TJ, RIDGEWAY SO.
6 **R** at road then **L** up hill.
7 **R** at road then after farm **L** down Smeathe's Ridge. RIDGEWAY
8 **R** at road. SO at corner for RIDGEWAY/ or **L** at corner for village.
9 **L** then 1st **R** after fly-over. NO THROUGH ROAD.
10 **L** to rejoin RIDGEWAY.
11 SO onto **BW** heading for Liddington Hill.
12 **L** at B4192 (fast road). Then 1st **R** over M4.

Resource

BARBURY CASTLE
Wardens –
Lynne and Brian Simpson
Burderop
Wroughton
01793 845346
Camping, cafe, water.
Shepherds hut available for accommodation.

SOUTHEND
Mrs P Parkins
Elm Tree Cottage
01672 841408
Water & BB.

Mrs A Francis
Laurel Cottage
SN8 1SG
01672 841288

OGBOURNE ST GEORGE
Mr G Edwins
Foxlynch
Bytham Rd
SN8 1TD
01672 841307

Mrs Rostron
Parklands Hotel and Restaurant
SN8 1SL
01672 841555
BB & camping

SWINDON
Railway information
0117 9294255

The Rudge:
Overton Hill – Wanborough Plain

To DATE YOU HAVE RIDDEN ACROSS OR ALONG NINE RIDGEWAYS BUT ONLY NOW are you on The Ridgeway. Confusing isn't it, and it gets more confusing in 40 miles (63 km.) when suddenly it changes into the Ridgeway Path and is nowhere near a ridge. It is also no right of way for a cyclist, and those who try following it end up pushing a long way. Before that it splits into the Ridge Way and the Ridgeway and before you even arrive here you will have noticed you were riding the Ridgeway Link, so let's start from scratch.

It was first suggested the track along the northern edge of the Marlborough Downs merited special attention back in 1948, during the formative stages of the National Parks Act. Twenty four years later the Countryside Commission finally 'opened' a byway from Overton Hill to Ivinghoe Beacon in Buckinghamshire. The line of the route west of Goring and the Thames Gap to Overton Hill was straight forward, clearly marked by a green road along the ridge, occasionally metalled but never obscured. East of Goring to Ivinghoe Beacon any ridgeway had long been smothered under tarmac or re-routed around rural developments in what is the London commuter belt of the Chilterns. Weaving through the tangled mess, different bridleway and footpath routes were mapped and in places actually do travel the ridge. More frequently they follow the line of the Icknield Way, Swan's Way or no particular way and dispute still rages as to precisely which is what.

Nobody is too sure why the full 82 miles (132 km.) was called The Ridgeway. The officer in charge suggests the name might have been a hangover from the Middle Ages, though our research indicates it was then known as the Hiycaweg, a hangover from the Anglo Saxon and probably a little too Germanic for the zenophobic post-war Brits. While there can be little doubt the green road to Goring follows a fairly remarkable run of escarpments, The Ridgeway has attracted a disproportionate outpouring of superlatives from a disproportionate number of famous scribes. Kenneth Grahame (*Wind in the Willows*), Thomas Hughes (*Tom Brown's Schooldays*), G. K. Chesterton, Richard Jefferies, Sir John Betjeman, the ubiquitous Mr Hardy, even *Private Eye* and *The Oldie* editor Richard Ingrams has a tome on the subject. All of them lived or live within spitting distance of the chalk edge and one wonders of the definitive name isn't somehow linked to the arrogance of a southern intelligensia whose principle contact with the great outdoors was a regular weekend hit of *their* ridgeway. Certainly since the seventies it has become the off-road playground of Londoners, featured in copious art and travel books, magazines and supplement articles, T-shirts and mugs.

Travelling the Chalke Way from start to finish we have the advantage of context and while The Ridgeway is good, even brilliant in places, it falls short of many of the qualities previous ridges possess. The literary oozings lauded up on Liddington Hill and the Marlborough Downs are equally deserved by Win Green and the North Dorset Downs. For my own lyrical waxings, I prefer to call The Ridgeway by its local name, the **Rudge**, not through any nostalgia for Rudge bicycles, but because it frees us to reappraise the unbroken string of byways to the Thames Gap, for if there is such a thing as an off-road motorway, this is it. On a weekday in high summer parts of the Rudge can be packed, but mostly it is a continuous dribble of "Good morning", "Afternoon", "Think it will rain?". At weekends you give up the pleasantries such is the crush. It sounds awful but after miles of lonesome cycling it can be fun pootling amongst fellow voyagers, and just think, if they weren't here, they would be someplace else, blocking your breeze in one of those deliciously isolated spaces we've discovered.

Of course the popularity of the Rudge does mean that for most of its length the track is well maintained. Find a quiet day and you can fly down it without distressing anybody but the bugs. This is one of its draw-backs. While it deserves to be savoured, the tendency is to bolt. Just like a motorway, it is excellently signposted with the National Trust acorn, and there are plenty of wayside attractions. Just like a motorway it appears to run dead straight, parts of it are boring and the hypnotic effect of pedalling on and on means few think to swing off and explore the more interesting Downs. While plotting the entire ridge, we recommend four scenic diversions from the duller sections of the Rudge. They are a more challenging ride up and down dale, but you don't half appreciate the ridgeway when you return to it.

Like all popular lines, the Rudge comes in small, medium and large. In parts, particularly climbing Liddington Hill from the south, it is no wider that a footpath. Elsewhere, notably east of the Ridgeway Youth Hostel, it expands into a multi-lane carriageway where equestrians can frolic with their 'sulkies' or lightweight racing traps. For most of its length however the width of the Rudge is pretty much that of the Old Salisbury Way, either flanked by gnarled hawthorns or open to the breeze, with wire fences delineating private farmlands. Despite ploughing between fields thick with wheat or dotted with sheep, much of the surrounding area feels barren, a wilderness of plenty with the occasional oasis of ancient beeches that huddle close by but rarely across our path. On a still evening, riding high and vulnerable across it's exposed back, the solitude would be oppressive were it not for the rhythmical strains of the chainwheel reminding us we are not alone. When the wind is up, it wuthers something rotten through the field fencing and in sheltered areas stirs the leaves into an agitated clamour that suggests predators are on the loose. Hit a hot spell and the shimmering haze off the distant track can induce a white line fever that sends the mind spiralling down to explore the deepest recesses of the soul. Whatever the elements throw at you and it, the Rudge has a way of turning the traveller in on themselves, the long chalk ribbon never deserting the explorer, always in front, showing the way home (or at least to Holme).

Our first diversion is to **Fyfield Down**, past Overton Down where the building blocks for Stonehenge and Avebury are thought to have originated. This is not really a diversion since the Saxon named Herepath has as stronger a claim to being a prehistoric road as The Ridgeway. It at least connects with Avebury and more than likely carried the Wide Load bearing the sarsen stones which still litter the combe, where they were deposited by the melt waters of glaciers way back in the darkness of time. From a distance they apparently look like grazing sheep, earning them the name 'Grey Wethers', though a comparison with modern hybrids roaming the valley suggests either the early flocks were filthy or whoever dreamt up the metaphor suffered acute colour blindness. Thinking back to the long dry track across Salisbury Plain and the two steep escarpments boxing the Vale of Pewsey, one has to be impressed by the haulage problems overcome by the builders of Stonehenge. What were the secret qualities of sarsen stone that spurred them to undertake such a muscle-twanging task? A little further on lies Fyfield Down, a well preserved Celtic Field system whose humps and hollows can be seen from the track, but not visited. It is now an important nature reserve, rich in its population of butter-flies and wildflowers, and a place to stop for a breather before climbing up onto Hackpen Hill to face the Rudge at its rawest.

Once again this is classic ridgeway, with no cover, the odd beech outcrop where you least need them and splendid vistas each side of a clear straight track. Beneath the chalk the spring line is marked by pockets of settlement linked by a main thoroughfare that once was the Port Way (Bronze Age) and later the Icknield Way (Saxon), or so it is believed. Ahead is **Wroughton Airfield**, an old WWII airbase, now an outpost of the Science Museum with a large collection of transport aircraft. To your right the downs slip away like tributaries off a chaotic catchment area that splits and divides, disguising where the main torrent runs. Always the shapes are rounded and flowing, scarred by occasional byways that leave a trail of hawthorns in their wake.

Barbury Castle is one of the great chain of hillforts, last defended by the Romano-British against the Saxons as they surged south to face a stand off with the true Brits. In 1985, while laying an oil pipeline, engineers found 'Erica' here, the remains of a woman from the Roman period who was buried with her boots on. Traces of leather fixed with bronze studs and a quantity of hob nails were found around her feet, suggesting Erica worked the fields in clod-hoppers rather than the dainty open sandals depicted in romantic artist-impressions of the times. Today the earthwork is better known as a Country Park that pays homage to the local 19th century writer **Richard Jefferies.**

Jeffries is not a man many of us will have read, but if you like your literature to be inspired and inspiring, and have a healthy scepticism of the rural idyll, I recommend dipping in. He was a tormented young man who died in 1887 at the age of thirty eight after a five year struggle against tuberculosis. Son of a Wiltshire farm labourer, he came to prominence in his early twenties when he wrote a pragmatic contribution to the letters page of *The Times*, which was then debating the situation of agricultural workers and Joseph Arch's intention to unionise them. This piece was spotted by the editor of *Fraser's Magazine*, a sort of *Spectator* of its day, who invited Jeffries to contribute occasional copy on country matters. Thus was born the Country Diary column that is now a feature of possibly every reputable broadsheet in the world. In one such contribution Jeffries drew the public's attention to the Rudge, then a poor, overgrown reflection of its earlier and present self. His writing had a deeply spiritual slant, nothing religious, more soulful, and he was a great influence on the urban bourgeoisie searching for beauty away from the smoking stacks of the Industrial Revolution. As he wrote, "It is morning on the hills, when hope is wide as the world . . . let us get out of these indoor narrow modern days." They did and we still do.

Eight o'clock in the morning, the sky yet to decide on the manner of the day, a tingle in the air and in the limbs, no telephone or line manager for miles and you are cruising down **Smeathes Ridge**. This is the Rudge at its best. When winter blurs the panoramic sweep across Chiseldon, you could be riding the Cairngorms, great glens swooping off the saddleback, sucked into the billowing peat mists of an unseen Scottish bog. In the clarity of high summer, bold splashes of colour hit you from below in Ogbourne Down, from above, the sky, ahead, everywhere. Even the grey that is Swindon has a shine to it. But always the experience of Smeathes Ridge is about space, and as Jefferies pointed out "The heart looks into space to be away from earth." If ever you get the desire to just take off, like the BMX kids in *ET*, it will be here, but the experience is short lived before we clatter down to earth and **Ogbourne St George**.

The map would suggest the Rudge originally passed through Ogbourne, and that its current route is an off-road bypass. In comparison with villages we have already encountered, you won't be missing much to stay on the rough except maybe sustenance. The Old Crown and the famous Shepherd's Rest at Foxhill are the only two watering holes on the Rudge until Streatley. For provisions you will need to drop into Ashbury at the foot of the edge, or Lambourne in the Downs, both mapped on the second leg of our journey across the ridge. Water is easier to come by, oddly enough, and we have plotted the taps thoughtfully provided for two and four legged travellers.

Liddinton Hill is another of those vantage points from which locals swear they can see what's on Icelandic TV. The second highest point on the Chalke Way after Win Green, I've only ever managed to see an awful lot of Swindon from here, but the view back along the bulging chalk edge we've ridden is excellent. To give a famous scribe his head, the poet Edward Thomas wrote of these hills, 'There is something oceanic in their magnitude, their ease, their solitude - above all in their liquid forms, that combine apparent mobility with placidity, and in the vast playground which they provide for the shadows of the clouds. They are never abrupt, but flowing on and on, make a type of infinity. A troop, a clump, or a sprinkling of trees, a little wood, a house, squares of wheat or newly ploughed land cannot detract from them – not even when the air is so clear that all sounds and sights and smells are bright and have a barb that plants them deep, and the hard black rooks slide in crystal under the blue.'

It is all of that.

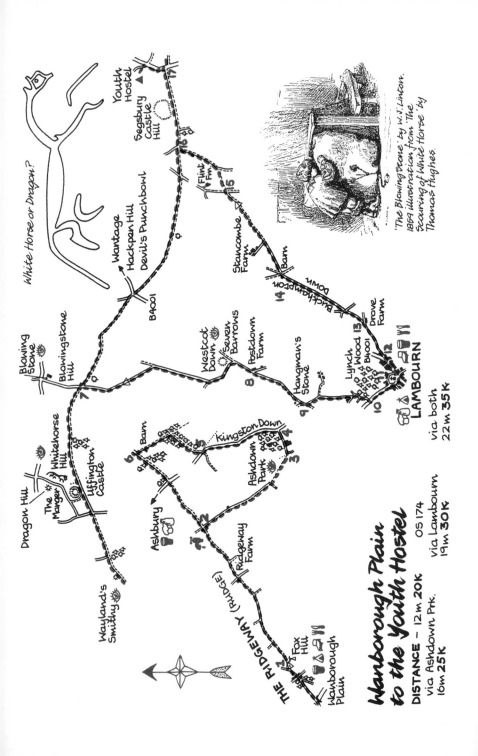

White Horse or Dragon?

Youth Hostel

Segsbury Castle
Hill

17

Wantage
Hackpen Hill
Devil's Punchbowl

16

Flint Fm.
15

Blowing
Stone

Blowingstone
Hill

Staucombe
Farm

Barn

B4001

Buckhampton
Down

14

Westcot
Down

Seven
Barrows

Postdown
Farm

Dragon Hill

Whitehorse
Hill

The
Manger

Uffington
Castle

7

8

Hangman's
Stone

9

Lynch
Wood

13

Drove
Farm

12

Wayland's
Smithy

Ashbury

Ridgeway
Farm

Barn

6

5

Kingston Down

4

3

Ashdown
Park

10

B4000

LAMBOURN

'The Blowingstone' by W. J. Linton.
1854 illustration from 'The
Scouring of White Horse' by
Thomas Hughes.

Fox
Hill

2

THE RIDGEWAY (RIDGE)

Wanborough
Plain

Wanborough Plain
to the Youth Hostel

DISTANCE — 12m 20k   OS 174

via Ashdown Prk.   via Lambourn
16m 25k   19m 30k

via both
22m 35k

Directions

1   R into car park RIDGEWAY.

Via Ashdown Park

2   R at barn where sign points left for Idstone.
PUBLIC RIGHT OF WAY **SO** down track then onto **BW** between fields.

3   L at gravel road.

4   L at TJ.

5   After bend **R** FOOTPATH. Follow track (not path) up to brow of hill then **L**.

6   R onto RIDGWAY.

Via Lambourn

7   R at road SEVEN BARROWS.

8   R onto BYWAY opposite Postdown Farm.

9   L at fork then branch **R** at farm drive.

10 L at TJ.

11 L at MARKET PLACE.

12 R MMB WARREN FARM.

13 L MMB WARREN FARM.

14 R at barn, off concrete onto tarmac.

15 SO up track between posts. Keep barn in field to left.

16 R onto RIDGEWAY.

17 L after cottages then **L** again for hostel, otherwise **R** then **L** for RIDGEWAY.

Resource

FOXHILL
The Shepherds Rest
Foxhill Crossroads, SN4 0DR
01793 790266
BB, camping & food

Ashdown House
01494 528051
Open April to end Oct: Wed & Sat
2-6pm. Closed Easter & every Bank
Holiday. Woodlands: all year: Sat to
Thurs dawn to dusk.
Fee.

LAMBOURN
Mrs J Warr
The Downs House
High St, RG16 7XW
01488 71637

The George Hotel
High St, RG16 7XU
01488 71889

Mrs F Rutherford
Alvestoke
Sheepdrove, RG16 7YU
01488 71737
BB & camping

The Rudge:
Wanborough Plain – Youth Hostel

AT A SQUEEZE THE RUDGE FALLS INTO THREE DISTINCT SECTIONS. AFTER THE unnerving exposure of Hackpen and Liddington Hills, the length from Foxhill to the Youth Hostel is positively friendly, snuggling between bushes and trees, even the odd wood, calming the cyclist after the neurosis of all that open space. The final 14 miles (23 km.) to Streatley are different again, but here, along this middle length round the Vale of White Horse, there is the drawback that you don't get to see much through the foliage unless you go out of your way.

The diversion down to Ashdown Park is short, sweet and quirky. Aside from the superior riding, on and off-road, the attraction is **Ashdown House**, a strikingly symmetrical tower of a building for a country house, and somehow oddly familiar. 'It is the perfect doll's house, proof of a longing for neatness and all-round order typical of the years after the Civil War.' So wrote the historian Nikolaus Pevsner, and he's right, you do find yourself looking up the line of the brown-stone corner dressings for the catch that will release the whole front of the building to swing open and reveal the floors and dolls furniture inside. Curiously we don't know when it was built or by whom, though Dutch influences in the design are self-evident. It was originally at the heart of an extensive forest with four long straight avenues leading to each of its four identical sides, presenting a clear view of any unwelcome visitors. This might relate to the story that its original owner, Sir William Craven, the Lord Mayor of London, fled the city during the great plague, and rode and rode until he was far enough away from all sources of infection to build himself a pad, Ashdown House. Unfortunately Sir Will was Lord Mayor 54 years before the plague decimated London, but such is the blur we call history.

Back up on the ridge, huddling under a copse, lies **Wayland's Smithy** serene and secure with a row of four magnificent blocking stones guarding the entrance to the long barrow. It is said to be named after an Anglo-Saxon blacksmith called Welland who possessed supernatural skills. He was captured by King Alfred, set to work for the cause and lamed so he couldn't escape. A subtle variation on this tale is that Wayland was actually a Saxon god who worked nights as a blacksmith. If you left a coin on the lintel stone and tied your nag to one of the beeches, legend had it you could return the next morning to find Dobbin sporting a brand new set of shoes. In the gloom of an autumn evening, as the dead leaves flutter down and the sighing earth breathes out its mist, all this sword and sorcery seems quite plausible against the backdrop of the Smithy. I left a 50 pence piece and a torn inner tube, and returned at sun-up to find a 50 pence piece and a torn inner tube. Since the long barrow is dated sometime around 2,800 BC, I hadn't great expectations of a fable that didn't give its name to the tomb until the 10th century AD. This century there have been two excavations of the site; the first in 1919 revealed eight skeletons, one a childs'; the other in 1962 uncovering a further 13 with broken arrow tips amongst the bones. This dig also established that there are two barrows here, with a thousand years between them. Business evidently picked up.

A short ride down and up, and a sign on the left informs us we are at the Uffington Castle complex. Walk your bike up to the edge, lay it down, and sit and ponder on the White Horse, or what little you can see of it. As with the Cerne Giant, the best place to view this marvellous chalk carving is from a hot air balloon. If they are both Celtic in origin, this suggests early pagan religion had a concept of hierarchy, gods up above, mortals down below, and that hill carvings were for their divine eyes only, all of which gels with the 18th century theories about the religion worshiped at Avebury. Certainly Celtic gods and godesses take on equine form in other media, on ceramics and in stone, and from the Iron Age, coins have been unearthed bearing a similar design to the Uffington White Horse. Several pubs in the Newmarket area display photographs of Iceni coins unearthed at Freckenham. Horse motifs figure prominently, several surprisingly close to this earth carving. A different theory has it that the horse commemorates King Alfred's victory over the Danes at the Battle of Ethandune (now Edinton) in 870. Another that it was cut by Hengist, the Anglo-Saxon leader, in 5 AD. Whenever it was executed, we know the carving is the youngest of all the features around the hill fort.

'The White Horse is in another category from the rest of the great chalk figures, for it has the lineament of a work of art. Seen on its own hill, it becomes an affair of violent foreshortening or tapering perspectives more or less indecipherable. But it is precisely this aspect of the Horse design that I found so significant. Once the futile game of "picking out" the Horse is abandoned, the documentary importance of the site fades, and the landscape asserts itself with all the force of its triumphant fusion of natural and artificial design. You then perceive a landscape of terrific animation whose bleak character and stark expression accord perfectly with its lonely situation on the summit of the bare downs.' The landscape painter Paul Nash writing in 1958.

Without a doubt the earth formations surrounding the artwork are extraordinary, part moulded by humans, predominantly by nature. To the east is **The Manger**, looking more liquid than pastoral, as if the floor of the wide gully is grass lava draining down the slope, leaving a rim of scum at intervals where it choose to rest and cool a little. Why The Manger? "'Cos that's where the horse comes to eat" (Trad.). Ahead is a much smaller, squashed version of Silbury Hill, this time built by the elements. **Dragon Hill** is named after King Alfred's father, Uther Pendragon. There again Dragon Hill is so named because here St George fought and killed either *a* dragon or *the* dragon, depending on who you read. Where the beast's blood gushed to the ground, the grass was destined to wither in perpetuity. Unfortunately it does, or at least it doesn't grow very well, but I suspect that has more to do with the actions of too many Nike trainers. None of this area is properly chronicled until the time of Henry II. The names and associations we guess were Saxon or before. It is possible therefore we took the wrong root and that Dragon Hill actually relates to the chalk carving which should be entitled the White Dragon. Think of a giant lizard and the image begins to make more sense.

The fullest description of the ritual maintenance of a chalk figure is *The Scouring of the White Horse* by Thomas Hughes. Writing in 1859 he describes how it was cause for jugglers, wrestlers, musicians, stalls and people to come together, to wine and dine, scrub and pull grass until the carving gleamed. They played catch the pig, chased cheeses down the slopes of The Manger, scrabbled in a tub of flour to 'Find the Bullet'. Up at the earthworks, at the Castle, tents and platforms presented entertainment for a donation. They were busking. These were 'festies'. In 1780 over 30,000 people came to see the scouring and some probably even scoured. Today the monument is maintained by the National Trust, but there is a White Horse Committee who still look for volunteers to lime wash the carving. Over the years its shape has changed slightly, though, unlike the Cerne Giant, it has not lost any of its essential features. At odd times it has fallen foul of vandals who have usually been more creative than destructive. Using black polythene bin liners and wall-paper paste, one inspired bunch transformed the horse into a zebra for the day. In February 1995, using the same optical dating technique applied to the Turin Shroud, researchers from Oxford University revealed the White Horse was dug somewhere between 600 BC and 1400 BC. More interestingly they discovered the outline was not originally scoured but was cut into trenches, then back-filled with rammed chalk quarried from the hill site.

We are now sweeping around the **Vale of Whitehorse**. Echoing our curve but making hard work of it near the foot of the scarp is the Upper Icknield Way or B4507 if you prefer. A more fluid curve is proscribed in the middle distance by Brunel's Great Western Railway or GWR, an acronym that came to stand for God's Wonderful Railway. Opened in 1841, it was the engineer's magnum opus, a high speed line from Bristol to London with no curve less than a mile radius and so few gradients it was nick-named 'The Billiard Table'. Cutting across everything is an invisible line running north east through Uffington Church, the tower you can see up the road from Dragon Hill. This is the Old Salt Road, one of Alfred Watkins' leylines, an old straight track linking a handful of farms with 'wick' in their names, Ruffinswick, Chapelwick, etc. Alfred made the connection from salt to white to whit to wick and bingo, he had another line ruled on his map. Chalk is also white and farms called something – 'wick' are dotted all over the area, but this is probably a mere technicality, eh Alfred?

Of the four diversions we recommend, the loop round Lambourn is the longest and most exciting to ride. It starts on tarmac with a long fast freewheel down the south side of Blowingstone Hill. You might be tempted to challenge your lungs at the actual **Blowing Stone**, located at the foot of the northern escarpment, accessible but in the corner of a private front garden. The stone is a block of sarsen perforated by numerous cavities where tree roots once tunnelled in, and it has possibly been relocated from Uffington Castle. Tradition states that King Alfred blew through it producing a bugle-like sound to summon his Saxons against the Danes. Though I have never been successful, it does work if you completely cover the hole with your mouth, then blow. The knack is having a cake-hole the size of Vesuvius, and leaving yourself enough puff to honk back up to the Rudge.

Towards the bottom of the freewheel south, on your left as you cruise along Westcot Down, is what looks remarkably like a spaceship parking lot. There are over 40 Bronze Age barrows around **Seven**

Barrows but the field on the corner is of particular merit as a Site of Special Scientific Interest, principally for its natural history. Currently controlled by the volunteer wildlife trust BONT (Berkshire, Buckinghamshire & Oxfordshire Naturalist Trust), Seven Barrows has possibly never been ploughed and is one of the few untrodden and uncultivated areas of the Downs where spring heralds a swatch of bright colours splattered amongst and fluttering around the barrows. Orchids, bellflowers, different vetches, field scabious, cowslip - over a hundred species of plant attracting squadrons of butterflies - marbled white, speckled wood, common blues and the occasional painted lady on vacation from North Africa. In fact what is most appealing about this diversion to Lambourn is the continual flappings, flowerings and paddings that pass before your eyes. On one occasion I quietly pedalled behind a vixen for a good five minutes as she padded up the lane near Hangman's Stone. Finally she heard a gear change and bolted. A blood curdling feline shriek then cut through the air, followed by the blur of a domestic moggie darting across from where the fox disappeared to. By the time I drew parallel, the vixen was sat amongst the scrub smacking her lips and definitely smiling. If you give it the time, the Chalke Way is full of such wildlife cameos.

Then of course there are the gee-gees. If you took the plunge into Overton Down you will have already crossed a gallop, but from here until dropping off the Rudge into Streatley you are in the thick of equine country. While vast tracks of the Berkshire Downs have been turned by the plough, most of the gallops are virgin territory, mown, and chomped by sheep but not churned, leaving the kind of well-draining springy turf that is ideal for exercising mares and stallions worth a fortune. While horses have been ridden and bred around here since the 18th century, the Downs didn't come into their own as a training area until about sixty years ago, when Sir Hugh Nugent encouraged local landowners to forsake the fickleness of sheep farming for the more lucrative horse trade. There are now over 60 stables and studs on the Downs and it has become the centre for the National Hunt, but you have to be up early to see any more than the occasional line of thoroughbreds exercising. At seven in the morning, horses and jockeys outnumber the birds.

While its' origins are in the point-to-point races promoted for hunt riders, the **National Hunt** is nothing to do with blood sports. Steeplechasing began in 1811 when the Clerk of the Course at Bedford erected a quartet of fences specifically for the hunters' race that was a feature of most flat meetings. By the 1830's the idea had taken hold at several courses and was proving more of an attraction that the rest of the programme, not surprisingly, given the thrills and spills of races where anything up to thirty fences had to be jumped. It wasn't until 1866 that the Jockey Club, the ruling body of horse racing, welcomed representatives of steeplechasing onto its' committee. By then the sport was riddled with corruption and a long way from the amateur ethic that first enthused it and point-to-point meetings. Todays participants are thoroughbreds and bear little relationship to the mongrel hunters that populate the dying blood sport. Their big events in a calendar peppered with valuable races are the Cheltenham Gold Cup and the Grand National at Aintree, but if you want to register an entry it's the Red Lion Hotel in Lambourne you head for.

Lambourn takes you by surprise, skulking as it does in a hollow at the confluence of a number of downs and bottoms, camouflaged by tall trees. Despite emerging onto the main street opposite the Valley Equine Hospital, the town is nowhere near as horsey as you might expect. In fact, on entering the market place, the shopfront that first catches the eye is a launderette and it is not full of little men washing brightly coloured, grass stained strips. Long before the big money moved in, Lambourn was the main market town for the area, hosting a weekly market and three annual sheep fairs. The word Lambourn actually means 'stream where lambs are washed,' and it is here in Lynch Wood, that the River Lambourn seeps from the chalk. The precise location of the spring drifts, according to the amount of rainfall that has soaked into the downs above, but as the closest source of constant water the town was a natural focus for sheep farmers watering flocks that grazed between here and the Rudge.

Lambourn was then known as Chipping Lambourn and had the unusual distinction of being home to the King's mistresses ('meretrices'), though which King is unclear, except that the priest who noted this was writing in the Middle Ages. Local historians, outraged at the thought of their beloved town being labelled a royal knocking-shop, are adamant this was a slip of the quill and what the cleric meant to write was 'meritorii' or 'lodgings'. The only possible royal lodgings in Lambourn were built on the site of the current Estbury Almshouses, close by the church, but this was a Saxon palace , and probably more myth than fact.

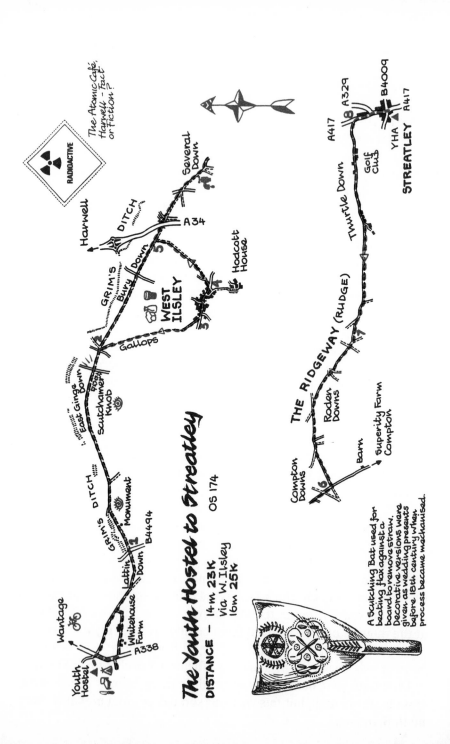

The Youth Hostel to Streatley

DISTANCE — 14m 23k
Via W. Ilsley
16m 25k

OS 174

RADIOACTIVE

The Atomic Café, Harwell - Fact or fiction?

Wantage

Youth Hostel

Whitehouse Farm
A338

GRIM'S DITCH

Lattin Down
B4494

Monument

East Ginge Down

Scutchamer Knob

Gallops

West Down

GRIM'S DITCH

Grim's Bury Down

WEST ILSLEY

Hodcott House

A34

Several Down

Harwell

THE RIDGEWAY (RUDGE)

Compton Downs

Barn

Superity Farm Compton

Roden Downs

Twurtle Down

Golf Club

A417

A329

B4009

YHA

STREATLEY
A417

A Scutching Bat used for beating flax against a board to remove straw. Decorative versions were given as wedding presents before 18th century when process became mechanised.

Directions

1   SO RIDGEWAY.

Via West Isley

2   In dip after car park,
    R between white posts **BW.**
    Follow left edge of gallops down hill.

3   **L** at cricket green.

4   After post office, **L** onto CART TRACK
    then branch **R.**
    Keep field on left until rejoin Ridgeway.

5   **R** to underpass.

6   Shortly after hitting concrete,
    L RIDGEWAY
    (old sign, easily missed).

7   Branch **L.**

8   **R** RIDGEWAY, **R** STREATLEY then **L** at **CR** onto B4009.

Resource

WANTAGE
The Court Hill
Ridgeway Centre
Court Hill
Wantage
OX12 9NE
012357 760253
BB & camping

Wantage Motor Cycles
8 Church St
01235 768643

STREATLEY
Hill House YHA
Reading Rd
RG8 9JJ
01491 872278
Ask warden for directions
to unofficial camp site.

The Rudge:
Youth Hostel – Streatley

AT THE TOP OF COURT HILL STANDS THE RIDGEWAY YOUTH HOSTEL, Scandinavian in appearance, blending with the landscape and an independent hostel custom built for the National Trail. You don't have to be a YHA member to stay here. If you hate kids, steer clear, because this is an educational centre as much as somewhere to rest weary limbs. But if you are keen to learn more about the chalk downs and the Rudge, drop into their exhibition room. Around the walls the National Trail is mapped and brightly annotated with the kind of snippets of information, photos and fables that appeal to all age groups. A large flip portfolio goes into greater depth and on one sheet actually dares to suggest that the worst erosion of our byways is caused by farmers and their working vehicles. In Britain, off-road cyclists take a real clobbering for the fat-tyre prints we leave on the landscape. There has been much talk of banning riders from our National Parks and introducing a license scheme for using the rough, so it is reassuring to know someone somewhere appreciates the truth of the erosion scare. More importantly, the exhibition is the first opportunity we have to learn what a pyramidal orchid or a speckled wood butterfly actually looks like. City-slickers will find the Chalke Way much more rewarding with a few ID's tucked under their belt. By the time you complete this epic voyage, you might confound yourself and return to the desk a budding ornithologist.

West of the A338, the Rudge has a different character again, with a broader ridge branching on heath, gallops running parallel to the track and far more cattle in the adjacent pastures. As the uplands drift down to the Thames Gap, any pretence of cover totally disappears and after a long dry spell, there is a real Spanish flavour to the dusty trail and white borders of the fields. The glare from a mid-day sun can be quite vicious, reflecting off the land. This is definitely a section where bareback riders reach for the factor-12 sunblock. It is also an area where there are two farms within as many miles with the name Starveall and one wonders if this is significant, considering how arid it can be out here.

At the foot of the ridge, best seen the other side of Scutchamer Knob, is the unmistakable line of **Grim's Ditch**, another prehistoric border that has been running parallel to the Rudge since Lattin Down. Described as the 'longest serpent of antiquity,' the ditch once ran for about 50 miles (80 km.) all the way to Dunstable. Today the remains dog our path all the way to Wiggington, near Tring. Recent excavations date its construction to around 4 BC, but it was the Saxon's who named it Grim, after the Devil. It might well have been the eastern edge of King Cuthwulf's domain, or had some connection with that irrepressible dyke-digger, King Offa, but the more likely theory is that it is much older and drew a line between Iron Age tribes. The ditch was probably designed to prevent sheep and cattle rustling, as well as protect the Icknield Way from raiders.

The monument that sticks out like a sore thumb is to **Lord Wantage** (1832-1901) or Robert Lloyd-Lindsay as Burkes Peerage called him. Bob received the VC in the Crimea War and was instrumental in setting up the British section of the Red Cross. He was one of those philanthropic land-owning aristocrats who was actually switched on. His conservation ideas had an important impact on his 8,000 hectare estate in the Berkshire Downs, initiating a policy of replanting indigenous trees, shelterbeds and hedgerows. One wonders if the old codger turned in his grave when he saw the blot on the landscape that was erected to commemorate his good deeds. It doesn't sit well with a man who tried to conserve the landscape, though the inscription says it was raised by his wife. No comment.

A little further on, hidden in the wood to your right, is **Scutchamer Knob**, or Cuckhamsley Knob, another ancient barrow where once a large oak stake was driven into the mound. This may have been a 'stapol' marking the medieval meeting places of the Berkshire Shire-moot, a group of nobs who met to discuss local affairs, much like a modern county council, except unelected. The Saxons had a similar use for the site and it is thought the name is a corruption of 'Cwichelmshlaew' meaning the burial place of Cwichelm, the King of Wessex in the 590's. The practice of holding court within earshot of the late greats is still a tradition amongst many aboriginal peoples.

A more popular reading attributes the name to the rag trade and the scutcher, the tool (and employee) used to beat out wet flax before it could be worked into yarn for the linen industry. At the foot of the scarp, flowing north, is the Ginge Brook that once powered a number of mills in the villages of West and East Ginge. Before starting the big scutching campaign, workers and families would hike up to East Ginge

Down with their hampers and flaggons and penny whistles, and have a regular beano on Scutchamer Knob. Once upon a time in this country it seems the prospect of flogging your guts out in a job of work was only palatable if it was preceded by getting blotted the night before. Nothing changes.

As you emerge from the woods, expect to be taken slightly aback. The last time we saw the full sweep of an escarpment we were cycling down Smeathe's Ridge and already the height of Round Hill Downs looked much reduced after the whalebacks looming out of the Vale of Pewsey. We are falling, only by tens of feet, but under the open expanse of sky it is noticeable. Ironically the worst climb is yet to come. To your right is the bridleway diversion to West Isley, initially bumping along the gallops but soon in the pretty little village. At any time of day this is a pleasant detour, but ridden early in the morning you will probably find yourself pushing, the better to observe the galloping stallions thundering across the turf beside you. West Isley is the most famous horse racing village in the Downs, but not because every cottage has a stallion stabled in their out-house. Many locals work for Her Majesty at Hadcott House, the Queens' Stables, where around 100 nags are housed, twelve of the beauties belonging to our Liz.

Any bike ride that takes in the South Dorset and Marlborough Downs, West Isley, and the Newmarket area is bound to put cyclists in contact with a bucket full of horseflesh. Not only will you see the equine equivalents of Sally Gunnel and Linford Christie being put through their paces, thundering across the gallops, but like as not you will turn a corner in the back of beyond and come face to face with the towering bulk of the more placid variety of nag. Many of these will be expensive pets, but some will be competition horses, bred for show jumping, dressage and eventing. Where the speed merchants are a bundle of nerves to steer well clear of, competition horses you can light a bomb under and they won't bat an eyelid. It is useful to be able to recognise the difference.

In Britain, competition breeding is very much the poor relation. The money involved in this side of the industry is small change compared to the millions invested in the blood stock of racing thoroughbreds, but the process of quality control should be no less exacting. On the continent, where governments have take a positive position towards standards control, young stallions are put through special test centres before being licensed as suitable for competition breeding. If they fail the 100 day M.O.T., it's straight down the knacker's yard for the snip. In Denmark this process is so rigorous, of 15,000 colts born in a year only four might survive to be sires by the time they are eight. This explains why, over the water, competition stallions can fetch more that a million pounds a head.

In Britain our stallions rise to the low ten thousands and the industry is more of a game. When the old girl loses her edge round the ring, she is trotted up the road to the local sire for a quick assignation, and whatever plops out breeders' take as comes. It's a far more traditional approach typified by the Hunter Improvement Society, whose annual Newmarket show is pure Loriston-Clarke, Prior-Palmer and probably Parker-Bowles. Here bowler-hatted chaps make delicate judgements about the 'confirmation' (the build) of high-spirited thoroughbreds trotted round the ring for a few minutes. Breeders are awarded the dizzy sum of £1,000 to keep prize-winning stallions in different parts of the country, to improve the local breeding stock. Since that barely covers the straw bill, competition breeders are justifiably miffed that the premium grand is the only help they get from the British government. The money comes from horse racing's Betting and Levy Board, who control a honey pot that has been hit by the recession but can well afford more. In France the government invests a mere £3 million a year in competition breeding from the racing kitty, and sees a sizeable return. In Britain we invest sod all and are experiencing a trade deficit to the tune of £30 million a year. More worryingly the quality of our breeding stock is beginning to suffer, in reputation if not in blood.

The village of West Stow also has a poor reputation in ecclesiastical circles for its wayward priests. During the reign of King James, one Marc Antonio de Dominis was the encumbent. He was also the Italian ex-Archbishop of Spalato, hiding out from the Pope after a lengthy and vociferous disagreement over certain scientific principles. Despite continuing to preach against Il Papa, he was finally invited to return home with a full pardon. True to his word, God's supreme representative on earth duly clapped Marc Antonio behind bars and poisoned the poor fool. Dr Godfrey Goodman's case was more complicated, largely because he was caught in the middle of major political upheavals. When Charles I was on the throne, Godfrey was thrown into prison for refusing to sign a number of canons relating to religious doctrine and discipline. A short time after his release, and after Charles lost his head, he was once again banged up inside, this time by the Parliamentarians. It turned out Godfrey had signed the canons after all.

Regaining the heights, you will see before you the ugliness that is the old Atomic Energy Research Establishment at **Harwell.** With a Nobel Prize winner (Dr John Cockroft) as its first director, it was set up in 1945 to research all aspects of atomic energy. A decade later it had four reactors and accelerators, a radio-chemical lab and more than 2,000 members of staff exploring the unknown. Since then its brief has expanded into areas of ecological and environmental research that the most fervent anti-nuke campaigner would have problems criticising, including ozone monitoring, industrial land reclamation and the development of car exhaust catalysts. It is the Achilles Heel of modern science that its discoveries are often commercially exploited before researchers have had time to iron out the short falls of the new technology. The chickens rapidly return home to roost it seems, and scientists who would rather be pushing back the boundaries find themselves mopping up the fall-out.

A couple of words of warning before we arrive at the Thames Gap. Just after **Several Down** you will hit a concrete road. Don't get carried away with the bliss of riding something smooth. There is a poorly sign posted left approaching. If you find yourself speeding passed Superity Farm, you have missed it. The final plunge into **Thurtle Down** is definitely one you can hurtle down, if no body or animal is around. Be careful. It is the main drainage channel for a large area of down, and the run-off has eroded deep grooves, that aren't always visible in the compacted path. Go wild but never take your eyes off the track, or go easy and enjoy the leafy splendour of the approaching Thames Gap.

Streatley – Risborough Gap

AT THE END OF THE LONGEST, MOST SUSTAINED LENGTH OF WILDERNESS IN southern England is a road that drones with computer cloned cars, a railway line that clatters continuously through night and day, a river plied by leisure craft big enough to sail the oceans, and over head, low flying jets from I care not where. This is the **Thames Gap**, slashing through the chalk, down which all roads lead to or from Oxford and London and points in between. At one time the river was considerably broader and would have been a formidable barrier between the Danish Vikings and the Saxons. As it silted up and the shallows appeared, it became a fording point for east-west traffic along the ridges, precipitating settlement along both banks, now Streatley in Berkshire and Goring in Oxfordshire. Neither is a particularly wowie place though each has its curiosities, like Goring's Post Office and The Miller of Mansfield Inn, but I recommend a stroll between them, around the lock and the mill weir.

Edwardian **Goring** was a fashionable holiday resort where the middle classes flocked to socialise on and off the water. There were marquees and tea-parties, picnics and soirees, and it was a particular favourite with the theatrical and arty world, who held court under the willows. Oscar Wilde was a big hit when he visited, and boarded for free. On the river there were summer regattas and spectacles of gaily lit boats, fireworks and fancy-dressed punt processions. The razamataz has gone but the county border is still a mooring for the Ted Heath set with their blue canvas pumps, captains hats and keys to the boat hung around their neck with a bit of cork. Amongst the fibre-glass cruisers and plastic tubs you should find some marvellous examples of boat building tied up, with clinker built hulls and teak decks that cost an arm and a leg today. The famous Thames Steamers, worth upward of £700,000 a piece, are a particular joy to behold, immaculately preserved and lovingly maintained right down to the brass screws whose grooves all point in the same direction. And then there is the incongruous, like the boat house moored on the Streatley side, half Balti Restaurant, half Brighton Pavilion, totally out of keeping.

In the harsh winter of 1850-1, the Thames froze thick, so thick 'velocipedists' were able to pedal upstream to Wallingford on their penny farthings. Having tried pedalling across frozen wastes with

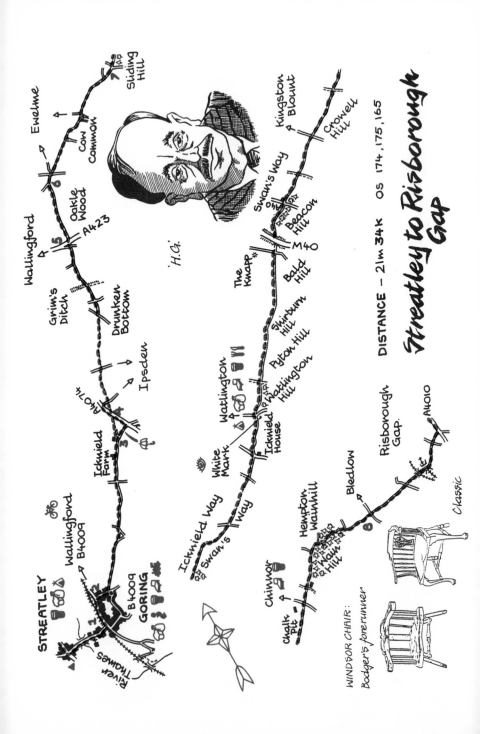

STREATLEY

River Thames

Wallingford
B4009

Wallingford
B4009

GORING

B4009

1

2

3

Ickwield Farm

A4014

Ipsden

Drunken Bottom

Grim's Ditch

Wallingford

A423

Oakle Wood

5

6

Cow Common

Ewelme

Siding Hill

7

'H.G.'

Ickwield Way

Swan's Way

White Mark

Watlington

Ickwield House

Watlington Hill

Pyton Hill

Shirburn Hill

Bald Hill

M40

The Knapp

Beacon Hill

Swan's Way

Kingston Blount

Crowell Hill

Chalk Pit

Chinnor

Hempton Wainhill

Wain Hill

Bledlow

Risborough Gap.

A4010

Classic

WINDSOR CHAIR:
Badger's forerunner

DISTANCE — 21m 34K   OS 174,175,165

Streatley to Risborough Gap

Directions

1 L at TJ B4009.

2 R then **L** IPSDEN.

3 After 'The Barn' **L** through gap.
  Follow **BW** up over hillside.

4 SO over A4074, through gap in hedge into field.

5 SO all the way.
  SO EWELWE.

6 **R** at TJ, **L** EWELWE then **R** SWYCOMBE.

7 SO onto SWAN'S WAY.

8 SO onto UPPER ICKNIELD WAY,
  PRINCES RISBORO'.

Resource

GORING ON THAMES
Information Helpline
Goring Community Centre
01491 873565

Mrs Wiltshire
Leyland Guest House
3 Wallingford Rd
RG8 OAL
01491 872119

Railway Information
01491 872822

WALLINGFORD
Castle Cycles
45 St Mary's St
01491 836289

WATLINGTON
Mr Crawford
The Well House
Restaurant & Hotel
34 – 40 High St
OX9 5PY
01491 613333

Mrs M Roberts
The Cross
48 High St
OX9 5PY
01491 612218

Mrs Hilton
White Mark Farm
82 Hill Rd
OX9 5AF
01491 612295
Camping
Adjacent to Icknield Way.
Tea making facilities for back-
packers and cyclists.
Open Apr to Oct.

CHINNOR
Mrs D Steel
Chinnor Hill Manor
OX9 4BG
01844 351469

pneumatic tyres, I must presume there was a good covering of snow and frost for their solid wheels to adhere to. A further cycling connection comes in the shape of the Beetle and Wedge Hotel, Goring, which was the model for the Powell Inn in *The History of Mr Polly* by H.G. Wells, essential reading for all pedal pushers interested in their heritage. 'HG' was a keen cyclist at a time when the vehicle was causing a minor social revolution in this country. The lower middle classes were becoming mobile. People who had never been further then the end of a shop counter, or maybe a railway line once a year, were now out and about on the highways and byways of Britain, rubbing shoulders with both toffs and plebs. Snared in his dull haberdashers world of mediocrity and frustration, Mr Polly escapes on his push-bike and discovers adventure, trouble and happiness in the arms of the landlady of the Powell Inn. He sets fire to his old life and starts anew as handyman, ferryman, fisherman and dossing-under-the-willows man at the riverside hostelry. The film version is possibly the best of the HG transpositions, with John Mills playing a blinder in the title role and some classic scenes in glorious black and white that successfully capture the feeling of freedom and challenge made possible by the humble bicycle.

Despite what the signs say, we are now travelling the **Upper Icknield Way**, a prehistoric route that, to the west, possibly mirrored the Chalke Way right down to the south coast. There is certainly one farm in the Vale of Blackmoor, north of Cerne Abbas, bearing the name Icknield. To the east we slip on and off it as it follows the spring-line all the way to Swaffham in Norfolk, passing numerous Icknield Farms, Cottages, Houses, Studs and Halls. The name is possibly derived from the Iceni tribe of Celts, denizens of East Anglia, and since Dorchester has an Icen Way, it is more than likely there was a trickle of craftsworkers and traders who regularly travelled its full length 4,000 years ago. Though they never paved it, the Romans made use of the Via Icenia and, probably rationalised it a bit. Given their ignominious defeats at the hands of Boudicca's Celts, it does seem unlikely the colonialists would have celebrated their failures by naming a road after the enemy. Alternatively Icknield could be an old English word for Oxen or Oxfordshire. Whatever it means the first reference to the route is in an Anglo-Saxon charter penned by the monks of Monks Risborough in 903.

On and off road along the Chalke Way, and not a car in sight
Top – A splendid East Anglian thatch on Eagle Lane, Dullingham
Bottom – Bonhume Down, the plunge of Salisbury Plain into the Vale of Pewsey

Opposite Left – The beginning, middle and end

Top –
View across Chesil Beach and Weymouth
to the South Dorset Downs from Fortuneswell
on the Isle of Portland

Middle –
Silbury Hill, the mysterious giant cairn at the
hub of the prehistoric ridgeway system

Bottom –
Hunstanton Cliffs, where the chalk seam ends

Right –
St Mary's, Ashwell

Below –
The thatcher's craft, alive and busy in Melbourn

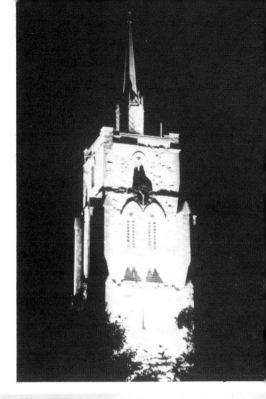

Right –
The naughty bits of Avebury's fertility symbol

Opposite Top –
Time out on Maiden Castle, Dorchester

Opposite Bottom –
Idyllic off-road cycling on the Peddars Way,
a Roman troop road

Below –
The crabman's crabby bicycle, Gore Point, Holme

Above Left –
One very frustrated stallion, the
National Stud, Newmarket

Above –
The Ridgeway, alias the Rudge, sweeping round
the Vale of Whitehorse

Left –
A Thames Steamer, Goring

Opposite Top –
The classic dolls house, Ashdown Park

Opposite Middle –
Norfolk's 'Bicycle Repair Man', appearing
at all reputable open-air markets

Opposite Bottom – Checkerboard flint work, Saturday
Market Place, King's Lynn

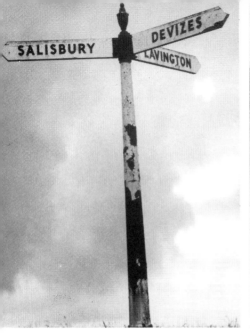

Top Left – The loneliest signpost in the country, beside the Central Range Road, Salisbury Plain
Top Right – The Chalke Way disappearing into the mists of the Ebble Valley from Win Green
Below – Breakfast in the Brecklands

We are bound for the **Chilterns**, an ill-defined area of 650 square miles (1683 sq.km.) that flows through Oxfordshire, Buckinghamshire, Hertfordshire, back into Bucks and then Bedfordshire. Again we are following a ridge, lower down the escarpment this time and sometimes in the Vale, but gone are the bleak whalebacks and sporadic clumps of ancient copse. By virtue of a thin covering of clay possibly deposited by a lake that drowned the area as the Ice Age retreated, the Chilterns are covered with extensive woods. Oak, ash, sycamore, wild cherry, holly, yew, but most of all beeches line our way and camouflage the curve of the ridge above us. On this section of the Chalke Way more than any other so far the seasons are brought into focus. In autumn the ride is coloured by a deep amber and a bike can get stuck in the drifts of dead leaves. Winter, and the bark is sodden black with a thick icing if snow dolloped on the branches . The pale green of the young leaves of spring are like the leaded mosaic of a stained glass window as the sun pours through to awaken those hibernating. And in summer a dense canopy shadows the track, providing welcome relief from the burning sun. Whatever the time of year, the throng of ancient green-woods shield the cyclist from the trauma of commuterland.

In the last twenty years, the population in this area has more than trebled. What were delightful villages have sprawled as tasteful estates have been bolted on willy-nilly, so desperate to be tasteful they are naff. Charming towns like Wendover have lost their historic character to the demands of the market place, or rather precinct, and the stink of exhaust from the perpetually queuing traffic. Power-shouldered drivers zip along the twisting roads in their first, second or third car, forgetting these are country lanes, one hand on their Vodophones. Having said that, it is commuter cash and commuter clout that has saved much of the Chilterns from even more development. Founded in 1965, the Chiltern Society is a conservation group dedicated to protecting the beauty and character of their back yard. With over 6,000 members, a quarterly magazine, eight specialist sub-groups and a slick membership form that goes straight for the Deed of Covenant, they bring the skills of the city to saving the country. While lacking the peace and solitude of Dorset, the Chilterns still deserves its designation as an Area of Outstanding Natural Beauty.

From Goring to Luton, this whole areas is serviced by a road and rail network that makes London easily accessible, but then it always has been, relatively, and historic links with the metropolis go back to the

Middle Ages, if not before. While the **Chiltern Hundreds** was originally a Norman administrative area (encompassing 100 'hides', an area of land capable of supporting a lord and his household), its fame owes everything to London. The three hundreds of Chiltern comprises Desborough, Burnham and Stoke Hundreds. Once the province of wealthy clerics and varying degrees of aristocrats, it was a mecca for brigands and highwaymen who plucked the rich, the only people who could afford to hire freelance bodyguards and travel. Often the guards took back handers off the raiders and deserted their charges at the first sign of trouble. The Chiltern Three Hundreds were unique in having a steward with sole responsibility for making the tracks and turnpikes safe from daring Dick Turpins. When the Hundreds were finally abolished, the Stewardship of Chiltern was retained by the Crown as a convenient desert island for embarrassing Members of Parliament they wanted shot of. In the event of public scandal, or if an MP needed to retire quietly to "spend more time with my family", they could apply for the non-existent office of steward. In theory, this was a paid civic position which would disbar them from being an MP. In fact it was somewhere for naughty boys to write their memoirs on a fat stipend.

But the camouflage of beech leaves works both ways, and somewhere along this stretch of the Chalke Way there is every chance you will peddle passed folk living in buses, vans or trailers who just want to be left alone to get on with their lives. Hidden from the road, their humble encampments conjour up romantic or pitiful notions, depending which movies you've seen, but the truth is far more disturbing. Gypsies I have always found open and friendly. New Age Travellers have been helpful in the passed, but seem nervous and unhappy. They both have a lot to fear from a government that in 1992 removed the statutory obligation on local councils to provide sites for the so-called itinerants, then in 1993 introduced the notorious Criminal Justice Bill increasing the states power to evict and prosecute for trespass. It also authorises the police to destroy their homes, should the whim take them. Whatever we might think of their life style, these are people who have been nomadic from birth, or who have sought or fallen into an alternative culture from that of the grey double-breasted money idolaters nurtured under Thatcherism. They are young and old, white and black, and they have effectively been denied four Articles of Human Rights by the Act, passed in 1994. Unwanted and alone, they are fighting a rearguard action to preserve their minority, and possibly save us all from the victory of blandness. There are times when you have to wonder if the Government isn't full of little Austrian Corporals hell bent on ethnic cleansing and wish that the Stewardship of the Chiltern Hundreds would gobble them all up.

Our ride begins on rolling foothills, through rich farmlands reclaimed from a dense forest whose remains cling for dear life to Ipsden Heath up on your right. Soon we pick up signs for the **Swan's Way**. To add more confusion, we haven't got to the bottom of this one. The original Swan's Way is an ancient byway, now largely tarmaced, that runs from Northampton to Knettishall Heath in Suffolk. This Swan's Way also starts in Northamptonshire, at Salcey Forest, but turns west near Princes Risborough and terminates at Goring. How much of this long distance bridle-route created by Buckinghamshire County Council follows the original byway I don't know. And does it matter?

Further down the road another good example of just how easy it is for us to muddy the waters of history can be seen at **Watlington Hill**. Cut into the escarpment (but poorly maintained) is a phallus that local historian H.J. Massingham dated at 500 BC. Mapped as the White Mark, H.J. deduced that the line of the erection pointed to where the sun rose on Midsummers Day and that the site was a prehistoric place of worship for a fertile future. H.J. argued his corner convincingly, though the image is actually of a church spire, carved into the chalk by one Edward Thorne in 1764. Ed had always felt Watlington church deserved to be crowned with a spire. From his window he could see over the church tower to the hill, so one fine day he took a spade and dug himself a proxy spire that visually fitted on top of the tower and made an English eccentric very happy.

Wathington is also the place where you will most clearly see the wave of chalk crashing down onto the clay beach of the Vale we are riding the edge of. The divide is most evident in the building materials employed in the older houses you will notice between here and Ivinghoe. Where flint was most prevalent, now it is red brick, once manufactured locally at Baldon and in other west Oxfordshire villages. Up on the downs there are other pockets of grey brick buildings, occasionally with some stone dressings and decoratively studded with the more expensive red bricks. Grey bricks were generally produced at a craft level on the site of the growing community, dug and fired in the immediate vicinity. Their colouring is a vitrified glaze produced during the firing of what is a poor clay, full of impurities, but perfectly adequate for brick making. Flint cottages are still in evidence however, and just before we plunge under the M40, to your left, is yet another landfeature called The Knapp. We have traversed Knapp Down, climbed Knapp Hill and passed several Knapp Closes, Copses and Farms. Time to explain.

Flint has been used as a building material for thousands of years, and providing water doesn't seep in through the mortar, it will last just as long. Freshly dug from quarries like the Neolithic Grimes Graves in Norfolk, the material is slightly moist and easier to work than surface flint that has hardened with exposure to the elements. Even then, cutting and shaping (otherwise known as 'knapping') is a skilled business, the secret of success lying in the craftworkers ability to 'read' a flint and determine its lines of weakness. Inside the white crust, the core is a grainless silica which is only slightly softer than a diamond and would take you or I hours of chipping away before we achieved a break. Skilled knappers first tap the stone to check it is sound and not frost damaged, the difference between the ring of a bell and a muffled thud that indicates it will disintegrate at the first heavy blow. Having found a suitable angle of attack (never a flat surface), they will strike it with clean blows until the flint has been 'flaked' into shape. The discarded slivers are often used as filler or 'gallets' between the larger knapped flints.

Todays craftsmen and women use coal hammers but because steel tends to produce a deep, bulbous shave they will also employ lengths of deer antler, just like Neolithic knappers. In construction work they tend to use lime mortar which seeps into the crust of the flint, creating a stronger bond than that afforded by modern cement mortar. As to the design of walls, our jaunt along the Chalke Way has already revealed something of the rich variety of possibilities, from checkerboard squares to fine flush work, from haphazard layering to intricate mixes where stone and brick are called into play along-side the black flint. And if you are wondering how recent repairs manage to look centuries old, the answer lies in a solution of fresh cowdung that is painted on the wall encouraging moss and lichen to take hold. "Just going to give the front of the house a lick of shit, darling . . ."

As you pedal through the exquisite ancient woods of Beacon and Chinnor Hills spare a thought for another group of craftsworkers, now no more, but whose name has become wrongly synonymous with cowboy builders and botched jobs. In fact, the 'bodgers' were a group of resourceful woodworkers who set up mobile workshops in temporary huts thrown up on site amongst the Chiltern beeches. Between November and March, when the sap was low, they would move into the forest, fell, chop and shave the branches on a draw-shave horse before turning the wood on simple pole lathes. The association with crude workmanship is probably more to do with their make shift accommodation than the chairs they turned out. Whilst nowhere as ornate as your Loui Quinze or Chippendale, a bodger chair was a sturdy piece of furniture, well made but strictly functional.

Each village had its own speciality. At Chinnor, for example, bodgers were known for their high backed rush-seated ecclesiastical chairs, but the greatest demand was for them to turn legs and rails for the Windsor chairs fabricated at High Wycombe. By the 18th century Chiltern chairmasters were turning out over 80% of the chairs made in Britain. Predictably the Industrial Revolution was to hit the craftworkers badly. Though never a full-time occupation, by the end of the last century bodgers were largely week-end bodgers, reduced to making wooden pegs for marquees. But all was not lost. The Chilterns retains its reputation as a centre for furniture production, or at least it does if you consider MFI snap-together kits fall into the category of furniture.

The past 21 miles (34 km.) has been all about trees, splendid great monsters that have seen it all before and bide their time. The best is yet to come but first we have to negotiate what Sir John Betjeman called 'Metroland'. BMW-land would be more accurate.

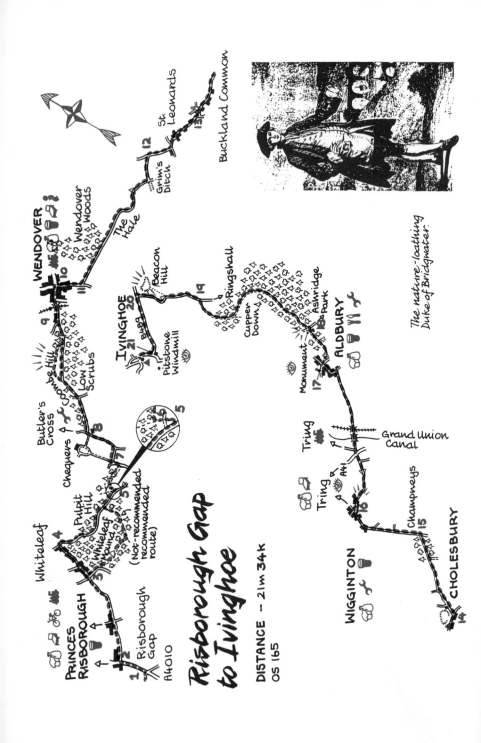

Risborough Gap to Ivinghoe

DISTANCE ~ 21m 34k
OS 165

PRINCES RISBOROUGH

Whiteleaf

Butler's Cross

Cheqvers

Pulpit Hill

Whiteleaf Mound

(Not-recommended recommended route)

Risborough Gap

A4010

Coombe Hill

Low Scrubs

WENDOVER

The Hale

Wendover Woods

Grim's Ditch

St. Leonards

Buckland Common

IVINGHOE

Beacon Hill

Pitstone Windmill

Ringshall

Cupper Down

Ashridge Park

ALDBURY

Monument

Tring

Tring

A41

Grand Union Canal

Champneys

WIGGINTON

CHOLESBURY

B489

The nature-loathing Duke of Bridgwater.

Directions

1 L onto A4010 PRINCES RISBOROUGH (busy road).
2 After speed restriction sign, **R** UPPER ICKNIELD WAY.
3 SO WHITELEAF on wall.
4 **R** at TJ.
5 After farm gate to Pulpit Hill, **L BW** (hidden entrance).
6 **R** at crosspaths. Blue and white arrows on tree.
7 **L** at road.
8 **R** DUNSMORE then at top of hill SO between bollards into Combe Wood.
9 **R** at road, over railway then SO into Wendover.
10 **R** at RA then **R** THE HALE.
11 **L** up hill.
12 **R** CHOLESBURY.
13 **L** WIGGINTON.
14 **L** WIGGINTON.
15 **L** WIGGINTON.
16 **R** ALDBURY.
17 **R** at village pond LITTLE GADDESDEN, then **L** off Tom's Hill Road to MONUMENT.
18 Pedal past Visitors Centre, **L** at car park back to monument then **R** along permissive **BW**.
19 **L** at road.
20 **L** at TJ IVINGHOE (fast busy road).
21 **R** at TJ IVINGHOE.

Resource

PRINCES RISBOROUGH
Mrs M Mercer
Black Prince
86 Wycombe Rd,
01844 345569

David Bolton Cycles
Lloyds Bank Gardens
Market Square
01844 345949

WENDOVER
Tourist Information
The Clock Tower
High St
01296 696759

Mrs H Biggs
The Hollies
Nash Lee Rd, HP22 6BG
01296 623089

Railway Information
01494 441561

TRING
Royal Hotel
Station Rd, HP23 5QR
01442 827616

Rothschild Zoological Museum
01442 824181
Open daily, fee.

IVINGHOE
Ivinghoe YHA
The Old Brewery House, LU7 9EP
01296 668251

Risborough Gap – Ivinghoe

ONCE UPON A TIME THERE WAS A SMALL BUSTLING MARKET TOWN CALLED Princes Risborough, an attractive place, not exactly place-mat material, but pleasant enough. It was originally called Great or Earl's Risborough but when Edward III`s son, the Black Prince, built himself a castle and moved in, local residents did themselves the honour and rechristened the community. They thought they would live happily ever after. Then, in the middle of the 20th century, a dogma called `modernisation' pounced on the town and ripped out the heart of the medieval streets, replacing charming flint and brick cottages with shuttered concrete and prefabricated blocks.

We steer you round the back of Princes Risborough. We similarly ignore the recommended bridle route through the woods encompassing Whiteleaf Mound. For those who like a challenge, we map the not-recommended recommended route, though it is largely unridable, particularly in the wet, and big on nettles, short on fun. Of the ten counties we pedal through on the Chalke Way, Buckinghamshire wins the cowpat for its lousy way-marking and singular failure to maintain public rights of way, and besides, the jaunt through the sleepy hamlet of Whiteleaf is far more entertaining.

Having finally climbed back up onto the chalk escarpment at Lower Codsen, be wary of the left hander into the woods of **Pulpit Hill**. Cycle passed all the obvious entrances. As the road starts to dip, look for a quick flash of an old wooden bridleway sign and a narrow gap in the bushes that goes back on itself. Pedal passed, carefully turn in the road and take a run at it from the opposite direction. Ignore the forestry tracks that almost immediately cross your path and look for a poorly defined crossroads of paths waymarked by tatty arrows nailed to a tree on your left. Hang a right and enjoy an enchanting down hill dodging the beeches around the back of **Chequers**, the Prime Minister's weekend retreat.

'Chequers' is a corruption of 'Exchequer,' a title gleaned from the chequered table on which the accounts of the land were once totted up. In the 12th century, one Elias Hostiarius, Usher of the Exchequer, acquired the estate and passed it to his son, Henry de Scaccio, who finally secured the title deeds to the land. 'Scaccio' is Latin for 'chequer' so the name of the estate was pretty well set in blood. In the

1560s William Hawtrey married into the Hostiarius line, built the current house and imprisoned Lady Jane Grey here for a couple of years. The estate then slipped through a number of famous fingers until, in 1909, Member of Parliament Lord Lee of Fareham bought the place and enjoyed its rural idyll so much he decided to bequeath it to the Crown. In his own immortal words, "The better the health of our rulers, the more surely they will rule, and the inducement to spend two days a week in the high and pure air of the Chiltern Hills and woods will, it is hoped, benefit the nation as well as its chosen leaders".

Hope he might, but the last few encumbents have certainly proved Lord Lee very wrong. The first PM to use Chequers, Lloyd George, wrote, "It is full of the ghosts of dull people". By now it must be overcrowded with grey spirits bumping into each other, but all the same it is interesting how many government leaders finally retired into the area. Ramsey Macdonald, Clement Atlee, Aneurin Bevan, Harold Wilson and our beloved Maggie the Hacker all settled quietly (or not in the case of Thatcher) into a Chiltern 'Dunruling'. If you spot a number of suits patrolling the perimeter looking like they've stepped out of *The Blues Brothers*, you can be pretty certain the boss is in residence. Don't leave your bike unattended. Ceasefire or no ceasefire, they are bound to think it's an IRA bomb and instantly have a SWAT squad crawling through your panniers. "Ah ha! A map!!"

Down and up, down and up. You have hit the hills, but none are particularly painful. **Coombe Hill** is the highest point in the Chilterns at a mere 832 feet (254 m.) and the last opportunity along the Chalke Way to stand on a distinct edge and peruse the vast flatlands disappearing north, in this case the Vale of Avesbury. When you arrive at the quagmire Buckinghamshire jokingly call a bridleway, keep to the left, amongst the trees, and at the first opportunity pedal through to the grassed tip of the scarp. The great wave of chalk is breaking up as it looses height, its smooth contours punctured by clay inlets that bore primeval rivers and now bear railways, roads, motorways and a canal funnelling into the big city. Down and up, down into Wendover and up the Hale, onto the heathland, and a gentle ride through rippling countryside and linear brick villages hemmed in by Green Belt.

Leaving Cholesbury we enter **Hertfordshire** and cross a thin peninsular of the county which really ought to be in Buckinghamshire, which we return to five miles (7 km.) later. Herts is an odd county, difficult to identify. It isn't known for its famous cheese, pies or brew.

There are no unique indigenous crafts or industries. Tourists don't flock to a Hertforshire village to get their photo taken on the set of a popular TV series. Sir Bernard Miles is the most renown example of Hertfordshire man, a rubber faced actor who had country wisdom etched deep in every crease and is best known for character appearances in black and white movies of a bygone age of great British studio productions. Barbara Cartland is the county's most distinguished writer in residence, but that doesn't explain why most people just tear through Herts in a mad dash to arrive at London.

All the famous roads traverse it, Akeman Street, Ermine Street, Watling Street, the A1 (M) and the concrete sections of the original M1. Its proximity to the 'smoke' targeted Herts as a laboratory for social experiments of the town planning kind, most particularly the Garden City and New Town movements to soak up human overspill. Its agricultural output found a ready market feeding the capital. In return, before the advent of motor cars, Herts took delivery of the city's waste – night soil and horse droppings, soot, ashes, horn shavings, fur clippings and all the other wonderful biodegradable crap that could be spread on fields. By the end of the 18th century the county was officially 'the best corn county in the kingom', and nearly every fertile corner that a plough could squeeze into was seeded.

Waste of a different kind is dumped at **Champneys**, on your right as you pedal along the straight into Wigginton. Here mounds of fat are pummelled and coerced into some semblance of the human form at the cost of a respectable weeks wages a day. Established in 1925 on a 69 hectare estate, this is Champneys the famous health farm where the indolent rich try to buy their way to fitness via medical consultants, dieticians, aerobics instructors, tennis coaches, water treatments and therapy classes. Its the sort of strawberries and slimmers cream place that deserves a visitation from the Carry On Team.

Champneys used to be one of the Rothschild houses, one of a clutch that now dot the planet. In 1872 Baron Lionel Nathan de Rothschild purchased Tring Park, squeezed between Tring and Wiggington, and successive Rothschild siblings made a success of running the estate. Walter, the second Lord Rothschild developed what was the largest private collection of stuffed livestock (deadstock?) into the public Zoological Museum. His commitment to the conservation of endangered species like the giant tortoise spurred him to lease the Aldabra Atoll in the Indian Ocean, a sympathy for the living that extended to human beings.

Unlike their neighbours at Pendley Manor, the Rothschilds were good landlords, and can take credit for building the delightful cottages in **Wiggington** which once housed their estate workers. At the foot of the hill on your left, the story of the Pendley Estate is about as philanthropic as the story of Milton Abbas, but far more sketchy. According to Daniel Defoe, in the mid 15th century a 'Mr Guy' wiped the village of Pendley off the map and developed for himself a sizable estate with 'a most delicious house'. Mr Guy then proceeded to enclose the common land of Wiggington Common. Twice he erected fences and twice the villagers tore down the obstructions and buried them. Finally Mr Guy gave up and had to make do with a back garden of a few thousand hectares, poor sod.

As you enter the village, pause at the T-junction opposite the first chapel on your right. Get off your bike, sit cross legged in the middle of the junction and run your hand under your bum Don't be surprised to find you are hovering a metre above the tarmac. You are slap bang in the middle of another leyline running E.S.E. to W.N.W. for 20 miles (32 km.), linking Akeman Street in the east to Berkhampstead Castle, Thomas 'Becket's old pad, in the west. Between the two lowland termini is a steep climb up the Wiggington spur followed by an almost immediate descent into the Bulbourne Valley and the Castle. At the risk of yet again pouring cold water on Alfred's inspired theory, if I was a Neolithic traveller I'd walk round the lump. Even Jack and Jill Ug had the sense to save their energies.

And so down the spur, over the Grand Union Canal and into the beautiful village if **Aldbury**, curled at the foot of the last clearly defined chalk ridgeway we will ride. With its bullrush pond, civic stocks and village green, Aldbury features in many a tourist's photo album and is a popular location for the sort of cinematic costume dramas British production companies excel at. The name is Saxon for 'old fortified place', though there is no record of a fort located hereabouts. Neither is there much evidence of it being a working village. James I introduced straw plaiting as a cottage industry that helped to supplement agricultural incomes, but this was largely a residential village, home to an emerging middle class of yeoman farmers who worked the estates. The 16th century manor house facing the pond bears the inscription BW for Benedict Winch, whose family of yeoman farmers occupied the house for over a hundred years.

Stocks House, by contrast, was occupied for a considerably shorter time by fluffy tailed Bunny Girls. Here the mesdames of the playboy Club taught Hefner's babes how to lay a tray of cocktails on an onyx table without bending at the waist. Who would have thought it . . . in Aldbury.

Today Aldbury's traders do well out of Sunday strollers who set off from here to climb up to the National Trust's **Ashridge Estate**, a climb you will also probably find yourself walking. At the time of the Crusades, Edmund Crouchback, nephew of Henry III and later Earl of Cornwall, created a deer park, built a palace and established a monastery up at Ashridge Park. The order of Bon Hommes were keepers of a gold box containing drops of the blood of Jesus Christ, apparently a gift from the Patriarch of Jerusalem to Edmund's father. Some three hundred years and countless pilgrims later, the monasteries were dissolved and the relic exposed as a fake. Whether the box was empty or the deductive skills of medieval DNA fingerprinting were employed isn't recorded. Anyway, the estate was confiscated, passed on to Henry VIII's children then sold to Sir Thomas Egerton, Lord Keeper of the Seal. As the Dukes of Bridgewater, Egertons remained in residence until 1921 when the National Trust acquired the building and the 1,619 hectares of parkland.

The most famous of the Egertons is commemorated by the **Bridgewater Monument** located near the information centre, though you will probably see the former before the latter. What it is with men and their monuments, or have I been reading too much Freud? This is the third ghastly column we have encountered, but at least this one can be climbed, affording a magnificent panorama across to Ivinghoe Beacon and probably Oraefa Jokull (Iceland) on a clear day. Francis Egerton, the Third Duke of Bridgewater, is commonly known as the father of inland navigation, the first of the great British canal builders. In 1761 he built the Bridgewater Canal linking the family's coalfields at Worsley to the markets and distribution points of Manchester, slashing the cost of the commodity by half (or doubling his profits). Of course, Francis didn't build anything. He simply had the idea and the cash to commission James Brindley, a man who could neither write nor draw yet somehow managed to undertake the greatest engineering feat of that century. I suspect somewhere there is buried a master builder who deserves to be recognised as the person who listened to Francis and James waffle on, then went out and got his hands dirty digging the damn canal the way that he knew best.

Francis Egerton was actually a pretty destructive character. A misogynist and all-round bastard, he hated the countryside, loathed Ashridge but had a soft spot for shooting furry creatures and ripping the heads of flowers. He neglected the estate so completely that the house fell into ruin and had to be demolished. As you ride along the ridge under the mighty bows of oaks, cedars, beeches and firs that have resided in the park for centuries, you can see poor old Frank's point. For a man who deserved to live his life in a cell, this profusion of nature must have been hell on earth. For myself the pedal round to Clipper Down, though short, is one of the most enjoyable lengths of woodland cycling along the Chalke Way. The permissive bridleway is easy riding and sufficiently root-free to allow the eyes to wander skywards, to catch the flickering sun light as it tries to penetrate the canopy and bring warmth to the damp undergrowth. Just occasionally you catch sight of a circling buzzard or hovering kestrel, maybe something furry scurrying along a branch, and then it's all over. You emerge opposite the golf course and come face to face with a lion.

The White Lion of Whipsnade Zoo is the most recent (1933) and last chalk carving we will encounter. Seen to your right on the Dunstable Downs as you pedal towards Ivinghoe Beacon, it is not the most imaginative rendition of the King of the Savannah, but no doubt serves its purpose. And before you ask, I have no idea where the Dulux dog is or was hacked out, the other classic example of hill carving as advertisement. Ahead a chalk track leads up to the headland of **Ivinghoe Beacon**, but cyclists are not welcome. For a final look back along the Chiltern ridges, secure your beloved against the No Cycling sign (to make the point) and walk up. Like Win Green, the Beacon is a launch pad for radio controlled gliders and kites, but come Sunday, it's a tight fit. Between the banks of the hill fort and the steep down to Ivinghoe there just isn't the space to cater for the throng of shell-suits that pour out of Luton and Dunstable. A better grand-stand seat for the aerobatics is to be found on the road at the foot of the hill, just before the junction.

But the view from the beacon is grand. I'm particularly taken with the delightful cement works, belching forth down at **Pitstone**. As a backdrop to the oldest windmill in the country, the 'Blue Circle Bastard' speaks volumes just in its contrast. Whoever agreed to the siting of this one must have needed a lobotomy to qualify for voting.

Possibly they are the same wise men who, as I write, are suggesting local residents would relish a rubbish tip locating on their doorstep. But for all our romantic notions of a golden age of windpower, benign technology also had its siting problems. Dated 1627 and 1749 (no explanation forthcoming), Pitstone Windmill is of the postmill variety, meaning the upper housing rotates as it is pushed by hand to face into the wind . Positioned at the mouth of the Bulbourne Valley, bordered by Ivinghoe and Pitstone Hills, this postmill was vulnerable to erratic wind changes. In 1902 a freak gale caught the mill from behind. The sails rotated in the wrong direction. Instead of locking up, the internal mechanism went into reverse, strained, then exploded under the stress, sending cogs and ratchets shooting through the roof. Pitstone Windmill hasn't worked since and in 1937 it was handed over to the National Trust for restoration.

Pitstone Mill has come to symbolise the end of the Ridgeway Path, the long distance footpath we have occasioned across since leaving Overton Hill. For us it represents a halfway point, not only in terms of miles or kilometres, but in the feel of the journey. You have pedalled 201miles (322 km.), largely across ridges linking vantage points that give a clear outline to the chalk. You, I hope, have visited many ancient monuments, some world beaters, and pondered the paradox of the highly sophisticated primitive. From here on north east the accent is on riding, on going with the flow of a landscape that is never flat but has definitely lost its edge. The historic sites are still there, but their impact is dulled by familiarity with the type. The pleasures to come are simple pleasures. Isn't that what cycle touring is all about?

And like all truly great cycling adventures, the Chalke Way has its low point, its black spot. You are about to enter the Twilight Zone of the Luton conurbation. Nightstop at Ivinghoe and steel yourself for a grizzly morning's ride. By tomorrow lunch time it will be all over, bar the rest of the adventure.

Ivinghoe – Telegraph Hill

ONCE INSIDE THE VILLAGE OF IVINGHOE THE INCESSANT WHAPPING BACK AND forth of traffic burning up the B489 is muffled, and the 'Blue Circle Bastard' (as a fellow tippler called it, though he wasn't sure exactly who owned it) is hidden. With its 17th and 18th century buildings, fine church and a village green that hosts an annual fun fair, the community has survived the pressures of Metroland remarkably unscathed. The nasties have been reserved for neighbouring Pitstone Green. Not much bigger than a large hamlet, **Ivinghoe** once held the status of a small market town. The Youth Hostel is housed in what was the Town Hall and it isn't hard to picture 15th century yeoman farmers, a pint of porter in hand, stood outside the inn on the green haggling over prices. (Today the King's Head is an exclusive restaurant you won't be dressed for, but go in and pig out anyway.) By virtue of the headland of Beacon Hill, the Upper and Lower Icknield Ways squeeze together here. Having left the ancient byway at Wendover, we rejoin it for a highly enjoyable cruise across open country to **Edlesborough** and the church of St Mary's that stands like a lighthouse on a low chalk outcrop disrupting the smooth horizon.

'Edlesborough' means 'Churchtown', and St Mary's is certainly one to visit, if you can get it in. To my knowledge the church ceased preaching The Word sometime back and shut up shop, presumably to deter vandals rather then fallen souls. Built of Totternhoe stone, the Perpendicular exterior has weathered badly, but the softness of the chalk made for excellent stone carving within. Until 1828, it was crowned by a reputedly 'gleaming spire', before lightening really lit it up and felled it. On the surface yet another bastillioned church with tower, inside St Mary's reveals a wealth of ecclesiastical artistry. The woodwork is superb, particularly the high screen and tall pulpit with its unusual four-tier canopy, but the place I always go for is the choir stalls, to study the misericords. These are the underside of the sloping seats where the clergy perch during the sermon, designed to keep them awake and miserable, hence misericords. They were traditionally sculpted by the apprentices whose choice of subject matter was designed to impress. Generally gargoylesque, in St Mary's they are more delicate. An owl, a bat, even a mermaid, and the wood carving is more skillful that many a pulpit makers'. Why such a modest parish

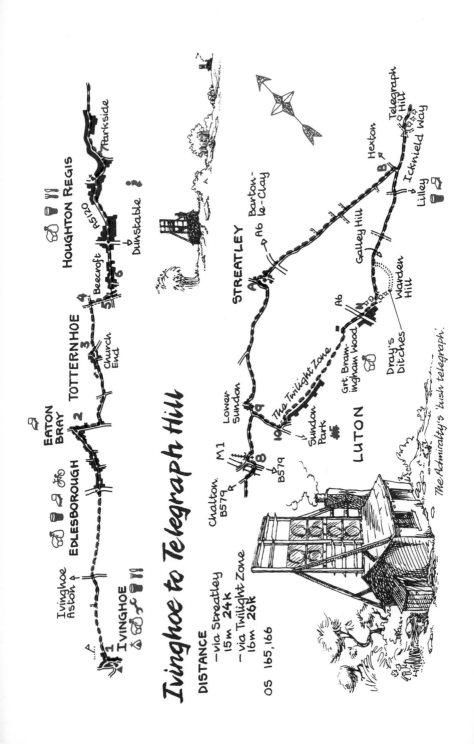

Ivinghoe to Telegraph Hill

DISTANCE
- via Streatley 15m 24k
- via Twilight Zone 16m 26k

OS 165, 166

IVINGHOE

Ivinghoe Aston

EDLESBOROUGH

EATON BRAY

TOTTERNHOE

Church End

Beecroft

Dunstable

HOUGHTON REGIS

B5120

Parkside

Chalton. B579

M1

B579

Lower Sundon

Sundon Park

The Twilight Zone

Grt. Bram-ingham Wood

Dray's Ditches

LUTON

Warden Hill

Galley Hill

STREATLEY

Barton-le-Clay

A6

A6

Hexton

Lilley

Icknield Way

Telegraph Hill

The Admiralty's 'bush telegraph'.

Directions

1. **R** on corner opposite church (or **L** if coming from YHA), then **R** at pub and **SO** past IVINGHOE GOLF CLUB.
2. **R** at TJ then **L** TOTTERNHOE.
3. **R** DUNSTABLE then **L** after pavilion onto track FOOTPATH.
4. **R** at crossways. Blue arrows.
5. **L** at overhead powerline into estate.
   SO over road onto paved footpath.
6. **L** at DROVERS WAY then **SO** over four **RA**s SUNDON.
7. **L** at **RA** opposite 'The Chequers'. SUNDON.
8. **L** at TJ CHALTON then **R** SUNDON.

Via the Twilight Zone

9. **R** LUTON.
10. **L** CHESTNUT AVENUE then **L** SYCAMORE CLOSE.
    Pick a course between fields and estate and past water tower to ruined barn.
    Join tarmac path to right of barn, follow it **L** then **R** down hill to A6.
11. **SO** onto **BW**, **L** along avenue of hawthorns, then **SO** onto track.

Via Streatley

A. **R** then **L** BARTON.
   SO over dual-carriageway LILLEY.
B. **R** LILLEY then **L** onto ICKNIELD WAY.

Resource

EDLESBOROUGH
Mrs J LLoyd
Ridgeway End
5 Ivinghoe Way
LU6 2EL
01525 220405

Janes Cycle Shop
2-6 High St
01525 220208

EATON BRAY
Ms R Hodge
Bellows Mill Cottage
01525 220548

Dunstable Tourist Information
01525 471012

Railway Information
01853 27612

LILLEY
Lilley Arms
01462 768371

church should merit workmanship worthy of a cathedral is unclear. There must be more to the parish of Churchtown, nay Edlesborough, than it readily reveals.

Routefinding can be immensely frustrating, particularly along bridleways and tracks that are at the bottom of the list of priorities drawn up by cash strapped local highway authorities. In a borough that makes its living out of the manufacture of Vauxhall cars, off-road demands have probably dropped off the list. For a number of years now, Mrs Elizabeth Barrett of East Anglia Trails has been pouring over maps searching for a horse friendly link between the Icknield Way at Telegraph Hill, north east of **Luton**, and the Ashridge estate we rode through yesterday. The course of the Icknield Way runs bang through the middle of the grizzly conurbation ahead of you, wedged in the bottleneck of the Lea Valley. For walkers, the Icknield Way Association has waymarked a path that takes advantage of a rusting branch line through **Dunstable** but then plunges our Vibram-soled cousins through the morass of the Luton districts of Leagrave and Limbury. It is a footpath, but if it wasn't it would still be unsatisfactory for cyclists and equestrians.

Mrs Barretts' current solution involves a broad loop round the south east of Motorcity, but negotiations are still going on. In places it is blocked, illegally of course, but the powers that be are unlikely to send in the 7th Cavalry. Elsewhere, while fine for bikies, certain intersections with fast roads are hazardous for horsies. It also misses out the Ashridge ridgeway, which is a shame. More importantly, Mrs Barrett's compromise diverts us a long way from our intention of following the chalk edge and the prehistoric encampments, so our solution is to go for the short sharp shock approach, getting you back on the rough as quickly as possible.

And the road through Beecroft and **Houghton Regis** is really not that bad. It is down hill on a busy but relatively slow suburban thoroughfare where parking restrictions reduce roadside obstructions, and abundant shops, pubs and 'chippies' entice you to relieve the trauma. For children, there is pavement all the way until you are spat back out into the countryside and over the M1. Should you opt to remain on tarmac, from here until Streatley the traffic speeds up and during the rush hour the lanes become the unofficial Luton bypass, chocker with semi-conscious commuters. At other times they are a pleasant detour. Alternatively, hang a right before Lower Sundon and venture into the Twilight Zone of Great Bramingham Wood Estate. Luton is growing faster than the Ordnance Survey can map it. On paper there is a bridleway running along the edge of Sundon Park and Great Bramingham Estates, but try and find it! Squeezed somewhere between new back fences and long established fields, it occasionally emerges but generally is lost under the dumps of garden waste, builders' crap and rusting whiteware. When I contacted the Borough Council, they were adamant the ROW was fully functional. A Mr Toprani assured me he had navigated it with his own fair feet back in 1992 and besides, there were far more pressing lengths of tarmac that demanded his attention, notably the official on-off on-off Luton bypass. The Countryside Commission expressed equal disinterest in the erosion of our right to travel, and short of taking direct action (all but outlawed by the Criminal Justice Act) there is frankly not a lot anybody can do. I could tell you that Luton Borough Council's phone number is (01582) 31291 extension 2275 and encourage you to give them earache, but that would be below the belt.

The good news is the Twilight Zone is still ridable, just, provided you occasionally adopt the scooting technique we employed as kids mucking about at the edge of urbanity where spent condoms go to die. Keeping civilisation on your right and picking your own course through, the experience can be good fun if approached with the right blend of cynicism and determination. Look on the bright side. You are within scooting distance of the Great Bramington Wood Sainsbury Superstore, should any campers wish to stock up on microwave meals. More seriously, those who dare win an excellent ride after crossing the A6, up passed Dray's Ditches to Galley Hill, site of a couple of Neolithic barrows and a 15th century gallows. Here we rejoin backpackers walking the Icknield Way. Of the two alternatives, I would opt for the Twilight Zone, but I'm a sucker for the ridiculous. Neither is A1 cycling and we will update *The Chalke Way* as the situation develops. Whichever you choose, within an hour of entering Beecroft you can be deep within the Bedforshire outback.

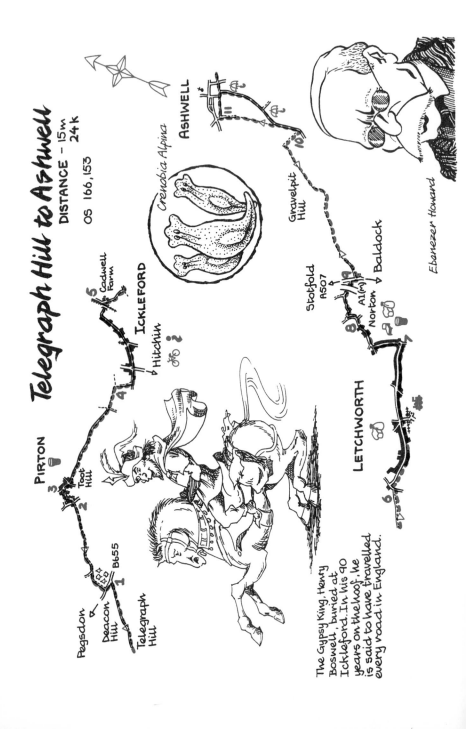

Telegraph Hill to Ashwell

DISTANCE – 15m
24k

OS 166,153

Crenobia Alpina

PIRTON

Pegsdon
Deacon Hill
Telegraph Hill

B655

Toot Hill

ICKLEFORD

Cadwell Farm

Hitchin

ASHWELL

Gravelpit Hill

Stotfold
A507

Norton
Baldock

A1(M)

LETCHWORTH

Ebenezer Howard

The Gypsy King, Henry Boswell, buried at Ickleford. In his 90 years on the hoof, he is said to have travelled every road in England.

Directions

1 **L** at B655 then **R** BRIDLEWAY.
2 **SO** ICKNIELD WAY.
3 **R** at TJ then **SO** onto HANBRIDGE WAY.
4 **R** ICKNIELD WAY then **L** at road and **SO** at **RA**.
5 After railway bridge, **R** ICKNIELD WAY, **SO** through farm then **L** at TJ.
6 **L** at road then **R**. Follow ICKNIELD WAY **SO**.
7 **L** at **RA**, up hill then **R** at TJ NORTON.
8 **R** NORTONBURY LANE then **R**.
9 **R** at A507 then **L** ICKNIELD WAY.
10 **L** at road, up hill then **L** onto **BW** ICKNIELD WAY.
11 **R** onto Ashwell Street track.

Resource

HITCHIN
Hitchin Library
Information Point
Paynes Park
01462 434738/450133

C & J Frost Cycles
94 Walsworth Rd,
01462 434433
(cycle shop)

NORTON
Three Horseshoes Inn
Norton Rd
01462 684890

Telegraph Hill – Ashwell

IT MIGHT BE HARD TO BELIEVE, BUT ONCE UPON A TIME THERE NO TELEPHONES. Long before electric telegraphs, semaphore messages were relayed by sight, be they via smoke signals or waving flags. Between Great Yarmouth and Whitehall, the Admiralty built a chain of tall huts, one every ten miles, to relay news of the Napoleonic war. Each hut was manned by a look-out who would monitor the message from the previous hut and pass it to a colleague for relaying on. The medium for the message was a series of shutters on the roof that opened and closed by hand operated levers and pulleys. Telegraph Hill was the site of one of a number of huts located along the Icknield Way. They worked well on a clear day, but when the fog set in it was a matter of who draw the short straw to put on their running shoes.

While we might seemed to have regained the chalk ridge at Telegraph Hill, from here until Hunstanton the topography is a poor indicator of the geology. The plunge of Pegsdon Common is the closest we get to the the divide, and the hills we now climb are like the ripples following on the back of a spent wave. The landscape is mellowing out, working down towards the prairies of Cambridgeshire. You will begin to notice the place names you have seen before, like Streatley, here pronounced 'Stretleh', and the route is now waymarked by the flint axe logo of the Icknield Way Path. As with The Ridgeway, we don't follow the Riders' Route to the letter, so keep your map handy. But before we can really stretch our legs and feel we are back in the middle of nowhere there is Hertfordshire Part II to negotiate and the vision of **Ebenezer Howard.**

In the 1900s Herts. had a population of around 25,000 rooted within its 700 square miles (1813 sq. km.). By the 1970s there were over a million. As London grew and grew, the over-spill developed into a flood that threatened to drown the county. As early as 1898, in his book *Tomorrow,* Ebenezer Howard had foreseen the problem and proposed custom-built urban sponges to soak up the torrent. The Garden City Pioneer Company was founded four years later to develop a handful of Hertfordshire villages into leafy modern metrolands for the commuting middle classes. Their success did not meet with everbody's approval. Sir John Betjeman had a poetic field day. In the mid Forties however, Ebenezer's idea was resurrected and given government assent in the New Towns Act that lay the foundations for such futurescapes as Stevenage and Milton Keynes. In 1949 that other, slightly better known work of vision appeared, *Nineteen Eighty Four*. Eric Blair (aka George Orwell) ran the village tuck shop in Wallington, down the road from Letchworth and a bit before Stevenage. He didn't have to go far to do his research.

"The most striking thing about Letchworth is that there is nothing striking to see." Lionel Mumby's observation on the first fruits of Ebenezers' dream is horribly accurate. The most interesting thing to say about our ride through is that the road is wide and, yes, leafy. Letchworth garden city was built to encompass the parishes of Norton, Willian and Letchworth. At the turn of the century their combined population stood at 566. Sixty years later it was 25,000, and the butt of many a joke. Residents who enthused about the place were stereotyped as jazz-types who wore open-toed sandals, spouted left wing ideals and toasted the new life over a steaming nut roast. In fact, in its early days, the town was a hot-bed of temperance where you were more likely to encounter wayside pulpits proclaiming "Be Sober, Be Vigilant" than revolutionary graffiti.

It was also an intelligent solution to the dreadful post-war housing shortage that threatened to sentence those who had fought for King and Country to a life on the streets. But like the rest of Hertfordshire, Letchworth still struggles with its identity. Too sprawling to capture the warmth of a village, the wide boulevards and profusion of greenery are equally too open to generate the adrenaline that makes for a town. Its heart seems to lie closer to small town mid west USA and the pulse of the *Little Picture Show*. We are soon through it though and heading into Norton *en route* for the thoroughly English parish of Ashwell.

So ends the grim section of the Chalke Way. In parts it has been truly beautiful, but the double whammy of Houghton Regis and Luton, hotly followed by Letchworth, has interrupted the muse and brought us back down to earth. This leg is a rude reminder of just how marginalised cycling is in this country, but as a transition between the two halves of our odyssey, the Twilight Zone serves to purge us of the high drama of ridge riding and monstrous megaliths and prepare us for the more subtle gentle wonders to come.

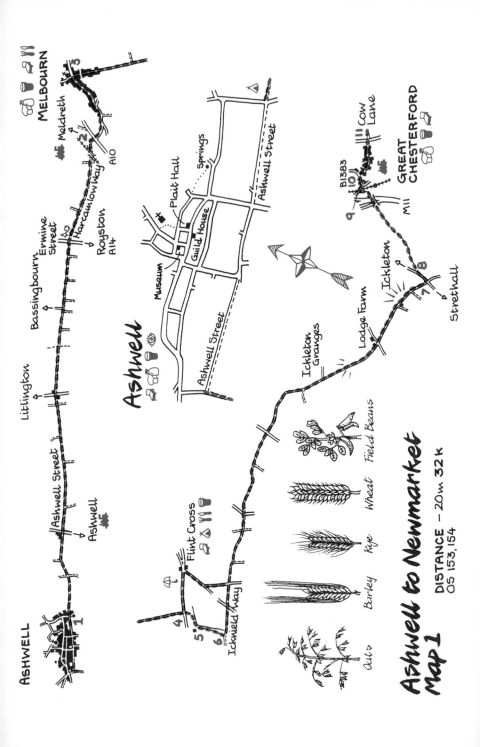

ASHWELL

MELBOURN

Meldreth

Harcamlow Way
Royston A14
A10

Erwine Street

Bassingbourn

Litlington

Ashwell Street

Ashwell

Ashwell

Springs

Plait Hall

Guild House

Museum

Ashwell Street

Ashwell Street

Ashwell

Flint Cross

Ickneld Way

Oats   Barley   Rye   Wheat   Field Beans

Ickleton Granges

Lodge Farm

Ickleton

Strethall

GREAT CHESTERFORD

Cow Lane

B1383

M11

Ashwell to Newmarket
Map 1

DISTANCE — 20m 32k
OS 153, 154

Resource

ASHWELL
The Three Tuns Hotel
High St
SG7 5NL
01462 742107

Ashridge Farm Camping
Park
1 Ashwell St
SG7 5QL
01462 742527

Village Museum
Open Sun/Bank Hols or by
arrangement.

MELBOURN
Goldington Guest House
1 New Rd
SG8 6BX
01763 260555

FLINT CROSS
The Flint Cross Motel
01763 208272
BB & camping

GREAT CHESTERFORD
Mrs J Day
July Cottage
Carmel St
01799 30315

Mrs J Chater
The Delles
Carmen St
CB10 1NR
01799 530256

Crown & Thistle
High St
CB10 1PL
01799 530278

Directions

1 SO on track past campsite, all the way to A10.
2 SO over A10 (fast busy road) MELBOURN.
3 R at CR onto Mortlock Street.
4 SO over A505 (fast busy road).
   Into field, branch R and follow line of ditch.
5 At electricity pylon, L through scrub. Follow
   blue arrow SO keeping ditch on left.
6 L at track ICKNIELD WAY, then SO.
7 L ICKLETON.
8 R diagonally across field ICKNIELD WAY.
9 R over level crossing, or if closed,
   L then R under railway bridge.
10 L at B1383 CAMBRIDGE, then
   R past church ICKNIELD WAY.
11 SO up Cow Lane.

Ashwell – Newmarket

IT IS SOME TIME SINCE WE'VE SUGGESTED A VILLAGE YOU COULD HAPPILY SPEND a full day exploring, and the fact that **Ashwell** once boasted 32 pubs has nothing to do with our recommendation. It is a liquid of a different kind that puts this community on the map, spring water, for here the River Cam rises, otherwise known in its early life as the Rhee. Visit the springs and taste the cold clear water to remind yourself of the pre-chemical nectar we used to enjoy, but be careful not to swallow a *Crenobia alpina*. This small flatworm thrives in fresh water below 11° C (52° F) and is thought to have flourished here since the Ice Age. Where other places celebrate their ponies, dolphins or ospreys, Ashwell is proud of its unique prehistoric worm, and why not?

Thanks to the springhead, this area has been settled since at least the Bronze Age. Make arrangements to visit the **Village Museum** and you can trace Ashwell's history through the many artifacts ploughed up over the years in the vicinity. Between the 11th and 17th centuries the village was a town and one of the most important boroughs in Hertfordshire, hosting a weekly livestock and produce market and four annual sheep fairs. Farmers were well lubricated by a pub on most corners, which in turn were well served by the villages' own brewery. The maltings and Dray House still stand. Straw plaiting for the Luton hat industry brought in pin money, as it did in Aldbury, but at Ashwell they had a school, probably housed in **Plait Hall**, where the young learnt their craft. Quarrying for stone and coprolites was also relatively big business, both within the outskirts of the community. Chalk pits on Ashwell Street now provide sheltered sites for inconspicuous developments, and the imposing 14th century church was hewn from local white limestone and clunch.

St Mary's has the tallest tower and spire (known locally as a 'spike') in the county. It is said to have been the battle ground for a local corn plaiters' competition to see who was the fastest worker. Stood feverishly plaiting 112feet (34 m.) up on the tower, the winner was the person whose plait first touched the bottom. You will notice the clock has only three faces. This is possibly explained by the objections of a farmer to the north who felt his workers would while away the day clock-watching if the fourth face was installed. Inside also the common people have had an impact on St Mary's. On the north wall of the tower and elsewhere you will see some remarkable 14th century Latin graffiti commemorating the Black Death and a `tempest full and mighty' that flattened many an East Anglian barn in 1350 but also purged the plague. One of the scribblings appears to be a piece of architectural criticism scrawled by some medieval Nikolaus Pevsner. 'The corners are not pointed correctly, I spit at them.' Please do not add your own contribution, even if your name really is Baz.

But the simple delight of Ashwell is to stroll along its medieval streets and study the old houses. No longer an agricultural village, the community of in-comers is rich enough and proud enough to invest heavily in preserving the fabric of its historic buildings, a tradition that goes back to the 1930s when villagers were catalysed into action to save the condemned 16th century town house that now stands as the Village Museum. The **Guild House** on the High Street is particularly striking for its ornamental plaster-work of scrolls and dolphins dated 1681. Before it became fashionable to chip off the rendering and reveal the structural woodwork, many wattle and daub buildings were literally plastered top to bottom with this type of decoration ('pargeting'). It served to hide the multitude of sins stuffed into wall cavities and to weather-proof woodwork. Only the wooden brackets and bargeboards were left exposed and these were often ornately carved. We will see more exuberant pargeting as we cycle through Cambridgeshire and on into Suffolk, but for the time being I strongly recommend picking up a map at the Field Study Centre opposite St Mary's and having a good root around Ashwell.

As we roll into Cambridgeshire, down the long straight green track of **Ashwell Street**, there is every reason to believe we are following a Roman road. All the familiar features are there, if not of a cobbled road, then at least of an ancient byway that has been straightened and rationalised by the colonialists. On the Ordnance Survey map it is labelled 'Icknield Way Path' in modern type, indicating it is a part of the Regional Recreational Route surveyed by the Icknield Way Association and opened in September 1992. Two miles (3 km.) to the south and shadowing Ashwell Street roars the A505. In Gothic type, this is labelled 'Icknield Way', and is the route identified by the Survey's first archaeology officer, OGS Crawford back in 1912. Given this is wide open, gently undulating country, it is likely the zone of movement would have been quite broad here and that both roads can justifiably claim to be Icknield Ways. Ashwell Street runs parallel to the northern spring line and would have been the preferred route on a hot summer's day.

But the line of Ashwell Street we ride owes more to the enclosures of the last century than any Imperial intervention. As late as the 1800s, much of the Midlands, south and north east England, and the mountains of Scotland and Wales were still common lands or ill-defined arable lands, and while there were plenty of 'rights of common' covering who could do what where, on the ground it was open country. Tens of thousand of acres were gradually broken down into fields and allotted to landlords in proportion to their current holdings or long-standing rights of common, such as grazing rights. In the process thousands of miles of medieval roads that meandered across the landscape had to be rerouted into new rights of ways running between rather than across the now private fields. Because surveyors find it easier to work in straight lines, many new drove roads were mapped with a ruler and change direction at a high point that made for easy alignment on a sighting post. (Here Alfred Watkins went off at a tangent.)

Though Ashwell Street is overgrown in places, its full width conforms to the 30 to 40 foot standard for that period of enclosure. It is a great ride of 7.5 miles (12 km.) through to Melbourn, carving a path between fields thick with corn or bulging with sugar beet. I've encountered lost little Bambis along the way, though my enquiries failed to establish if there was a venison farm nearby or if wild deer roamed this very (for them) inhospitable parish, and after one refreshing downpour, I stopped to dig up what looked like a flint arrow head embedded in the mud. It probably wasn't but keep your eyes peeled. Though only a few barrows still bulge above the prairies, your way is littered with prehistoric sites and a number of relics have bubbled to the surface of Ashwell Street.

At Melbourn, the OS map informs us we are now riding the Harcamlow Way. This is a venerable title for a walking route that isn't even as old as my granny. Devised by a Mr Fred Mathews, the Harcamlow Way is a figure-of-eight walk centered on Newport, Essex, taking in parts of Hertfordshire and Cambridgeshire. It is one of a number of recent tourist trails Ordnance Survey have seen fit to annotate in the same way that the Wiltshire and Norfolk Cycleways are. Considerably older and not worthy of a mention in the map is Cow Lane, your route out of Great Chesterfield. This is the no-frills name for a historic drove road up to Burton Hill Common. Along this villagers herded the household cow to pasture, then herded it home at night to a mucky yard off a dark narrow street in an impressive walled town. While the Roman battlements of Great Chesterfield had been recycled into houses by the 18th century, the present state of the old drove road suggests ghostly herds still trudge up the hill to where a ruin of a farm fittingly creaks in the wind.

Throughout our long journey we have been in the midst of agriculture, predominantly pastural to start with, but since Ivinghoe the open landscape has increasingly been monopolised by corn crops. The dearth of hedgerows and wide rippling horizon now bring these to the fore, as does the odd duck to avoid a field spray or dive to dodge a harvester. Cambridgeshire joins Hertfordshire in its reputation as 'the granary of England'. Over 85% of the county is devoted to agribusiness of which all but 12% is under the plough. You will mainly see vast tracks of wheat and barley interspersed with beet fields, and these are often heavily irrigated or sprayed to bring into fruition. You might also notice several malting towers in the distance, signs of a once flourishing local brewing industry (now studio apartments), and on the ridge to your right a line of windmills used to grind speciality flours for village bakeries. Today conglomerates with famous subsidiaries like Spillers-French and Rank Hovis McDougall gobble up the thousands of tons of grain East Anglian farmers produce each year. Just before Linton we pass a shiny new example of one of the numerous commercial grain silos in the south of the county. Between the prairies and these great glittering cans, you could be in Little Canada.

Like all industries, farming has to keep moving. Largely due to its climate, soil and a wealth of academics beavering away in university departments, Cambridgeshire has become the national centre for botanical research and development. The Agricultural Advisory Service, National Institute Of Agricultural Botany and the Plant Breeding Institute, all have husbandry farms in the country, bringing scientific principles to what has increasingly ceased to be the empirical process of getting food from the land. They study aphids, crop varieties, seed quality, cross breeding, chemical stimulants, anything and everything that will keep British farmers ahead of the game. Each year they publish revised lists of the best and latest varieties, a sort of *Farmer's Which?*, so if any readers are that way inclined, keep a sharp

Ashwell to Newmarket
Map 2
DISTANCE — 18m 29k
OS 154

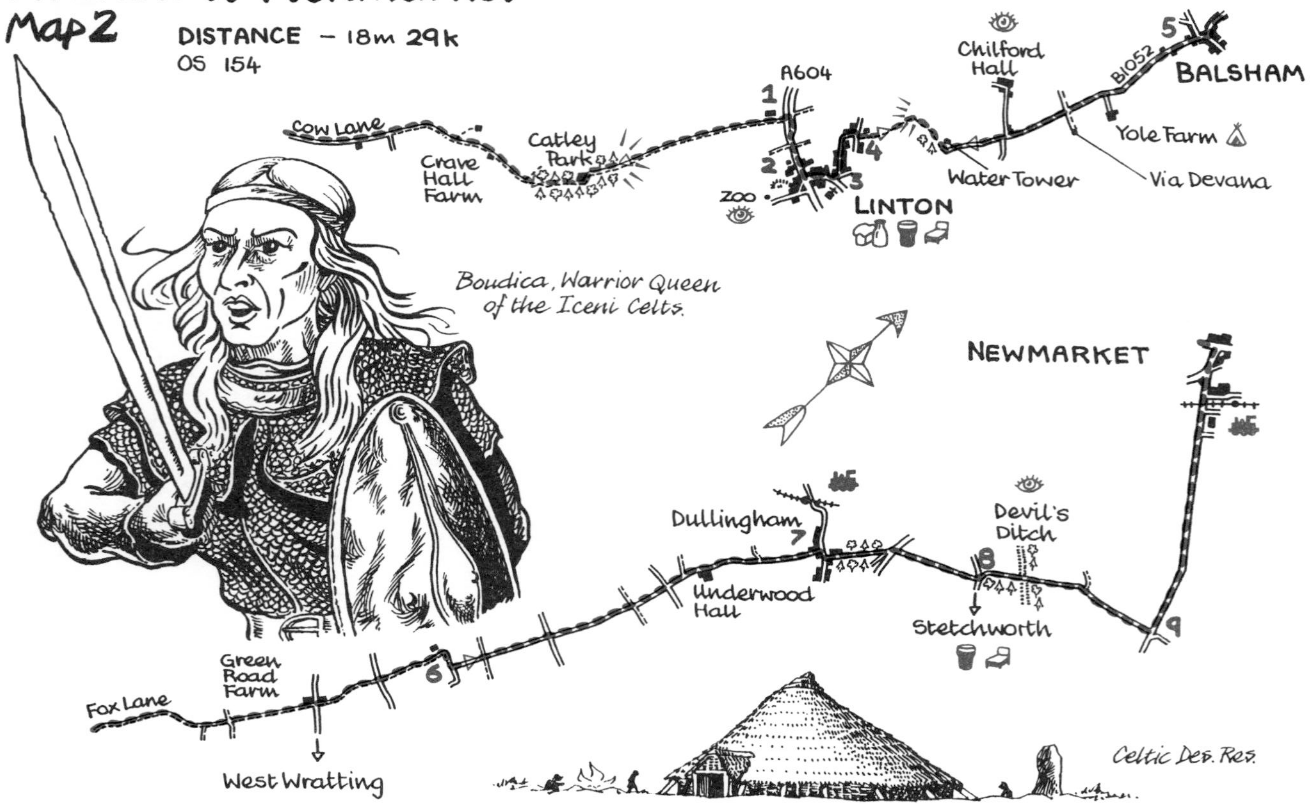

BALSHAM

Yole Farm

Via Devana

B1052

5

Chilford Hall

Water Tower

LINTON

4

3

A604

1

2

ZOO.

Catley Park

Crave Hall Farm

Cow Lane

Boudica, Warrior Queen of the Iceni Celts.

NEWMARKET

Devil's Ditch

8

Stetchworth

9

Celtic Def. Res.

Dullingham

7

Underwood Hall

6

Green Road Farm

West Wratting

Fox Lane

Directions

1 Cross dual-carriageway then **R** along cycle path (fast busy road, so stay on pavement if unhappy about road).
2 **L** opposite Green Hill pub, along High Street.
3 After bridge, **L** ICKNIELD WAY. Follow road round.
4 **R** at TJ then **L** onto **BW** after telephone exchange RIVEY HILL.
5 **R** WEST WRATTING, then **L** ICKNIELD WAY.
6 **L** onto road ICKNIELD WAY.
7 **R** STETCHWORTH then **L** up Eagle Lane.
8 **SO** at an angle.
9 **L** NEWMARKET. Turn to town map.

Resource

LINTON
Mrs A Peake
Linton Heights
36 Wheatsheaf Way
CB1 6XB
01223 892516

The Crown Inn
The High St
01223 891759

Linton Zoo
Cambridge Wildlife
Breeding Centre
Hadstock Rd
01223 891308
0839 222003 recorded info.

Chilford Hundred Vineyard
01223 892641

YOLE FARM
Ms S Kiddy
Balsham Rd
Linton
CB1 6HB
01223 893280
BB & camping

STETCHWORTH
Mrs Herbert
Prospect Villa
Tea Kettle Lane
01638 665021

look out. If there is a new strain of barley threatening to revolutionise the market, you are likely to see it here first. Unfortunately the second place you are likely to see it is the grain mountains of the European Community's Common Agricultural Policy.

While it is a joy to trundle along peaceful green roads and country lanes that haven't seen a car all morning, the intensity of arable farming has had a noticeable impact on the amount of wildlife you *won't* see between here and Newmarket. Butterflies are everywhere, but the green road we are riding is the wildest strip in the landscape, bordered by a tangle of vetches, worts and grasses that struggle to survive wafting herbicides. Worse than anywhere in the country, the east has been raped of its hedgerows. In the 1970s, 4.500 miles (7.240 km.) of hawthorn thicket was being uprooted each year, along with the animal and plant life that called it home. In the fields, mechanised harvesting techniques inadvertently herded young mammals and birds into the centre, culminating in a blood bath. The corncrake that used to flourish in Cambridgeshire is now Britain's most endangered bird.

And it is not just the impact of modern farming methods over the last 25 years. Barn conversions and the trend to convert old maltings into character cottages have removed the dark dry crevasses that provided breeding spots for many of East Anglia's birds and mammals. For example, the barn owl population has plummeted by 70% since the 1930s, largely because modern farm buildings are devoid of cross beams and cosy roof cavities, and only one in 25 owners are conscientious enough to install nestboxes. My encounter with deer is unusual, though they do roam free in many of the county's larger woods. More likely you will be brought to a standstill by a squadron of tortoiseshell or comma butterflies parked up on the white line of the track, twitching their flaps like fighters on a runway awaiting the all-clear.

Towards the end of this leg, **Devils Ditch** is a prime example of strip wilderness, but blink and you will miss it. Running from the natural water defences of the Fens near Reach to what used to be thick forests south east of Stretchworth, this is another formidable earthwork whose true origin lies buried deep in its overgrown banks. It is definitely post-Roman, possibly built by the Saxons to contain the vanquished after the Battle of Mons Badonicus in 500 AD. Equally it could be 7th Century Anglo-Saxon and the limit if the kingdom of

Anglia, dug to defend themselves from the rampaging King Penda of Mercia. It didn't do the trick. Today the section we cross is a mass of roots and branches that shelter a number of rare plants and species like the pasque flower, *anemone pulsatilla*. If you have the time, weave your way along the footpath a short distance. It is still very impressive and decidedly creepy, in both meanings of the word.

Before the ditch, and if you are travelling with children, a visit to Linton Zoo is probably a must. As these places go, Linton's approach to containment is a long way from the grim featureless concrete pits many of us (let alone the animals) find so distressing. The Simmons family that owns the zoo have been at the forefront of conservation and education for many years, and have a reputation for successfully breeding exotic species that should not or cannot be obtained from the wild. As early as 1977 they successfully bred in captivity the first Indian eagle owl. The Asian binturong, a large long haired fruit eating mammal with a prehensile tail for climbing, is another of the more obscure species they have had great success rearing. With so much of the world's natural heritage under threat, zoos like Linton provide an invaluable service to those who will inherit our mistakes, and they deserve a better press than is fashionable these days.

On the other hand, Mum and Dad might be more interested in a pit stop at **Chilford Hundred Vineyard**, over the hill from Linton. The actual vineyard is a short distance from the Hall, situated on a south west facing slope of the chalk edge. Here the soil conditions and sheltered position are not a million miles from those found in the Bordeaux region of France, producing a table wine with a 'good clean flavour, fragrant nose, fruity body and good acidity'. As a whiskey man, it's all lost on me, but I always enjoy a stroll round the Hall. Chilford is another family affair. Simon and Rebecca Alper have been in the wine business since 1972, but long before that father Sam fancied himself as a sculptor. The grounds are peppered with interesting examples of his work and those he's collected of other sculptors or from such high art markets as Brick Lane, London. The *pieces des resistance* are inside the great barn that is now a conference centre decorated with an impressive display of ye olde agricultural equipment. Head and shoulders above the scythes and spades is a superb collection of steel tractor seats, lovingly restored by Sam Alper and repainted in the manufacturers original livery. They are hung on the walls and lit like a gallery might a Dadaist found object. Clearly Sam is one of the great British eccentrics who have made so much of the Chalke Way a Pandora's box of the weird and wonderful.

Towards the end of this section we re-enter **stud country**, but not the quaint whitewashed stables type of stud, set round a farm courtyard with a couple of paddocks between it and the road where you can go and stuff grass in the face of a friendly Flikka. All you will see here is a grand entrance, tight security and an immaculate driveway disappearing off into the estate somewhere. Close to the gate there are a handful of staff bungalows that flank the avenue like Hussar huts guarding Buckingham Palace. Deep inside the CCTV perimeter are managers, secretaries, grooms, trainers, riders, vets, stable bods and all kind of computers whose sole objective is to serve the every whim of their royal charges and guarantee the line. These are the new breed of stud farms, on land reclaimed from agriculture, in buildings designed exclusively around the horse. Hygiene, security, disease control, fire containment, economy of human contact – the extreme vulnerability of these precious lumps of horsemeat dictates an architecture and a layout that puts them well beyond the public eye. Like tourists cruising the Balmoral estate on the eve of the Highland Games, you are highly unlikely to see the main event.

And some of these four-legged studs (and mares) are indeed royal, owned by Sheiks and Maharajahs, European crowns and the *nouveau riche* of America and Japan. At the height of the boom, in the mid eighties, you had to have oil gushing out of your back pocket to buy into this highest of high-rollers game, to afford the gamble of purchasing a mule. Offspring of the 1964 Kentucky Derby winner, Northern Dancer, were fetching a cool $3.5 million when, in 1983 Sheik Mohammed Maktoum of Dubai outbid Vernons Pools magnate Robert Sangster for the purchase of the colt Snaafi Dancer. He paid a trifling $10.2 million for a nag that never ran a race and on the training ground struggled to beat bushes. Two years later, Sangster broke the record and coughed up $13.1 million for a son of the great Nijinsky. Seattle Dancer was a good little runner but never great, and never likely to recoup his price.

The big studs produce brochures featuring pin-ups of their prize sires and dams with comprehensive records of their performance on the track and genetic characteristics. Blood lines are minutely detailed and traced back at least four generations. Then there are the critic notices – 'The compact, good-quartered Rock City, was effective at six furlongs to a mile and he acted on any going A more genuine and consistent individual would be difficult to find.' Finally there is the price tag, not only for him to sire or her to foal, but what the breeder can expect to get at auction for one of their sprogs. Always the tag is in guineas, an archaic hangover from pre-decimalisation that used to be 21/- (shillings) and is now £1.05p. Around Newmarket, siblings from the loins of Northern Dancer dominate the pedigrees and it can cost as much as 100,000 guineas to get a successful one of his line to 'cover' (i.e. hump) your mare. In any one year a stallion can be called on to cover over 100 mares, which as one flea bitten old dobbin said to another, is "Nice work if you can get it".

Newmarket is one of the biggest horse trading centres of the world. The Tatersalls auctions are the culmination of a busy six week round of autumn sales that whisk trainers from Doncaster to Kentucky to Fairyhouse to Newmarket to Newbridge (in Ireland) and back to Newmarket. Thousands of yearlings (one horse year equals roughly four and a half human) change hands after their pedigrees have been analysed, their physique assessed, gait scrutinised, looks studied and their movement around the auction ring dissected. As racing journalist Grahame Rook explains, "The eyes have it. The trainers and bloodstock agents who advise potential purchasers measure the stock on offer against a theoretical model of perfection and guide their clients through the maze of crooked legs, curbed hocks, wonky knees and blind eyes which trap the unwary. Scoring the next Nijinsky is an inexact science that largely comes down to aesthetics and hunches."

All of which is a lot of horse talk for a bike book, but we are nearing Newmarket and it helps to know a little before entering this strange urban strip where there are concrete bridleways wider that the roads. Before discovering the Chalke Way, I knew and cared little about things horsey, but you have to work damn hard not to be infected by these beautifully sleek and extremely neurotic critters. Hopefully you are about to become smitten.

Newmarket to Shelterhouse Corner
Map 1

DISTANCE
– 11m 18k
OS 154

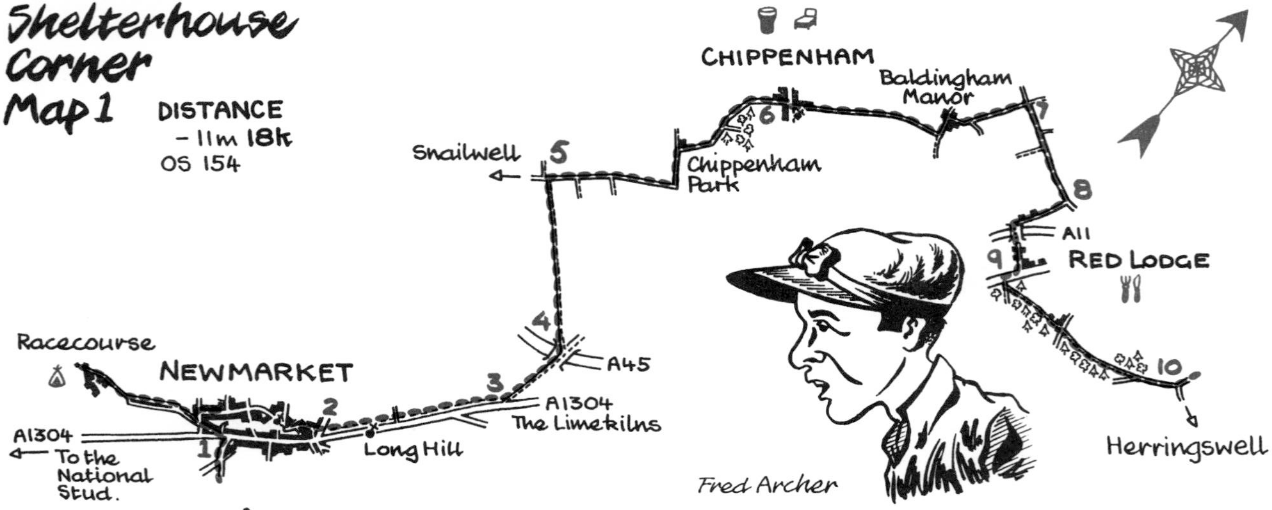

CHIPPENHAM

Baldingham Manor

Chippenham Park

RED LODGE

A11

Herringswell

10

8

7

6

5

Snailwell

A45

A1304
The Limekilns

4

3

Long Hill

2

1

NEWMARKET

Racecourse

A1304
To the National Stud.

Fred Archer

Clocktower

National Horseracing Museum

Tattersalls

Monument

Racecourse

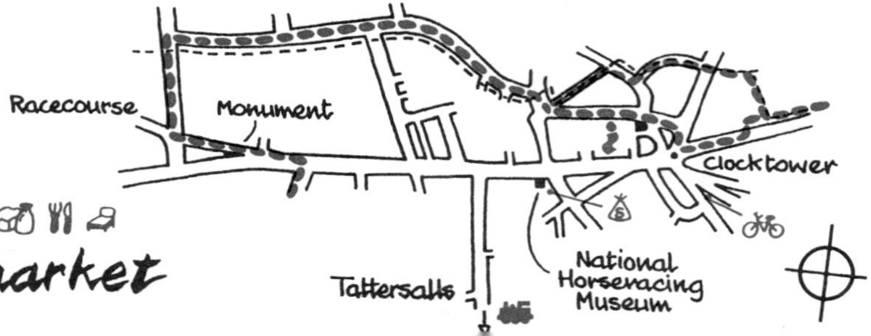

Newmarket

Directions

1 L then **R** up slip road to right of monument.
   SO to racecourse and campsite, or
   R along Hamilton Road then **R** again
   following concrete **BW**.

2 Opposite Heath Court Hotel, **L** along
   BW following A1304.

3 **L** to Al Bahathri Gallops ICKNIELD WAY.

4 **L** ICKNIELD WAY.

5 **R** at road.

6 **R** at Tharp Arms then **L** BADLINGHAM.

7 **R** at TJ ICKNIELD WAY.

8 **R** along Bridge End Road.
   At end dismount, over bridge, remount then **SO**.

9 **R** then **L** DEREK COOPER Ltd.
   Branch **L** GREENHAYS CHILDCARE CENTRE.

10 **L** at monument.

Resource

NEWMARKET
Tourist Information
63 The Rookery
01638 667200

Mrs D Champion
The Beechers,
Hamilton Rd
01638 666546

Mrs V Ward
Warren Hill Cottage
27 Bury Rd
01638 661103

Marleys Camp Shop
Sun Lane
01638 662466

Trax Campsite
Rowley Mile Racecourse, CB8 8JL
01638 663235
Open Easter to Sept.

Moons Cycles
1 Station Rd
01638 664897

The National Stud
July Racecourse
01638 663464
Open Mar to Oct, fee.

National Horseracing Museum
99 High St
01638 667333
Fee.

Newmarket Races
Clerk of the Course
01638 663044

Horse Training
Jockeys and horses go through their
early morning paces and can been
seen from the Trax campsite between
6am and 12.30.

Railway Information
01223 311999

CHIPPENHAM
Ms D Fuller
Enoch Cottage
01638 720429

Mrs S Blazey
The Maltings
Yard Cottage
20 High St
01638 720110

Newmarket – Shelterhouse Corner

NEWMARKET IS NOT SO MUCH A TOWN, MORE OF A PHENOMENON. IT IS THOUGHT Queen Boudicca had a stud at Exning, north west of the town, but there is no evidence to suggest the borough's reputation as a centre of horse breeding excellence was what enticed settlers until the 17th Century. In fact, before the 13th Century there is every reason to believe Newmarket was just a sheltered hollow of scrubland along the route of the Icknield Way and that Exning was the nearest local community.

The early Middle Ages saw a rapid expansion in trade and industry in the country, with the knock-on effect that scores of local markets suddenly sprang up on old or virgin sites. Between 1227 and 1310 no fewer than 70 new markets appeared in Suffolk. These tended to be roughly seven miles (11 km.) apart, the distance it was judged a villager would happily walk to go a-trading. At Exning it was decided to exploit the through traffic along the road to the south, and the stalls were set out at the turn of the century in the dip of the High Street to your right as you first enter the town. Temporary erections were soon replaced by permanent standings and the aptly named Newmarket began to take shape. With a history like that, it could be said Newmarket grew out of one of the first out-of-town shopping malls, and one wonders if, 700 years hence, the Happy Eaters, Trust House Fortes and Esso garages that cluster around today's A1(M) round-abouts will form the nucleus of equally charming future townscapes. I think not.

Horse racing has possibly been an organised sporting pursuit in this country since 2000 BC. Certainly the Romans were keen competitive equestrians, with and without chariots, but it wasn't until the 16th Century that the importance of breeding was emphasised and given royal patronage when Henry VIII imported 'warm' blood stock from the Middle East to enhance British genes. At the time there were some 12 towns that hosted regular race meetings, including Newmarket, but these were pretty chaotic corrupt affairs that included hawking, harrying and tilting amongst their events. It was James I who really appreciated the unique location of the fledgling town, set amongst the clean sleek lines of the well-drained chalk downland, ideal going for the sprinters. He built a palatial country house here, instigated the first royal sweepstakes in 1619 and began what was to become a long relationship between the crown and Royal Newmarket.

Charles I spent so much time here Parliament had to petition his Majesty not to put the gee-gees before his affairs of state. Charles II attempted to clean up the sport and introduced rules and regulations. There is then a slump in royal interest until the Prince Regent arrives on the scene, since when the town has enjoyed an unbroken succession of regal patronage. Even during Queen Victoria's reign, a woman who had no time for the turf, the momentum was maintained by Prince Albert. While other country towns have experienced mixed fortunes in their development, Newmarket has bounced along quite happily on the back of horse racing, though in recent times the council did express some concern about the constituents of their borough. It appeared to be a tad top heavy, class wise, so in 1961, along with a handful of other Suffolk country towns, they mounted an attractive campaign to lure 10,000 new residents, and built a nice new council estate to house them.

Today the most noticeable feature of the town is the height of its people. Flip, yes, but you have no idea how disconcerting it is to find yourself in the local chippy queuing behind a row of thirty-something midgets. Shagged out, ruddy faced and up to their waists in threadbare jodhpurs, these are the factory workers of Newmarket and they will be on again at day break, mucking out. Inevitably the town's pulse is dictated by the heartbeat of the industry, from traffic lights activated and giving priority to horse riders, to a single floor public library where a quarter of the space houses racing literature under lock and key, to the local hot spot called, of all things, 'The Sweaty Saddle'. Peeking between W.H. Smith and Currys on the High Street is the stern frontage of the Jockey Club headquarters. Around the corner, the splendid rotunda of Tattersalls, the Christies and Sothebys of blood stock auctioneering rolled into one. The problem with Newmarket is to know where to start, but if you are as ignorant about all this as I am, I suggest starting with the animal.

Campers are at a distinct advantage here. The official site is right next to the main stands in the centre of the **race course**. To enjoy the early morning spectacle of glistening horse hide being put through its paces simply throw back the flap and carry on schlepping out in your sleeping bag. Failing that, you are allowed anywhere on the race course to view, provided you maintain a safe distance between yourself and the riders (and are not walking an untethered dog). The jockeys are generally very friendly and love the attention . The horses are totally strung out, itching to let rip and get freaked by falling leaves. Considering the amount of inter-breeding, incest and unnaturally molly-coddling that goes into these thoroughbreds, it is not surprising their fiery-eyed demeanour suggests a cross between Norman Bates and Sinead O'Connor. Steer clear, particularly if you decide to watch them crossing town. This is a great photo opportunity. In how many suburbs can you turn a corner to find the road between terraces blocked with a wedge of advancing cavalry? Do not ride the bridleways before midday. By then the precious darlings will have stretched their legs and be tucked up in the stables being pampered.

Did I mention Newmarket is in Suffolk, or at least most of it is? A great headland lapped by the sea of Cambridgeshire, Newmarket juts out of Suffolk like Portland juts out of Dorset with the result that half of the racecourse is in one county, the other half in another, and the border runs right through the main stands. In 1839 the sister country celebrated this quirk by establishing the now famous Cambridgeshire Handicap Race, run over nine furlongs along the Rowley Mile on their own turf. To the south west the course is bisected by the northern continuation of Devil's Ditch and on the other side of it lies the National Stud. If you want a shifty behind the security fences of a modern breeding ground, this is the cheapest and most accessible of the limited stud tours on offer.

No longer a state industry, the National Stud arrived in Newmarket as recently as 1967. Built on land leased from the Jockey Club, it is housed in state-of-the-art premises designed to a brief devised by Director Peter Burrell after a fact-finding world tour of similarly prestigious establishments. The bloodstock originates from that of Colonel Hall Walker who offered a job lot to the government in 1916 on condition the nation also bought his Irish stud farm. At the time there was a big demand for quality light horses for the Army, but by 1943, when the bloodstock was transferred to this island and split between Gillingham (in Dorset) and West Grinstead, the internal combustion engine had transformed the cavalry into the tank corps and the aims of the National Stud were changing. In 1963 the decision was made to concentrate exclusively on class stallions. The mares were sold off, leaving the paddocks to a succession of superstuds who strutted their stuff like over-sexed Sean Connerys. Names like Mill

Reef, Never Say Die and now Suave Dancer - all big Oscar winners in their day.

Our next stop needs to be Tattersalls, up the avenue from the High Street, and worth a poke around the facilities even if the auctions are a month away. Arrive mid-October to November and there is a good chance the sales ring will be awash with the auctioneers' indecipherable motor-mouthings. The proceedings are open to the public but stand rigid unless you wish to become the proud owner of a 300,00 guinea psychotic. A nod, a wink, a scratch or a twitch is all it takes. When the 1993 Grand National winner, Minniehoma, was recently auctioned, the successful bidder clinched it by sticking his tongue out. The owner of the tongue was comedian Freddie Starr, but if you are into people-watching, this is the place to observe mice become mammoths and serpents become shoestrings. A stroll round the unloading 'stations' when the trucks are in is like reading a tour guide of the Chalke Way, with vehicles from Salisbury, Lambourne, West Isley and the Chilterns.

Last but by no means least is a trip to the **National Horse Racing Museum**, housed in the deceptively large Regency building of the former Subscription Rooms. Where once frock-coated gentleman settled their gambling debts, the story of the development of horse racing is now laid out neatly and interestingly, with all the hallowed respect you would expect of this sport. Amongst the trophies and effigies is a corner devoted to the career of Fred Archer, sports hero and sad person who is remembered in the name of the road we take leaving Newmarket. Fred was a giant amongst jockeys, a Mohammed Ali of the turf, who ran 8,086 races and won 2,750. Of the 17 years he spent in the race game, Fred was Champion Jockey for thirteen of them, and in 1884 he set a record that survived nearly half a century by winning 246 races in one season. His name slipped into common usage. 'Archer's up' was a colloquial expression for 'All's well', but for Fred, all was not well.

There were no executive jets in those days. Fred and his wife had to criss cross the country (and presumably abroad) on horseback. They were continually on the move, from one race meeting to the next. This and Fred's unending battle to keep his weight down took its toll. His wife died young and Fred slipped into a crippling melancholy. He grew fat, while 19th century marketing men grew fatter plastering Fred's beaming face onto pipes and plates and tinder boxes (and you thought merchandising was a recent horror!). In 1886 Fred blew his brains out in a cloud of despair. He wasn't the first violent casualty of the sport that used to attract hookers and pimps and duels at dawn, and he certainly won't be the last.

As we ride away from Newmarket across the Al-Bahathiri Gallops, and head off into farming country once again, it is hard to shake of the experience of that unique town. Every horse nibbling in a field or trotting down the road we view with alert interest and from a different perspective to ten miles earlier, but gradually another phenomenon starts to register. Sand is beginning to appear at the side of the road. Where a track turns off onto what you would expect to be flint speckled clay there are now deep furrows in soft grey sand and the agriculture is turning to coarse pasture. We are miles from the coast but sandsedge sprouts from the verge, a plant more at home on beaches. You can be forgiven for thinking we must be on a run in to the sea. In fact we are entering the **Brecklands** of East Anglia, 94 square miles (243 sq. km.) of heath, pine shelterbeds and forestry land like nowhere else in Britain.

Strange to tell but not so very long ago, 300 square miles (777 sq. km.) of Britain was a virtual desert. The land was a dust bowl, arid and shifting, where farms and villages had long given up the struggle and lay deserted, half buried under slithering dunes. As recently as 1872 Skertchly wrote, "From Thetford to the Fens, so barren is the land that one is often reminded of the deserts of Africa – hardly a drop of surface water - and for miles, neither a ditch, pond nor spring." Those on the fringes that could still farm weren't too sure where they should plough. "Sometimes my farmland is in Suffolk and sometimes in Norfolk. It blows back and forth." The irony is that the cause of this dereliction was precisely what the West now accuses Third World countries of ignorantly pursuing.

It might have been a couple of thousand years ago, but our ancestors blithely deforested this part of East Anglia, and slashed and burned their way to clearing the land for agriculture. Without an understanding of crop rotation or manures, they worked the top soil dead and then moved on, allowing the plot to revert to heathland where their sheep could graze. The 'breck' of Brecklands could be derived from the Norse word 'braec', meaning 'land newly broken for settlement', but by the 13th century the soil had become so impoverished little of it stood still long enough to settle on. Over the next couple of centuries, the population drifted away as rapidly as the sand drifted in. At least 24 villages were deserted. In places their scattered remains still peak above the surface, an eerie reminder that when it comes to exploiting the land, nature doesn't take kindly to short-term goals.

When the people moved out the **rabbits** moved in, and it is coneys by the score you will see casually bobbing across Cavenham Heath. The avenue out of Tuddington is like the tunnel in *'Alice'*, plopping you into the middle of an enormous cat litter riddled with rabbit holes. This is what most of the Brecks looked like until the turn of the century. It is a surreal landscape, like a lunar sea carpeted with stubble. Isolated clumps of heather and bracken interrupt the bumpy profile of the heath, and here and there clumps of birches thrive in the sandy soil. There is a harsh beauty to the desolation that takes on an haunted quality at dusk. Cycled at night and the mind plays tricks with the eyes. The Hound of the Baskervilles has definitely lunged at my throat along here, accompanied by an ear-bursting roar I later discovered was an F-15 coming in to land at Mildenhall USAF base up the road. The hound was probably a startled muntjac deer, but it might not have been.

Cottontails are not native to Britain. They were introduced by the Normans, not without some problems. By the Middle Ages however they had settled in and become a staple part of the English diet and wardrobe. Breckland soil was ideally suited to their burrowing instinct and the area became a commercial centre for rabbit breeding and skinning, though all along the Chalke Way we have encountered woods and downs with 'warren' in their name. Rabbits only tend to stray when there is a food shortage, consequently the early warrens were ill-defined open areas and catching them was very much a sport for ferrets and lurchers. By the 18th century the industry had become so demanding sophisticated traps were employed, rabbits were fed and warrens enclosed, patrolled by warreners on the lookout for wily poachers.

Poaching was a successful industry in its own right, encouraged by bill posters that invited Tom, Dick and Harry to bring their booty to traders at the 'Market Overt 'in Newmarket, who would legitimately sell it on to furriers and butchers in London. But get caught nicking a bunny and in those days you could look forward to anything from a public whipping to transportation to Botany Bay. And the obstacles to

Newmarket to Shelterhouse Corner

Map 2   DISTANCE – via Shravedell Heath   – via The King's Forest   – to Campsite

OS 154, 155, 144

20m 32k   20m 32k   1¾m 2·5k

TUDDENHAM

Tuddenham Heath

Cavenham Heath

Cavenham

1

Prince Duleep Singh

River Lark

2

Canada Farm

Deadman's Grave

ICKLINGHAM

Weatherhill Farm

A1101

Lackford

B

C

West Stow Country Park

WEST STOW

River Lark

Shravedell Heath

3

Berner's Heath

Icknield Way

Queen Mary's Avenue

The King's Forest

Hall Heath

Elveden

B1106

4

Shelter-house Corner.

Between March + Mid-June

1

Stone-Curlew

Stone-Curlew

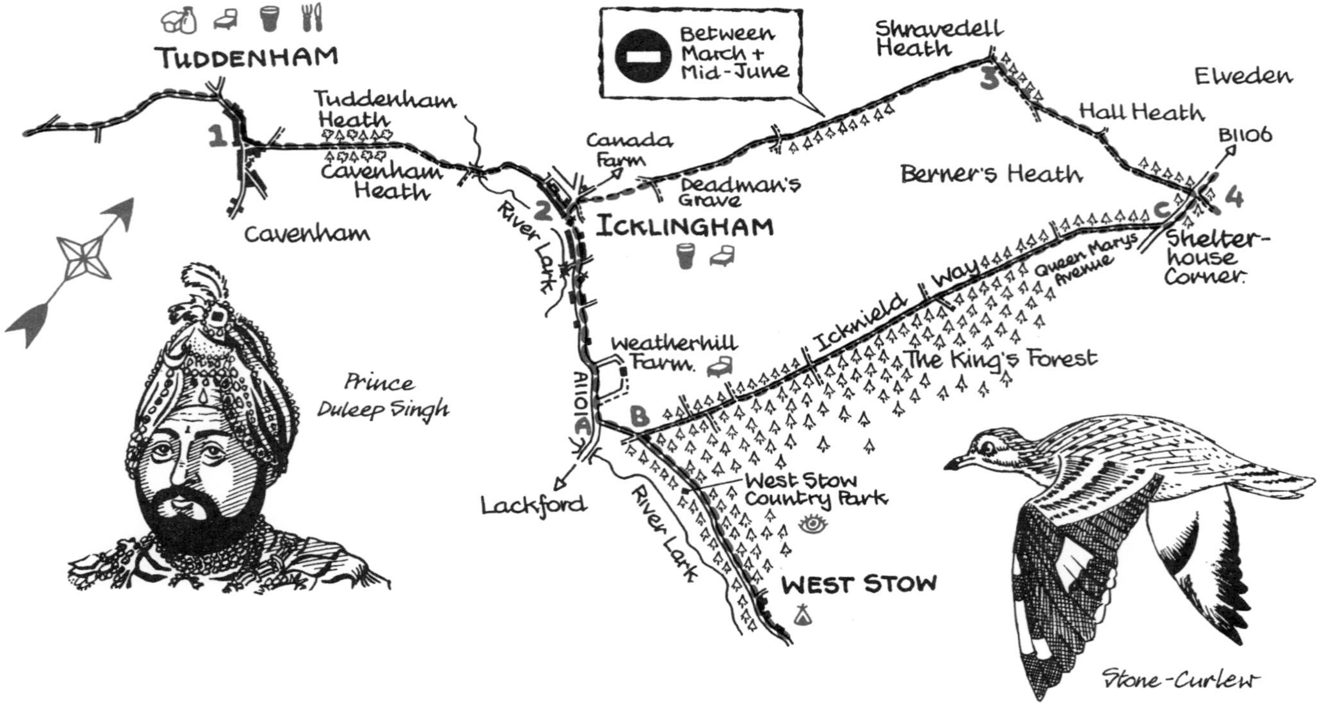

Directions

1 **L** at phone box THE GREEN.

Via Shravedell Heath

2 **L** at TJ then
R at next corner onto **BW** behind hedge running parallel to Canada Farm Road ICKNIELD WAY.
Branch **R** at farmgate BYWAY.

3 **R** BYWAY then **L** following telegraph poles.

Via King's Forest

2 **R** at TJ LACKFORD.
A **L** WEST STOW.
B **SO** for West Stow Country Park & camping.
L at cottage BYWAY.
C **L** at B1106.

4 Decision time – via Grime's Graves or via Barnham?

Resource

TUDENHAM
Mrs J Titcombe,
Oakdene
Higham Rd
01638 718822

ICKLINGHAM
Mr M Browning
Weatherill Farm
IP28 6PP
01284 728839

WEST STOWE
West Stowe Country Park
Visitors Centre & Anglo
Saxon Village
01284 728718
Open daily.
Fee for Anglo Saxon Village.

Cow Wise
Meadow farm
IP28 6EL
01284 728862
Educational dairy farm with camping too!

a successful kill were formidable. Warreners would strew dry twigs over paths and keep an ear out. They would rig up trip wires tied to shot guns, dig and camouflage holes, lay trapnets - anything to get one over the professional poacher who was often earning four times a warrener's wage. It was a war, complete with castles and armies.

Warrens were usually in isolated spots where it made sense to have the warrener and his family living over the shop. Their lodge was often a substantial premises with a tower for a vantage point and secure rooms where skins could be dried and meat salted. Because they were prime targets for gangs of marauding poachers, these home from homes were designed more like fortresses, with battlements, slit windows and strategic orifices where missiles could be dropped onto assailants. On the next leg of our journey across the Brecklands, a 15 minute detour takes us to the remains of **Thetford Warren Lodge**. This was at the heart of a 1200 hectare estate owned by the Prior of Thetford, and is most impressive for walls almost a metre thick that suggest warring poachers attacked with a darn sight more than sticks and stones. If all this seems a lot of fuss over a few Thumpers, bear in mind that in the 19th Century Thetford Warren was yielding 30,000 carcasses, and canal barges and wagons were crossing the country stuffed with furs and meat.

By the turn of the century the wild population was at pest proportions and the commercial breeding was on the decline. Then in the Fifties myxomatosis struck, a lethal disease that wiped out 99% of British rabbits and had a marked impact upon the natural ecology of the Brecklands. Without nibblers to chew back the undergrowth, heather, bracken and gorse took hold and smothered the natural flora of these ancient heaths. But that remaining 1% of survivors weren't slow to live up to their reputation. Today, in parts of the British Isles, rabbits are again a pest to farmers and foresters. In the Brecklands they are a mixed blessing. Off the record some landlords are calling for the reintroduction of 'myxie'.

It is the land of one particular Lord you may choose to traverse after Icklingham, but first I should explain why there are two routes across the heath to the B1106. The Brecks are a very rare and highly sensitive area. 72% of British heaths have been destroyed in the last hundred years, more in the Brecklands, which are particularly rich in unusual and unique species. For example the list of birds you might see in the woods, on the land, in the sky, paddling across the mere is extensive, but some populations are precarious. There are now only a handful of breeding pairs of goshawks, and the pairs of stone curlews has dropped from 1,000 in the 1940s to 92 in 1993. Those that work the Brecklands are sensitive to the situation and have noticed a peculiarity that might offend some cyclists' idea of their own environmental-friendliness. As it was explained to me by Simon Hooton of the Brecks Countryside Project, the fowl of the air are unruffled by loud, lumbering farm machinery, but extremely disturbed by the sight of the world's most predatory mammal, us humans. Stone curlews are particularly anxious and will abandon the nest, never to return, leaving their chicks wide open to animal predators. Simon understandably asks that we do not take the Shravedell Heath option between the March to mid-June nesting season. This is a plea to be respected rather than a prohibition.

If you do take this option you will be crossing the Eleveden Estate, the largest arable self-contained estate in the country, so extensive it is noticeable on a road map for its singular lack of population. In the 18th century, Lord Albemarle took on the 1,619 hectares of `barren, windswept, rabbit infested estate' and began the process of reclamation by planting sainfoin and lucerne to improve soil fertility and smother the weeds. A boost in the demand for food fired by the Napoleonic wars, encouraged his lordship to seed turnips, barley, oats and rye. He planted shelterbeds to diffuse the wind and grazed sheep and cattle to preserve freshly cleared heath, but with the peace came the depression, and in 1813 Albemarle had to sell up.

Elveden was then bought and sold through a number of wealthy owners, including a Punjabi Maharajah, Prince Duleep Singh. Duleep arrived in Britain in 1849 with a fat pension from a grateful colonialist power to whom he had resigned his sovereign rights on the subcontinent. He bought the Estate in 1863, by then 6,880 hectares, mainly to indulge his passion for hunting, and took it upon himself to expand Elveden Hall into 'an Oriental extravaganza unparalleled in England'. Although you won't see the place, it helps if you can picture a little Brighton Pavilion (or its interior, at least) plonked in the middle of the Brecklands. Difficult, huh?

Finally the Estate was bought by Earl Iveagh, whose family still control what is now more than 10,117 hectares of Breckland, partially sublet to the Forestry Commission, partially leased to tenant farmers. The first Earl was more into the game side than the agricultural, but throughout the estate's recent history more and more wasteland has been brought into arable and pastural production. The estate has always welcomed royal guests, notably Victoria, Edward VII and George V, and lavished them with pomp and ceremony. It is not quite so friendly towards commoners. To a person, everybody we asked about Elveden prefixed their response with a grimace and a groan. Although I haven't heard it from the horses mouth (after eight unreturned phone calls to the Estate Office, I gave up), the word is they don't like anybody crossing their territory even on an ROW, but stick to the correct path and you'll do fine. It is a wonderful ride, one to savour, and keep your eyes peeled for bounding wild life.

The alternative route is the equally impressive **Icklingham Belt**, following the line of the Icknield Way as it heads off towards Thetford. Unfortunately there is a short section of the busy A1101 between us and it, but there are compensations along the way, like the lovely rush roofed Church of All Saints, Icklingham. It is no longer saving souls but a key is obtainable should you wish to explore inside. There is also the living museum at **West Stow Country Park** erected as authentically as possible on the site of an Anglo-Saxon settlement excavated between 1965 and 1972. The River Lack was a magnet for these in-comers, a source of water, a medium of transportation and a good place to bury their dead. On the south bank near Lackford, a sandy spur offered up to archaeologists over a thousand cremated souls buried in ceramic urns. At Weatherhill Farm field workers are still sifting the soil to shed light on the Dark Ages, while at West Stow a more empirical approach is being explored.

In 1973 volunteers erected the first of a number of wooden post-houses that now form the museum. Each reconstruction tested different theories and was built using local tools and techniques of the period. Some erections are unashamedly inaccurate, but had to be built to discover why. Throughout the year the village stages events and demonstrations acted out by 20th Century Anglo-Saxons wearing the wardrobe department of *Conan the Barbarian*. These can be good fun and educational for children, but between times the museum employs an interpretive approach to your stroll round the site, equipping visitors with a Walkman and highly imaginative sound track. Perhaps of more interest to us journey men and women is the ice cream shop and visitors' centre. Combine the two and you can spend a pleasant half hour refreshing mind and body, taking in their neat little wildlife display.

From there, back to the cottage and up the Icklingham Belt to test your new found knowledge. You are riding through the King's Forest, one of a number planted around Thetford, partially to stabilise the top soil, partially for commercial reasons. This one celebrates the Silver Jubilee of George V and Queen Mary. Aside from calling on your powers of observation, the Belt is also a test of your riding technique on sand. Remember, select as low a gear as is comfortable, keep the legs turning smoothly apace, and apply as little pedal pressure as possible. Happy sand surfing.

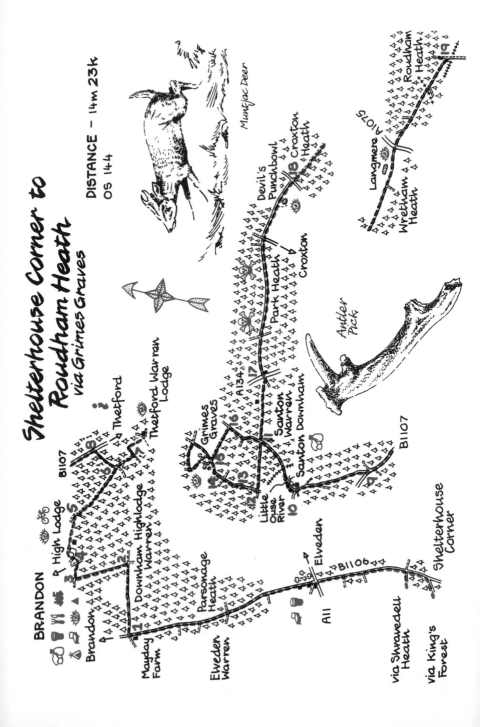

Shelterhouse Corner to Roudham Heath
via Grimes Graves

DISTANCE — 14m 23k

OS 144

Muntjac Deer

Antler Pick

BRANDON

Brandon

R High Lodge

B1107

Mayday Farm

Downham Highlodge Warren

Parsonage Heath

Elveden Warren

Thetford

Thetford Warren Lodge

Grimes Graves

Saxton Warren

Saxton Downham

Little Ouse River

Elveden

A11

B1106

Shrawedell Heath

King's Forest

Shelterhouse Corner

Park Heath

Croxton

Devil's Punchbowl

Croxton Heath

B1107

Langmere

A1075

Wretham Heath

Roudham Heath

Directions

1   R at Mayday Farm sign 10.
2   L HIGH LODGE then **SO**.
3   R at TJ HORSESHOE.
4   At sign 34, branch **L** following yellow BICYCLE sign round edge of car park and past High Lodge.
5   R at forest road.
6   L in valley at tarmac road, or via Thetford Warren Lodge — **SO** up hill. Sign 23.
7   L at TJ then **R** following red posts to the Lodge, on your left, through gate. Return same way — **R** at **6**.
8   L at TJ onto B1107 BRANDON.
9   R SANTON DOWNHAM.
10 R at Forest Offices then **SO** SANTON WARREN.
11 L sign 23.
12 At crossways joined on left by track up from railway, turn **R** past barrier, up hill.
13 At top of hill, branch **R** at red post, then **R** again.
14 Go **R** to follow perimeter fence round to Grime's Graves entrance opposite. Return same way.
15 Before bend, **L** then **SO** down **BW** to road.
16 R at road then **L** at 11. Sign 23.
17 SO at **CR**.
18 SO onto track.
19 L at white house. TJ sign 70 PEDDARS WAY.

Resource

ELVEDEN
The Elveden Inn
Brandon Rd
IP27 0SD
01842 890378

High Lodge
Visitors Centre
01842 815434

High Lodge Cycle Repairs
01485 540642.

BRANDON
Riverside Lodge
78 High St
IP27 0AU
01842 811236

Bridge House Hotel
79 High St
01842 813137

Foord Farm
Chalk Rd
IP27 0SD
01842 812246
Camping

Brandon YHA
Heath House
off Warren Close
Bury Rd, IP27 0SD
01842 812246

THETFORD
Tourist Information
Ancient House Museum
21 White Hart St
01842 752599

GRIME'S GRAVES
English Heritage
01842 810656

Daily from Easter to Oct
Nov – Mar, Weds to Suns
Fee.

Shelterhouse Corner – Roudham Heath via Grime's Graves

HERE WE GO AGAIN, MORE DECISIONS. THE ORIGINAL COURSE OF THE ICKNIELD Way would have forded the rivers Thet and Little Ouse at Thetford, then turned due north to Swaffham. Now that traffic has been diverted onto a bypass, Thetford is an attractive peaceful little town with an individuality that owes a lot to the rivers, but it is sited like a huddle of covered wagons surrounded by circling warriors who continually threaten but never attack. Slipping in and out of the encampment past war painted trucks and cars isn't easy on a push bike, so we give you two choices for skirting the whole shooting match.

Our northern route is across Forestry Commission land, through plantations similar to the King's Forest, though the under tyre surface is now well compacted and easy to sprint down. For a country where once upon a time you couldn't see the wood for the trees, Britain was remarkably inept at commercially and intelligently exploiting its forests. When the First World War interrupted imports from Europe it was the Canadians who pulled us out of the crisis, overseeing the felling and training up of local labour. In 1919 the government established the Forestry Commission to continue the good work and ensure there would never be another shortage of trench supports (in the event of another war), pit props, telegraph poles and railway sleepers. In 1922 the Commission bought the first hectares of **Thetford Forest**. Land was going cheap during the recession of the 1920's, particularly marginal farming land like the Brecks where some tenant farmers lived rent free simply to keep their lordship's property tilled and clear of rabbits. Now extended over 20,000 hectares, Thetford has become the largest lowland forest in the country and is the headquarters of the Forestry Commission.

Riding through the regimented lines of conifers can be depressing unless you know something of their story. Establishing a new forest is no easy task, and the Commission had to develop new techniques, employ hundreds of labourers and build innovative equipment to bring Thetford Forest to life. They started with cones, acorns and masts collected from the native Scots pines, oaks and beeches that already grew in Breckland copses or as long wind breaks (shelterbeds). 80 hectares were devoted to nurseries producing seven million seedlings a year. Some introduced species didn't take, notably Douglas Fir and European larch. Others flourished, like the Corsican pine. The ground had to be prepared, fenced off against rabbits, planned out in ten hectare blocks with fire breaks, beautified by planting broad-leafed species either side of public roads. Camps were built to accommodate the army of workers who built roads, cleared scrub and planted an average 1,500 seedlings per person per day. It was an enormous project that 16 to 20 years later produced one of those dark lifeless plantations that are forestry at its worst.

Then the thinning out began, a precise task with the axe that initially removed a quarter of the trees but would eventually reduce a plot of 2,000 seedlings to a mere 150 mature giants. By the 1960s Thetford Forest was in full production, felling and reseeding 250 hectares a year, with its own mill at Brandon where timber was stripped and sorted before distribution to manufacturers of wall-board, pit props or paper pulp. By 1989 the Conservative Government had consigned the coal industry to the grave and the Brandon Depot had gone the way of all other ancillary industries to mining.

But a new era of on-site timber processing rose out of the ashes, one that is far more entertaining for the passer-by. Cycle through in autumn and vicious machines called 'Grapple Harvester' or 'Forwarder' can be seen from a safe distance zipping through trunks and ripping off branches either side of you. If you happen upon a sign saying 'Forest Harvesting: No Access' proceed with caution. On our route they have to let you through, but be instructed by the forest workers exactly when. These great mechanical Goliaths move like Matchbox toys amongst the mighty pines but they are the cutting edge of a modern, mechanised and highly profitable industry that now exports coals to Newcastle in the shape of timber to Scandinavia. No wonder the Conservatives want to privatise the Forestry Commission.

Compared to a lot of plantation riding in this country the pedal through to Roudham Heath is remarkably bright and breezy. There is room to breathe between the conifers, space for a thick ground cover to flourish, where native or introduced mammals can have a good romp. It is a rare day if you don't see at least one member of the herds of fallow, muntjac, roe or red deer that roam the forest. Scan the woods at night with a power torch and you might be surprised how many pairs of eyes have popped out to watch you make a fool of yourself trying to negotiate the rough in the pitch black. Bats are common throughout the Brecklands and encouraged by nest boxes and hibernation tunnels, but you have to be quick to catch one in your beam and track it.

The relationship between trees and squirrels is an interesting one in Thetford Forest. Grey squirrels are prolific and audacious enough to take food from your panniers. They were introduced into this country from North America in the 19th century and have become as ubiquitous as blue jeans. Over the same period, home-grown red squirrels had become a pest and in some places were hunted to the point of extinction. Thetford Forest is one of their last refuges, but the numbers are alarmingly small and subject to special attention from the Species Recovery Programme. Grey squirrels are antagonistic to red, if only in spreading disease and crowding out their European cousins. They actually have very different requirements, greys preferring deciduous woodland, reds preferring conifers, but here the greys have muscled in. The original plantation of mainly Scots pines produced a rich crop of cones for the the red squirrels to pig out on, but when the Commission changed to Corsican Pine, a tree that produces fewer cones less frequently, food hoppers had to be installed to supplement their provisions. Greys are omnivorous scavengers that adapt to their surroundings. They are big, fat and heavy so the food hopper has been designed with a weight-loaded trapdoor. The greys fall through while the lighter reds scurry across to raid the larder. I guess it's a kind of justice.

Although it is on tarmac, the sweep passed Thetford Lodge into **Santon Downham** is possibly the most glorious artificial avenue of trees we ride on the Chalke Way. With its broad bridleway verges between the forest and lines of beeches enveloping the road, this is one to be experienced on a crisp autumn morning when the deep blue wash of the sky throws into contrast the shinning copper of back-lit leaves on the turn. Santon Downham is all but an artificial village, developed glove in hand with the forest. More than 300 homes were built for forestry staff but we skirt all that, preferring a route passed the attractive little church and the shop, where once again you can fulfil your craving for munchies if you missed out on choc ices at the Lodge. In the 17th Century the village was at the centre of the old wasteland, deserted and up to its neck in sand. Even the Little Ouse was obliterated in places, a river that a few centuries before was buzzing with shallow-draught lighters, horse-drawn back and forth to

Thetford, often with imports from or exports to Kings Lynn. Those who were excited by the ancient monuments and enigmatic sights of the first part of our odyssey will want to visit **Grime's Graves** and thus automatically plump for the northern bypass. It is not a dramatic site like Avebury, more of a gentle thrill, but it is probably more important in developing a picture of prehistoric society than any of the megalith masterpieces. There is nothing mysterious here. It was a flint mine, possibly a very big flint mine that shipped quality floor-stone products the length and breadth of the country down, amongst other ancient tracks, the Chalke Way. It is also a BMX track, much to the horror of English Heritage and any right-thinking cyclist. The idea of bung-heads on MTBs shooting around the 4,000 year old dips and dives of this ancient monument makes me ashamed I'm a cyclist, but to some extent, English Heritage ask for trouble.

The southern entrance to Grime's Graves isn't, despite their welcoming sign and flimsy barrier. They are happy for walkers to enter, but we have to go round and approach from the north, a five-minute ride that allows us to inspect the site before taking the plunge below ground. Looking a lot like a WWII bombsite, each flower speckled hollow marks an infilled shaft that bottomed out in a radius of galleries cut through the sand, clay and chalk to the flint face. There are hundreds of them. This is the oldest site in Europe, worked by the Neolithics, hacked out on hands and knees with antler picks. When you reach the bottom of the 30 foot (9 m.) visitor's shaft it can be difficult to get a feel for the flint miners' working conditions. Historian Anthony Burton was fortunate enough to crawl where tourists can't, past abandoned antler picks and chalk rubble, along a three foot (1 m.) high gantry that suddenly broke through to another deeper shaft. Unfortunately his light then gave out.

"I sat in the total, impenetrable blackness, surrounded by the memories of men who had toiled here in the so distant past. If there were ghosts here, none returned to haunt me, in fact I felt curiously comfortable in the dark cave. If my imagination failed me when I tried to conjour up images of the old Breckland, it certainly did not fail me then. I really felt I could understand something of what it must have meant to men with such primitive equipment to create this under-ground world: the reason for placing a little votive offering at the foot of the pit as a charm. But equally I felt that these men had been the masters of their underground domain. I was alone under the earth for a while, and I can only describe it is a friendly place." Fortunately Mr Burton wasn't working in air thick with chalk dust and the fumes of primitive oil lamps.

Turning due east across Park Heath we pass on our left the fenced in, strictly off-limits, MOD Personnel Only, Stanford Training Area (Stanta). Unlike Salisbury Plain Training Area there are no public right of ways across this 17,000 plus hectares of Brecklands, much to the chagrin of conservationists and the relatives of those who used to live there before the 1940s, but more of Stanford later. To the south, hidden in a deep pit, is the stagnant water of the Devil's Punch Bowl, a natural feature called a 'mere' but as unexpected in this arid land as Ashmore's village pond is in *Cannock* Chase. Meres are probably the result of underground water dissolving away a layer of chalk to form a subterranean cave that then collapses, leaving a tell-tale hollow on the surface. Water levels fluctuate according to the height of the water table and quantity of annual rainfall. Langmere (on your left as you cross Wretham Heath) has been known to flood its banks one year but by the end of the next be completely dry.

Predictably meres are important breeding sites for the Breckland water fowl population, though exactly what you will see depends totally on the unpredictable level of water. Langmere is one of the numerous nature reserves along the Chalke Way where travellers' binoculars come into their own. Gadwall, teal, pochard, and tufted ducks with their slick hairdos are regular visitors, as are great-crested and little grebes. Not exactly a rare species, but certainly scarce on lowland waters, garganey ducks have taken to breeding on Langmere, distinguishable by their go-faster white stripe that sweeps back from the eye. If you are a keen twitcher, better access can be gained by pedalling a short distance up the A1075 to the Norfolk Naturalist's Trust shop and hide.

Shelterhouse Corner – Roudham Heath via Barnham

OF THE TWO DIVERSIONS ROUND THETFORD, OUR SOUTHERN LOOP TAKES YOU through a more varied landscape than just the monoculture of forestry. There are still the plantations, though only a couple of miles of them, and still the odd long metalled straight where the lycra lads and lassies can burn rubber. But there are also leafy tunnels to honk up, sandy pastures to plough through, country lanes to dawdle down.

The line we take follows the Rider's Route of the **Icknield Way Path**, or would do, except following an official government-sponsored publication by the Countryside Commission, I discovered, is no guarantee of a definitive right of way. Map No. 3 of the route indicates a bridleway across West Calthorpe Heath that cannot be traced on an Ordnance Survey map. In itself this is not unusual, since there are other permissive routes along the Icknield Way Path that are not mapped by the OS. Armed with highlighted possibilities, I set off west down Dukes Ride to check out the lie of the land. After Barrow Clump Buildings, the Riders Route waymarks suddenly vanished, replaced by tatty paper notices stapled to a tree trunk that talked about some enquiry or other, signed by some Inspector in the Department of the Environment. They were illegible.

The following day I tried finding the Countryside Commission's recommended route from the eastern access to the Heath. Again the path petered out. From across the fields a cloud of dust heralded an approaching Range Rover driven by one very irate gentleman farmer, be-suited, and packing a mobile phone and shot gun. You can imagine the exchange of heated words, me defending my rights of access backed by, I thought, the full authority of the Countryside Commission, him denying all knowledge of the Riders Route, and chuntering about public enquiries and the scourge of pig rustlers. Having reassured him I didn't have one of his prize sows stuffed up my bike pump, I was shepherded off his land with tail between my legs, vowing to take this to a higher authority.

After a lot of letter writing by both parties it transpires the right of way was defined, mapped and published by Suffolk County Council before it was an agreed right of way, presumably in the belief that the powerful Elveden and Euston Estates would gleefully throw open their

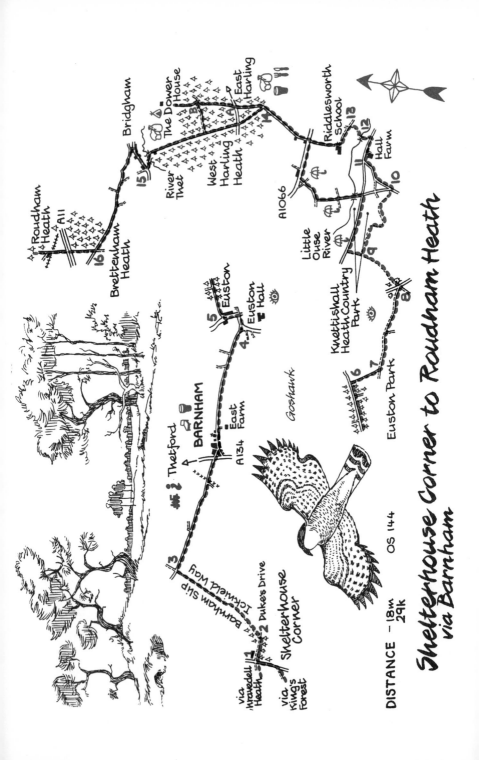

Roudham Heath
A11
Brettenham Heath
16

Bridgham
15

The Dower House
East Harling
West Harling Heath
River Thet

Riddlesworth School
13
12
A1066
Hall Farm
11
10

Little Ouse River
9
8

Euston
5
Euston Hall
4

Knettishall Heath Country Park
Euston Park
7
6

Goshawk

Thetford
BARNHAM
East Farm
A134
3

Ickham Way
Bartham Way
2 Dukes Drive
via Mavedell Heath
via King's Forest
Shelterhouse Corner
1

DISTANCE – 18m 29k   OS 144

Shelterhouse Corner to Roudham Heath
via Barnham

Resource

BARNHAM
Mrs M Heading
East Farm
Euston Rd
IP24 2PB
01842 890231

KNETTISHALL HEATH
Visitors centre.

WEST HARLING
The Dower House
Touring Park
NR16 2SE
01953 717314
On-site shop sells basic supplies.

Directions

1   Follow ICKFIELD WAY past Barrow Clump Buildings.
2   L BYWAY.
3   R at road.
4   L at TJ THETFORD.
5   R RUSHFORD.
6   R ICKNIELD WAY.
7   Keep branching L.
8   SO onto BW.
9   R at Information Board. Follow HORSESHOE signs.
10 SO onto left fork.
11 R at TJ, past farm, then L onto BW.
    Curve round Little Ouse.
12 Cross bridge or through ford, through farm gate then round right edge of field to farm gate.
13 L at track, through school, SO.
14 L at corner onto BW then SO over road. Sign 76.

Via The Dower House
A   SO following signs to campsite.
B   To continue journey from campsite, return along forest road then R onto BW. Sign 10.
15 R at TJ then L in village and L again HIGH BRIDGHAM.
16 Opposite BRETTENHAM HEATH R onto track. Blue arrow. SO. (Beware of crossing A11 – very fast road.)

arms to the public after several hundred years of firmly keeping them crossed. The farmer who confronted me, Mr James Stamper, deserves a humble apology and the Countryside Commission and Suffolk County Council deserve a severe wrap across the knuckles. Incredibly, a number of august organisations are still sending out Map No. 3 of the Icknield Way Path Riders Route.

Public enquiries to delineate a byway across West Calthorpe Heath are in the pipe line, but it is a long tunnel that might be blocked at the far end. As with the Twilight Zone round Luton, we will monitor progress and update accordingly. For cyclists and equestrians it does make sense to create an off-road link through to Euston village, cutting out the uninspiring blacktop passed Barnham, but there are problems to do with the spread of pig and crop diseases that make these negotiations more complicated than simply trying to wrestle access out of wicked land-owners.

Rhizomania is a soil borne disease that attacks sugar beet. It was first detected in East Anglia in 1987 on a farm in the vicinity of West Stow. Immediately the Ministry of Agriculture, Fisheries and Food (MAFF) quarantined the area and placed crippling restrictions on the movement of agricultural machinery that might carry the spore abroad. Since then the disease has spread, but it does not fan out in a predictable pattern. Carried by birds, deer, squirrels, whatever, there are now isolated pockets of rhizomania on isolated farms throughout East Anglia. Aside from having to work with one hand tied behind his back, Mr Stamper's son estimates the disease could cost them more than £60,000 this year. But while the Ministry can invoke all manner of limitations on the farmer, they cannot close the right of way across his or her land. In fact there are recently cases of the authorities removing 'No Access: Rhizomania' signs and chastising landowners. Understandably the agricultural community believes this makes a mockery of their containment efforts and the MAFF restrictions. Not surprisingly they are ill-disposed towards any suggestion of opening up new public byways across West Calthorpe Heath.

Euston Hall is the second of the great estates we slip through. For a couple of hundred years it has been the stately home of the Dukes of Grafton, but the core of the Estate, the Park, was originally the country seat of the Arlington family. Earl Arlington was the Secretary of State to Charles II. In 1616 the Arlingtons had less than 3,000 hectares of gently undulating, pleasantly wooded parkland. In the 18th Century, by when Euston was the property of the Graftons, the measure of an aristocrats status was the size of his huntin', shootin', and fishin' estate. The rich and powerful pursued a predatory policy of buying up holdings in neighbouring estates until they were in a position to make the lord of the manor next door an offer he couldn't refuse. This had nothing to do with a burning passion to nurture the land. Then as now, the majority of the landed gentry took little interest in affairs beyond their game parks, except to check the books. They were politicians, diplomats and military types. Then as now, working the land was left to tenants and farm managers like James Stamper.

By 1873 Euston Estate had a circumference of over 40miles (64 km.) and encompassed six full parishes and parts of a few more. Today just one of the farms is four times the original size of the Arlingtons' property. Beyond that I can't tell you a lot. The landed aristocracy are a closed book in this country, unless you want to know who sired who and which battle they bravely fought from a hill overlooking the fighting, but the Hall is open to the public in summer, all profits to the Duchess of Grafton's pet charities.

As you ride up the leafy hollow towards **Knettishall Heath**, keep an eye out for the stone waymark on your left. According to this, the Ridgeway or Rudge is 106 miles (171 km.) off to the south west, but that is by the walker's route. I estimate you are now 150 miles (241 km.) from Streatley, approaching the Peddars Way, one of a number of ancient and modern trails that converge on or pass through Knettishall Heath Country Park. Leased from Riddlesworth Estate, the park is 152 hectares of heath, grassland and mixed woods managed by Suffolk County Council. Like Cavenham Heath and Seven Barrows, it is an SSSI, but in summer the Little Ouse attracts scores of families togged out in bathers and equipped with truck inner tubes. Feel free to take a dip yourself. Should you prefer to take a *siesta*, be careful where you lay your head. It does nothing for your karma to open your eyes and find you have been curled up next to a couple of basking adders. Grass snakes are also common here, but perhaps the most beautiful creature to look out for is the green woodpecker. They are often seen on the ground, hunting for ants, and don't think twice about burrowing underground to plunder a juicy nest.

Again, somewhere round here the infamous Map No. 3 routes riders across a ford, but could I find it!? The route I always followed was over a footbridge too narrow for horses, spanning banks too overgrown with nettles for cyclists. Then, all of a sudden, the banks were shorn and a neat ford appeared next to the bridge. It is still under construction as I write, but better late than never I guess. Pedal over or through then up passed **Riddlesworth School**, famous as the *Alma Mater* of Princess Diana, the Princess of Wales. There isn't a lot to see that sets this aside from any other posh school in the country, but by comparison with Milton Abbey School, the place looks distinctly underachieving. Then, at Brettenham Heath, we hang a right onto the Peddars Way and at the railway crossing on Roudham Heath, join those who took the northern loop via Grime's Graves.

As to which of the two options I recommend, this is one occasion where the character of each ride is so totally different it is impossible to make a choice. Though neither is exactly brimming with places to stay, the southern leg is slightly better served by Bed and Breakfasts and campsites. If you have the time or are doing the Chalke Way in weekend bursts, I suggest holing up for a couple of nights and exploring both as a Breckland circuit. Thetford Forest and West Harling Heath offer a myriad of legitimate cycle trails (leaflet for Thetford Forest available at High Lodge), and there is no shortage of reserves in the area where a guy or gal can plant their bum and spend an enthralling couple of hours watching nature do its thing.

Roudham Heath – Castle Acre

IN 1986 RONALD REAGAN SAW FIT TO BOMB THE LIVING DAYLIGHTS OUT OF Libyan civilians in reprisals against Colonel Khadafi. The aircraft carrier used to launch the F-111s was anchored solidly on *terra firma* not a million miles from here at Lakenheath. Because France wisely refused the Americans permission to fly over their air space, fighter-bombers had to take the scenic route and refuel in flight, from air tankers based at Mildenhall a couple of miles south of Lakenheath. The ferocious roars that occasionally wrench asunder the still evenings emanate from there, as do the Chevvies and Caddies that take up the full width of a country lane, and the crew-cut affable beefcakes you might meet in the pub.

Even before the first World War, British bi-planes flew training exercises over Lakenheath Warren, dropping dummy bombs by hand from open cockpits. East Road out of Thetford became an impromptu landing strip, although in those days any length of level ground was liable to find itself suddenly commandeered. Through both World Wars, the Thetford region played a crucial role in air defence and attack, as well as for espionage activities, flying in sabotage squads. Cavenham Heath for example was home to a decoy airdrome or K-station where wood and canvas were imaginatively lashed together to create the illusion from the air of an operational airfield. North Pickenham, which we pass on the next leg of our journey, was an airbase specifically built for the B24 Liberators of the USAF's 492nd Bomb Group. In 1959, the station was in the command of the RAF and still operational as a launch pad for 60 Thor ballistic missiles. Four years later CND demonstrations were instrumental in getting North Pickenham closed. In 1943 the Liberators and Flying Fortresses of the American Eighth Airforce took over from the mashed up Blenheim bombers that the Luftwaffe decimated on the ground at RAF Watton. In one form or another the USAF have been based around Thetford ever since, though now the 'Russian Threat' has been exposed for the black farce it always was, one wonders why.

Land forces have also had a history of exploiting the thinly populated wilderness of the Brecks. In 1911 30,000 squadies camped in Thetford Warren and played war games. Five years later, Lloyd George watched tank manoeuvres on the Elveden Estate, but it wasn't until

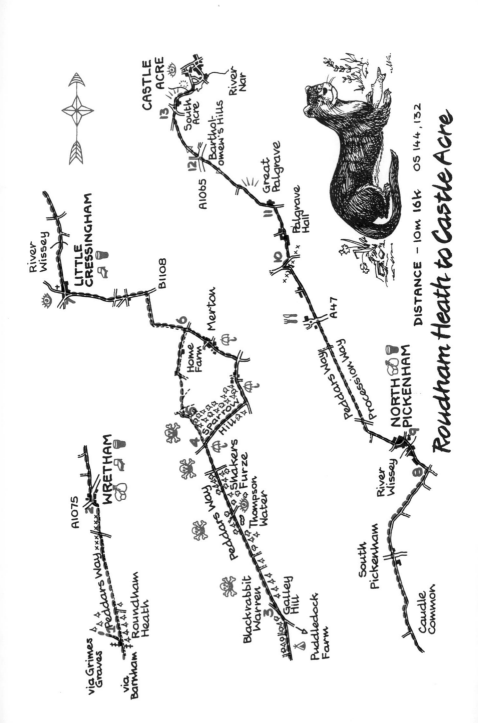

Roudham Heath to Castle Acre

DISTANCE — 10m 16k   OS 144, 132

CASTLE ACRE
13
South Acre
12
Barthol-omew's Hills
River Nar
A1065
Great Palgrave
11
Palgrave Hall
10
Merton
A47
Home Farm
Peddars Way
Processional Way
6
B1108
LITTLE CRESSINGHAM
River Wissey
7
Sparrow Hill
4
Shakers Furze
Thompson Water
5
NORTH PICKENHAM
River Wissey
8
A1075
WRETHAM
Peddars Way
Blackrabbit Warren
Galley Hill
3
Puddledock Farm
via Grimes Graves
via Bannham
Peddars Way
Roundham Heath
1
South Pickenham
Caudle Common

Directions

1 Follow sign 70 PEDDARS WAY.
2 **R** at road then **L** PEDDARS WAY.
3 Branch **R** onto track STANTA ACCESS.
4 **SO** onto **BW** in wood.
5 **R** at stile then branch **L** after first field to pick up PEDDARS WAY.
6 **L** PUBLIC PATH and **L** at TJ (fast road).
7 **R** LITTLE CRESSINGHAM then **R** SOUTH PICKENHAM.
8 **L** NORTH PICKENHAM.
9 **L** SOUTH PICKENHAM, then **SO** out of village, uphill past Manor Farm.
10 After bridge, **R** then **L**.
11 **L** at TJ.
12 **R** PEDDARS WAY then **L** staying on tarmac.
13 **R** FORD.

Resource

WRETHAM
Dog & Partridge
Main Rd
IP24 1QS
01953 498245

Mrs J Hazelby
Larkshill House
IP24 1RU
01953 498347

Puddlehock Farm
Gt Hockham
Near Thetford,, IP24 1PA
01953 498455
Camping

LITTLE CRESSINGHAM
Mrs J Wittridge,
Sycamore House
01953 881887

St Andrew's Church
People next door will gladly tell you all about it!

1942 that the War Office acquired 7,000 hectares in the Stanford area north of Thetford for battle training, specifically with live ammunition. In a rush of patriotic fervour, the 600 residents of the six villages that were to be evacuated cheered the military's announcement. They had to out in less than a month, and were rehoused in comparable property with the assurance that, come the end of the war, they could return to their homes, farms, pubs and schools. Sadly the War Office reneged on the agreement, arguing that unexploded ordnance was still a danger to life and limb. Presumably Whitehall had never heard of mine detectors, bomb squads or armoured mine sweepers. They were possibly more interested in securing another peace-time training area. In 1950 the MOD compulsory bought the **Stanford Training Area** (Stanta) and in 1990 expanded the military theme park to nearly 11,000 hectares.

In a cute little booklet on the Stanta published in 1979, Lt. Col. O'Leary (OBE, MC) explains that though Stanford is the smallest training area in the country, " . . . it is one of the most important as its terrain closely resembles the topography of that in North West Europe, where the bulk of the British Army is deployed facing the Warsaw Pact forces across the Iron Curtain". With the Cold War won and Russia bidding to become a player in NATO, the anachronism of Stanford is further highlighted by a £4 million replica of an East German village erected on site at the turn of the nineties. Complete with wrecked Russian tanks, three storey buildings and a church (Russian Orthodox?), the village was completed just in time to be overtaken by Glasnost. It is now called 'European Village', though the MOD aren't saying which EC country they perceive as the new bogey-man.

In 1977 the Nature Conservancy Council declared the Stanta "The one remaining piece of Breckland large enough to give the essential character of the district as it was before the 20th Century reclamation began – large unenclosed tracts of gently undulating, untilled, sandy and flint strewn prairie extending to the horizon, broken only by the occasional row of trees or larger wood". Again, it is an SSSI and its fringes are farmed, leased out to 16 licensees for crop growing. After myxomatosis decimated the rabbit population, a large flock of Beulah sheep were brought in to prevent the open heath becoming overgrown. Fluctuating around 10,000 head, the flock is broken up into smaller units that graze specific areas (or 'hefts'), much like their territorially limited moorland cousins.

Most of the Stanta's archeological wealth has long disappeared, submerged under the sand, but the flora and fauna abounds. The list of recorded birds alone runs to almost 200 species, including the Golden Eagle, though I suspect this sighting was an escapee. Other escapees, this time from nutria (fur) farms, were less than welcome. In the seventies, coypu and mink rampaged through the area, decimating root crops and cereals. They provided good sport for the khaki crew who willingly, if unofficially, joined in the turkey shoos to eradicate both species. In 1980, MAFF's 'Coypu Control' budget stood at a staggering £2.5 million. It paid off. In 1950 Britain (principally Norfolk) had the largest population of these South American rodents in the world. By 1988, the last one had become a muffler.

We are now travelling the line of the **Peddars Way**. The Icknield Way runs due north from Croxton slap bang through the middle of the Stanta, beyond which a clearly defined route to the coast is hard to pick out. Like the Peddars between Sparrow Hill and the old North Pickenham airdrome, the line of the Icknield was lost during the various land enclosures. We have ridden parallel to or upon it for nearly 160 miles (275 km.). It has become a firm friend, taking us to some wild places, to meet interesting people and see fascinating things, but it is time to move on and ride with a younger companion, a companion that has all the mellow, relaxed gentle attributes one looks for in the latter years of a journey's lifetime. The Peddars Way might represent our final dash to the coast but, without a doubt, it is the icing on what I hope you agree has been a truly scrumptious cake.

Approved by the Countryside Commission in 1982, the Peddars Way was officially opened by the Prince of Wales four years later as a long distance byway, the thirteenth in the country. Unlike the various ridgeways we have followed that evolved into a major cross country thoroughfare, the Peddars is one of those long straight masterpieces of Roman engineering that slice through the landscape regardless of contours and natural obstructions. Constructed in 61 AD, it is thought the road ran from Colchester up to Holme-next-the-Sea where the colonialists' possibly had a ferry link across the Wash. Its name could be derived from the Latin for foot ('ped'), but it is more likely to be a 16th century christening. Henry IV referred to the Icknield Way as the 'peddersty, alias saltersty', and in the 18th century Norfolk villagers held 'ped markets' where they would displayed their produce, much like rural Latin Americans and Arabs do today, in large semi-circular wicker baskets known as 'peds'. In 1845 there is a reference on a Royal Map to the 'Pedlars Way' and as recently as 1994 Christopher Taylor, Britain's leading road archaeologist, compounded the confusion by returning to a corruption of the Latin and calling it the 'Pedars Way'.

Whatever the origin of its name, the length from Brettenham Heath to Sparrow Hill gives you a taste of the excellent cycling to come. The surface ranges from tarmac to smooth bridleway as it carves a course through native woods and dark plantations. Where it tears free, the views never range far before a row of conifers blocks the low horizon. They are painted on a background with the deft strokes of a Chinese brush on damp cartridge. In the evening with the setting sun behind them, the colours are watery and still running. But what you see is tamed ruggedness. The mountains of Scotland with the mountains pulled out from under them so the carpet of shag pile drops in a crumple. If anybody ever told you Norfolk is flat, expect to be pleasantly surprised.

At **Galley Hill** (another hangman's job spot, like the one we passed north of Luton?) the Peddars turns a corner, one of two gentle realignments along its original 78 mile (125 km.) length from Colchester, but you need to be sharp to notice the bend. On the ground the Roman straight is full of kinks and curves where it has been deformed over the ages by more recent constructions like the now disused Thetford to Watton railway line we cross at Wretham. This was one of the many casualties in Norfolk of the swingeing policies of **Dr Beeching**, infamous Chairman of BR (then the British Railways Board) for a tempestuous four years beginning in 1961.

Running a national and nationalised rail network is no easy task, particularly if, like Beeching, you have no experience of managing a transport system and little understanding of the interdependence of that system. He was the Technical Director of Imperial Chemicals Industries (ICI), headhunted by the Conservative Government to make the railways financially viable and independent of the tax payers pocket (sounds familiar?). This was a recurrent theme of both shades of government, blue and red, and one that, to this day, perplexes our European partners who recognise their rail network as a sacrosanct part of the infrastructure, often more deserving of subsidy than their road routes.

In March 1963, Beeching presented his 'Reshaping' report to the nation and the press went bananas. Designed to save £13 million per annum on railfreight and £18 million on passenger services, it heralded the closure of 2,363 stations and halts, the withdrawal of 266 passenger services and massive track reductions, either by line closure or reduction to single track. Bearing in mind the age of these figures, it was a body blow to the industry from which certainly rail freight never recovered. The Tories definitely didn't recover from the storm of protest and by October 1964 they were out. Six months later Dr Beeching , now Lord (for his services to the nation?) was on his way back to ICI, leaving the bulk of his proposals to be implemented during the tenure of a very pissed-off Labour Government.

Even today, such cost cutting binges are based on the belief that somewhere deep inside the sprawling network is a tight, self supporting, hugely profitable system trying to get out. But rail systems aren't that simple and, as time was to tell, lopping off branches doesn't just dispense with the dead wood, it weakens the trunk. Beeching hadn't done his homework. That he and the Minister, Ernest Marples, were able to even propose such a debacle highlighted that within the corridors of power, the rail lobby was a beetle amongst elephants. Today it has shrunk to an ant. Perhaps it is a coincidence, but the pecs of the road lobby grew emphatically bigger in the Sixties, since when they have been flexing their muscles and driving wedges into any proposal remotely resembling an integrated transport policy.

If you are looking for somewhere for a break, hang a right at Thompson Water, otherwise know as 'Willie's Clump', and mutter a silent "Thank you" to the man who gave the lake its nick-name. It was J. F. Wilson who in the seventies first mapped the Peddars Way and produced the feasibility study for the Countryside Commission. Artificially created in 1845 and fed by the River Wissey, Thompson Water is possibly more important for the Ice Age 'pingos' that pock mark the common. These rare formations were created beneath the surface by frozen lenses of ice pushing up the soil which then tumbles back to form a rim. They look like little meres, and are buzzing with damsel and dragonflies the size of which I've never seen before.

After Sparrow Hill we swing away from the Roman road and wend along quiet country lanes that roughly mirror the course of the River Wissey. Until the ban in 1978, the river was the killing waters of the Eastern Counties Otter Hounds, a pack that consisted of a core of genuine rough haired otter hounds supplemented by casters from the Puckeridge Fox Hounds and Devon and Somerset Stag Hounds. If you are into a little 'sabbing', hare coursing occasionally still takes place in the area, with packs of beagles, whippets and Norfolk Lurchers, but otters are now a protected species and the lower reaches of the Wissey are a designated sanctuary.

The semi derelict church of St. Andrew's, Little Cressingham, deserves a quick look round, principally because the skeletal tower reveals much about 14th Century flint and chalk building techniques. It also gives you some inkling of how violent the elements can be in this part of the country, or were in the 18th Century when the tower and part of the nave were felled by a great storm that blew away half the village. Unfortunately restoration then was as crude and unsympathetic as it can be today. Ugly red brick walls were erected to seal off the main body of the church and allow it to continue as a place of worship. The tracery of the restored east window is similarly an abortion, but in all respects these make-do renovations are what give St Andrew's its unique character. It's not often you can look at a working church of any denomination and feel for its vulnerability. If you want to know more, the family in the house nearest the tower have a little leaflet they will be delighted to sell you, all proceeds to the church. When I last visited, they were in the middle of building work that revealed large blocks of clunch they believe were originally debris nicked from the ruins of the tower. Is nothing sacred?

On the corner of the North Pickenham air base, noticeable for its long lines of battery chicken barns, we rejoin the Peddars Way for a couple of miles of delightful off-road. This section is also known as the Procession Way, possibly a reference to medieval pilgrims travelling south to pay homage to a religious hermit holed up in North Pickenham. Nearby, but now gone, St. Paul's Chapel boasted a holy well, probably pagan in origin, where they sought to cure all manner of agues. Since a number of parishes converge here, it could equally be a reference to the old Protestant tradition of beating the bounds of the parish. This involves a procession of choristers, led by the local priest, walking the parish boundary once a year to redefine their manor. They beat the ground along the perimeter with willow sticks, though in parishes where it is still practised, I suspect they now pick a handful of strategic points and beat the ground with whatever comes to hand.

Given their isolation, their tribal mix and the harsh environment in which Norfolk people have struggled to eek out a living, one might expect the country to be rich in folk stories, morality tales and traditional yarns. One such is the regularly repeated legend of Swaffham pedlar, **John Chapman**. John had a dream in which he discovered an enormous pot of gold buried somewhere quite specific in London. One fine day he set off down the Peddars Way to dig up his fortune. Along the road, he bumped into a fellow traveller from London walking north. By a remarkable coincidence the Cockney had also had a dream, in which he discovered an enormous pot of gold buried somewhere in John Chapman's back garden. Each immediately returned home and acquired a spade. The story tells us nothing of the Cockney's success or failure, but John found his buried treasure and gave the lot to St. Peter and Paul's Church, Swaffham, to finance the building of the north isle. So if you have a dream and meet somebody walking or riding down the Procession Way, don't be embarrassed to stop them for a natter. They might have the winning number of next weeks National Lottery tattooed on the inside of their eyelids.

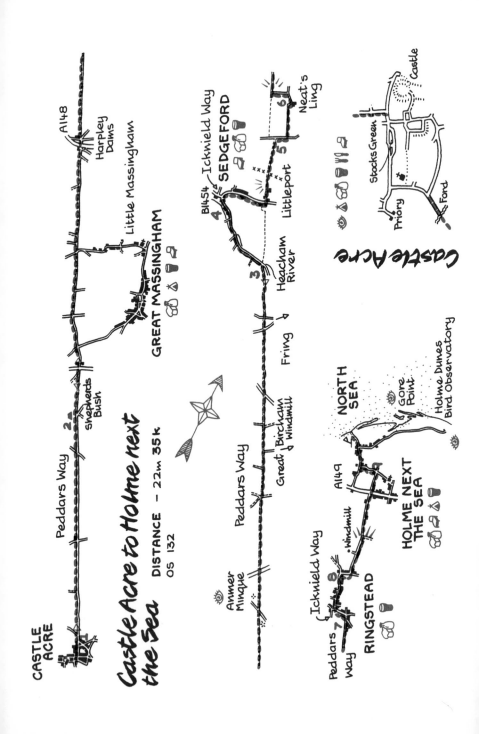

Castle Acre to Holme next the Sea

DISTANCE – 22m 35k

OS 132

CASTLE ACRE

Peddars Way

A148

Harpley Dams

Little Massingham

Shepherds Bush

GREAT MASSINGHAM

Anmer Minque

Peddars Way

Great Bircham Windmill

Fring

Heacham River

BI454 Ickwield Way

SEDGEFORD

Littleport

Neat's Ling

Ickwield Way

Peddars Way

Windmill

RINGSTEAD

A149

HOLME NEXT THE SEA

NORTH SEA

Gore Point

Holme Dunes Bird Observatory

Castle Acre

Priory

Stocks Green

Ford

Castle

Directions

1 Leave village up hill.
2 SO past trig point.
   Follow PEDDARS WAY SO all the way.
3 L at bridge. Ahead is a footpath only.
4 R at TJ FAKENHAM.
   At top of hill, L MAGAZINE FARM.
5 R then L at pylon before valley.
   Follow track through Neats' Ling.
6 L at chemical depot, then R at TJ PEDDARS WAY.
7 L HUNSTANTON, then R.
8 R then L following road to windmill.
9 L at Kirkgate Street, then L at TJ.

Resource

CASTLE ACRE
Willow Cottage Tearooms
PE32 2AE
01760 755551
BB & food

Independent Hostel
Ms A Loughlin
The Old Red Lion
Bailey St, PE32 2AG
01760 755557
Kitchen for preparation of own
food and concessionary rates to
YHA members.

GREAT MASSINGHAM
Mr Rae
Pleasant House, PE32 2HN
01485 520259

Rose & Crown
01485 520248
Camping & food

GREAT BIRCHAM
Working windmill with
tea rooms.
01485 23393
Open Easter – Sept, not Sats.

SEDGEFORD
Mrs J Frost
Parkview
Heacham Rd
PE36 5LU
01485 71352

HOLME NEXT THE SEA
Mrs Snare
Northgate House
46 Northgate
PE36 6DR
01485 533269

Inglenook Camping
Main Rd
PE36 6LR
01485 25598

Newholme Nurseries
Main Rd
PE36 6LR
01485 25269

Holme Dunes Nature Reserve
01485 240

Castle Acre – Holme next the Sea

WE ARE IN PILGRIM COUNTRY, AND I DON'T MEAN WHAT WAS. THOUGH THE numbers are unlikely to inspire a 20th Century Chaucer to rush home and pen a road novel, people still do the pilgrim thing in Britain. As recently as the 1980s over a 100,000 devout Anglicans and Roman Catholics annually travelled to Norfolk to make the sign of the cross. Their destination was and is the Priory at Little Walsingham, 17 miles (27 km.) up the road from Castle Acre. Just before entering South Acre we cross the A1065 at the seemingly unremarkable culvert of Bartholomews' Hills. No fewer that seven highways converge here, including a Roman road and an ancient fen causeway from Peterborough. Quite possibly this is where travellers from all points of the compass met and rested before the final push north east along the Picnamwade or Pickenham Way. Who knows, there might even have been a medieval Happy Eater here.

In the Middle Ages, Walsingham had an international reputation second only to Canterbury. The Shrine to Our Lady was erected in the 12th Century after the Virgin Mary dropped in for a chat with Richelde de Fervaques. It was modelled on the sacred cottages of Loretto, Italy, which were said to have been transported by angels from Nazareth. In the 1150's a Priory was built near the Shrine that attracted royalty, clergy and lay pilgrims in their droves (including Erasmus in 1511), but by 1538 it had ceased breaking bread and the Holy Brethren had surrendered to the crown. Three hundred years later the shrine was reconsecrated and open for business again.

All of which might appear to have nothing to do with Castle Acre, except it is hard to imagine pilgrims destined for Walsingham didn't take the opportunity to put in a little extra spiritual submission at the town's Cluniac Priory. The brick cross set in the flint walls of No. 8, Stocks Green, indicate the house was indeed a hostel for pilgrims, while the Priory itself accommodated illustrious visitors on the premises, above the stores, and the less illustrious in a separate building to the west of the main structure. As you turn the corner of South Acre and climb, the ruin reveals itself, picturesquely lying doggo in the Nar Valley. In its full glory it must have been an uplifting welcome to foot-weary travellers.

It is interesting to compare Castle Acre to the two other villages we recommend to you, Cerne Abbas and Ashwell. Unexpectedly, this is the hilliest of the three, perched on a northern buff overlooking the River Nar and flowing down to the flood plain where the Peddars Way crosses the stream. Once upon a time the river was navigable through here and the community was a thriving centre for trade and distribution. It was a wealthy town, with sufficient disposable income to profit theatre troupes that performed in Castle Acre's own Drury Lane. The body of the village is still contained within impressive earthworks and centred on Stocks Green, opening out from the 13th Century Bailey Gate.

Many of the houses are late medieval flint cottages that have stood the test of time and modernisation, but perhaps more noticeable is the almost total absence of thatched roofs. On the gable end of Watlington House on the south side of the Green you can still see the roofline of the old thatch, but throughout the Norfolk we traverse, organic roofs are surprisingly rare. I can only guess the cost of Norfolk reed and its vulnerability to high winds made pantiles a far more attractive proposition to the frugally minded East Anglians. And some of the pantiled roofs in Castle Acre are extremely attractive, particularly looking across from the top of Bailey Street.

The town was largely shaped by **William de Warenne**, first Earl of Surrey and son-in-law of William the Conqueror. In 1080 he built a fortified house overlooking the river crossing that the family developed a hundred years later into a splendid motte-and-bailey castle. The remains of the Norman keep barely merit ruin status, but the sloping site is impressive, with its sweeping prospect over the farming countryside to the south east and rectangular mounds that tell of dwelling places. William founded the Priory as a daughter house to the great Cluniac Priory of Lewes in Sussex. The considerable wealth and import of the Cluniac order can be gauged by the size of these buildings, even in their shattered state. On a 12 hectare site a mere 30 brethren resided. The Priory was well and truly Dissolved in 1537 but there is still plenty to see amongst the ruins. Pick up 'An Old Guide to Castleacre' at the post office. Written by Francis Highe in 1908, this neat reprint contains a detailed tour of the Priory and some excellent old etchings.

But Willy de Warenne had big plans for 'Castleacre', including shifting the town to a new location, lower in the valley, were he could keep a protective eye on it and improve the living conditions of his vassals. In its Norman time, the ramshackle wattle and daub hovels of the old community must have reflected badly on the de Warennes, surrounded by the opulence of their Priory and keep. But by the 14th Century the town had declined to a village, largely because trade routes had shifted and pilgrimages ceased. Today Castle Acre is a quiet little agricultural community and the pilgrims are now tourists, delighted by their discovery of such a gem of antiquity huddling so far off the beaten track.

Castle Acre also has its fable, this one concerning farm labourer John Jessop. It seems Norfolk men are always dreaming of buried treasure. Stealing into the Priory grounds in the dead of a broody night, John dug deep at the spot near the ash tree his vision clearly pictured. He worked feverishly while the wind "whistled rushed and roared". When he finally uncovered the leaden chest, the ground open up beneath it and the treasure plummeted out of sight down a deep deep shaft. Sudden a "head of hideous proportions" all horns and glaring eyes, lunged out at him in the dark. He shrieked and ran for his life and his bed, which he didn't leave for days. The story is told in the old guide book in full Gothic 'Tales from the Crypt' gore. As fine a piece of 19th Century horror writing you couldn't wish for.

We are leaving the Brecklands. As you climb out of Castle Acre, you might hope for a view of the North Sea across the flatlands of Norfolk, but there is a whole lot of riding still to do and this land is anything but flat. We are approaching the **Heights of Norfolk**. The topography has been quietly changing since Little Cressingham, gradually developing into the wonderful roller-coaster of gentle ups and downs that is our route to the sea. At a low of 92 feet (28 m.) Shepherd's Bush still deserves a trig point. It is the highest point along the Peddars Way, and here the old Roman road really comes into its own. Broader than any other imperial highway in the county (and it is the best preserved), it is thought the Peddars was specifically constructed to facilitate rapid troop movements deep into enemy territory.

These were the tribal lands of the **Iceni**. Originally a friendly rabble, they allied with the Romans in 55 BC to drive the Belgae out of South Anglia, but the relationship soon turned sour, probably embittered by the notorious greed of the Roman priesthood. In AD 47 began a series of uprisings that culminated in the Iceni giving Rome a taste of its own medicine, destroying the garrisons at Colchester and Verulanium (St. Albans). Finally quelled by the Roman governor Suetonis Paulinus, who was brought in specially for the task, the Celts responded positively to his reform of corrupt imperial structures, and to the stability and prosperity that followed in the wake of the revolt. Just in case, the Peddars Way was put in place by Suetonis to police the peace. The Icknield Way remained a busy highway, and became a service road for the various Roman establishments along it and the Peddars.

We know surprisingly little about the Iceni, except that their leader during the riotous years was the formidable **Queen Boudicca**, that her army numbered 120,000 and that their chariots did not sport flashing blades as the statue in London romantically displays. The warrior queen was "of the largest size, most terrible of aspect, most savage of countenance, most harsh of voice; having a profusion of yellow hair which hung down to her hips; and wearing a large golden collar, a parti-colour floating vest drawn close about her bosom, over this a thick mantle connected by a clasp, and in her hand a spear." Evidently not the sort of person one would want to tangle with, but this is a description by a Roman writer, Dion Cassius, who might have been a trifle biased. He goes on to describe how Boudicca massacred, tortured and crucified her prisoners, cutting off the breasts of women, stuffing them in their mouths and sewing up their lips. It seems Dion was the Quentin Tarantino of his age.

Whatever else you do between here and Ringstead, I strongly encourage you not to deviate from the course of the Roman way, but keep right on to the end of the road. The Peddars is entering its most remote stages. Along the next 16 miles (25 km.) of almost exclusively green road you will pass but a handful of houses. Either side hedgerows and rosebay tower above and where they don't, fields of beet sweep away to low valleys above which roofs, spires and tree tops indicate a distant community.

We are back to the wild ridge riding, but without the edge to emphasise your vulnerability. Here it is the sky that presses down and makes us feel insignificant. And what a sky! Memories of Salisbury Plain and the thunderous symphony. At times a Rimsky-Korsakov, bombastic and full of great crescendos. Other times a Bach piece, intricate and full of little cloud flourishes, with too many notes to pick out a particular aerial theme, but just enough to animate a heart-soaring concerto in white and deep blue. All the time, in the back of your mind, there is the expectation that at the next rise, you will see the heavenly melody playing over the ultramarine of the distant sea.

One more Norfolk tale to give you the creeps as you pound through the wilderness. In August 1577, the citizens of Bungay near Lowestoft were sheltering in St. Mary's, praying for deliverance from a terrifying storm, when the great doors burst open and a massive **black dog** came 'running all along down the body of the church with great swiftness and incredible haste among the people, in a visible form and shape, passed between two people as they were kneeling and occupied in prayer, wrung the necks of them both at one instant clene backward, insomuch that even at that moment where they kneeled they strangely died'. As big as a calf and silent on its paws, the **Demon Dog of Bungay**, aka Old Shuck , still roams the county far and wide in search of juicy wayfarers. He is sometimes invisible, the steam of his acrid breath, sound of his paw steps and two floating fiery eyes the only forewarning you are about to have your throat ripped out. Could this be the Hound from Hell that made a pitch for me on Cavenham Heath?

At any time of year, **Anmer-Minque** is an odd little corner. In autumn it is solid with wispy rosebay willowherb, tall and erect, with heads of long plumes that flow in the breeze like ribbons on a lance. It is the perfect setting for Macbeth's witches to hubble-bubble in, or for a black and white samurai movie. There are barrows here, probably the last you will notice, and distinct impressions that used to be marl pits. These were a creation of the 18th Century land improvers, who mixed a concoction of chalk and lime in the hollow for spreading on fields. A good marl dressing lasts around 20 years, but it needed to. It was back-breaking work and labour intensive. One acre of land (about half a hectare) required 100 cartloads to cover it, all mixed, loaded and spread by hand.

Past **Magazine Farm**, as you head across the last long straight of the Peddars Way, pause and look to your left. In the near distance, a hedgerow and trees delineate the line of the good old Icknield Way. It has returned to accompany us on our final run down to the sea. At Ringstead we rejoin it, but before taking up with our old friend again, on the brow of the hill before the village, there it is! The thin blue line, the end of *terra firma*, peeking through the trees and between the terra's folds. The sea! Then its gone, but by the time we emerge from the copse around Ringstead windmill, it has expanded to fill our vision. The excitement is tangible. It has been 370 miles (595 km.) coming but we have finally arrived at the end of the Chalke Way.

The temptation is to charge through Holme, scud across the sand and ride your beloved straight into the sea. It might be a classic photo call, but it would also be a classic mistake. Salt water and sensitive machinery don't mix. If you really must indulge the happy-snapper, return via the public loos where there is an outside tap you can wash your Rosinante down from.

Welcome to the beginning of the end.

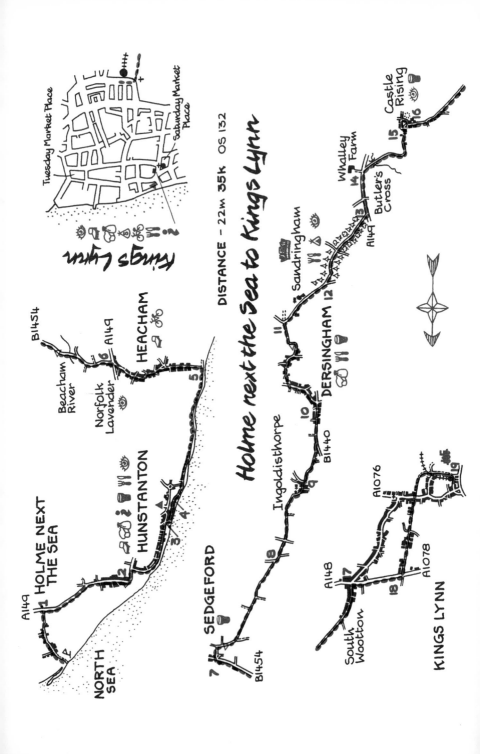

Kings Lynn

Tuesday Market Place

Saturday Market Place

DISTANCE – 22m 35k OS 132

Holme next the Sea to Kings Lynn

Castle Rising

16

15

Whalley Farm

14

Butler's Cross

13

A149

Sandringham

12 DERSINGHAM

11

10

9

Ingoldisthorpe

B1440

B1454

A149

HOLME NEXT THE SEA

1

2

3

4

5

HUNSTANTON

HEACHAM

Beacham River

A149

Norfolk Lavender

6

B1454

NORTH SEA

7 SEDGEFORD

8

A148

17

18

A1076

A1078

South Wootton

16

19

KINGS LYNN

Directions

1   R onto A149 (Very busy road).

2   R CLIFF.

3   R OASIS CENTRE. To visit cliffs, through the bollards to the promenade then R. To cycle along promenade, through the bollards then L. Otherwise follow road.

4   At car park R, dismount through pedestrian area then L and SO up and over levee to track.

5   L at wooden RA next to W.C.

6   R then L at Norfolk Lavender crossing fast busy road.

7   R SNETTISHAM.

8   L into narrow lane then SO.

9   R at TJ then L at B1440.

10 L at lights SANDRINGHAM.

11 R SANDRINGHAM.

12 L keeping fence on left.

13 L at TJ (fast busy road, keep to hard shoulder).

14 R at Whalley Farm Cottages (cross with care). SO along road BW.

15 L at TJ then SO for castle entrance on right.

16 L out of castle, then L again and SO to King's Lynn.

17 R at lights onto A1078.

18 L onto cycleway then SO all the way to rail station.

19 R at church. Station on right.

Resource

HUNSTANTON
Hunstanton YHA
15 Avenue Rd
PE36 5BW
01485 532061

The Lodge Hotel
Old Hunstanton Rd
PE36 6HX
01485 532896
BB & camping

Kingdom of the Sea Centre
& Seal Hospital
Southern Promenade
01485 534211

HEACHAM
Mrs P Glover
The Old Station
97 Station Rd
PE31 7AW
01485 70712
A must if you are a train buff.

A E Wallis Cycle Shop
36-40 High St
01485 71683

Norfolk Lavender
Caley Mill
01485 570384
Tea room & shop. Lavender in bloom
from mid-June.

SANDRINGHAM
Sandringham Camping
& Caravaning Club
Double Lodges
PE35 6EA
01485 542555

KINGS LYNN
Tourist Information
The Gaol house
Saturday Market Place
01553 763044

Maranatha Guest House
117 Gaywood Rd, PE30 2PU
01553 774596

King's Lynn YHA
Thoresby College
College Lane, PE30 1JB
01553 772461

Millets Camp Shop
143 Norfolk St
01553 773046

Cycle Lynn
120 London Rd
01553 769791

Railway information
01553 768455

Epilogue:
Holme next the Sea – King's Lynn

THE LAST TIME WE WERE BY THE SEASIDE WE WERE SURROUNDED BY CANDY floss, Mr Blobby and sizzling pink flesh. By comparison, Holme-next-the-Sea is very much chalk to Weymouth's cheese. A small residential village with pub, shop and riding stables, Holme attracts the beachcomber variety of daytripper, the dog walkers, bird watchers and shell collectors, and those who windsurf at Hunstanton but can't face a night on the town's all-singing all-dancing campsite. The razamataz here is limited to kites and beach balls strung up in plastic nets outside 'Hazel's Cabin' in the car park that is a field. You can get a cuppa at Hazel's, and a wicked slice of home baked cake, but that's about it for candyfloss.

Many moons ago, Holme was next the sea, before the port silted up, was dismantled and finally replaced by a golf course. Possibly it was a boarding point for North Seafarers undertaking the perilous crossing to the continent. We have no reason to suppose our prehistoric ancestors didn't regularly sail back and forth. Sturdy Bronze Age boats dated around 1300 BC have been discovered in Britain, notably at Dover. Made of twisted yew branches filled with packed moss, these curraghs were about 50 foot long (15 m.) and, were perfectly capable of carrying a dozen or so souls to the other side. More likely the port was a Roman ferry head for navigation across the Wash to Wainfleet. To the east of the Peddars Way, on your left as you leave the village, there are signs of an imperial 'colonia', 'where retired legionaires led a quiet life tending their allotments. To look at the village today, it is hard to picture a busy pier packed with foot soldiers being shepherded onto a spritsailed clinker-built cargo vessel, watched by wrinkled old campaigners reminiscing on their days fighting the dreaded Brit.

But it is the beach that is the lure at Holme, particularly for migratory birds *en route* to and from the Arctic. Along the miles and miles of rippled sand you will see avocets, spoonbills, sandpipers, redshanks and those rowdy oystercatchers who don't let the others get a word in edgeways. Depending on the time of the year, the beach can be thick with transit passengers waddling around amongst the resident great blackbacks and fulmars, but Holme Dunes Bird Observatory to the east is the best place to get a good look.

Towards **Gore Point**, soggy black lumps stick out of the surf, and bits of the stuff lie around on the sand. This is petrified wood, soaked for eons in seawater, the remains of an ancient forest and a good place to catch crabs the man with the crabby bicycle informed me. Before the dunes, a carpet of sea lavender, helleborins and orchids show off their rich summer colours amongst the marram grass. Between the dunes are wet areas known as 'slacks'. Here you will find samphire, a delectable free-food that comes to fruition in late July and tastes similar to artichoke. Campers should try it. Pick discriminately about five bunches per person, wash thoroughly to remove sand and salt, then bung them in a billy can of boiling water for a few minutes. Yummy with melted butter, and eaten by dragging the vegetable between your teeth to remove the bulbous bits off the stalk.

You really owe it to yourself to spend a day busily doing nothing on the vast emptiness of the sea shore at Holme. Tomorrow is soon enough to ride to Kings Lynn and jump the fast track back to the rat race. For now, stare vacantly at the closest God got to drawing a straight line, the curve of the horizon. But if all that gets too intense, pedal round the corner to **Hunstanton** and tuck into a slippery hot dog. Pronounced 'Hunston', this was once a choice Victorian resort for the intelligentsia, the Belle of the East Coast, and it is a shame to see distinguished 19th Century apartments standing derelict along the cliff, propped up by buttresses.

The original town was a creation of the 1860s and the idea of the Le Strange family, who resided for the summer at Old Hunstanton and appreciated the coast's potential for tourism. Spurred on by the rail head, a branch of the Great Eastern, the resort rapidly grew and went down-market to become *the* place go if you worked in the factory towns of the lower East Midlands. Many firms had 'Hunstanton Weeks' when the works closed down and the pen-pushers in particular trotted off to the Wash. Then Dr. Beeching had his bright idea, closed the railway and pulled the rug from under a community that relied on the custom of those who could afford a car or a holiday, but not both.

Today Hunstanton is neither a retirement town nor a holiday resort. It's a bit of both, but it shows its age. In summer trippers trundle in in convoy but the attractions are underwhelming, confined to a couple of blocks of souvenir shops, arcades and tea *shoppes* serving unhealthy menu and are definitely greasy-spoons. The beach is good but the swimming suspect, and the highpoint of your hols could be as thrilling as hiring a bike to pedal on the prom or pitting your wits against the Nintendo gladiators at The Pier Entertainment Centre. (The pier was swept away in 1970.) In winter the neon lights of the Entertainment Centre continue their ritual sequence and the tat shops remain open for that one shivering person who desperately needs a pair of flip flops. Here you can still get half-decent saucy seaside postcards, very un-PC but wonderfully English, and the town boasts the largest joke shop in the country, full of incredibly un-PC fun.

For all that, the town has character, possibly because the stores are still owned by shopkeepers, rather than faceless stockholders skulking behind designer chain-store shop fronts. The locals are happy to pass the time of day with you, nattering or just staring out to sea, and there is an air of conviviality in marked contrast to the freneticism of Weymouth. In many respects it seems Hunstanton lost a beat back in the Sixties and never quite caught up with the Nightmare Nineties. It is set in a gentle fold that emphasises this feeling of cosy insularity. At one end the bungalows are perched above cliffs of a mere 60 feet (18 m.), but it is the highest point in the area. At the other, swathes of trailer homes crouch below sea level, protected by a shingle wall on which higgledy-piggledy beachhouses have sprouted. The cliffs are a must because here, from the beach, you can see the very end of the chalk seam, sandwiched in a cake slice between the top soil and layers of red limestone, carstone and the blue-grey of Kimmeridge Clay. (You might have guessed the other place to find Kimmeridge is on the Dorset coast.)

When you leave the town, take either the promenade which can be a gauntlet of blotchy limbs, or the vibrant rouge beach road behind the sea wall (or a bit of both). Having spent all that time staring over the handlebars at a long white ribbon, the colour of this dirt track zings. For the first time since crossing the gault clay of the Vale of Pewsey, we are riding on something other than chalk. It shows, particularly in the buildings around Dersingham. All of a sudden, the villages glow bronze in the sun light, their walls constructed of row upon row of bricks the thickness of pantiles and the colour of bottled ginger. We prologued on the limestone of Portland, now we epilogue on **carstone**, still quarried at Snettisham, but since the standardisation of building materials has squeezed out the vernacular, the quarry is reduced to digging stone for ornamental ponds and facades of boring bungalows.

Norfolk Lavender, at the Heacham crossroads, might be somewhere to pick up a little something for friends back home, but don't expect to see long bushy rows of lavender blue, dilly-dilly. The fields are elsewhere, tucked out of sight on the Sandringham Estate. They take you there by the van load. If you are hungry, save yourself for the best fish and chip shop on the entire Chalke Way. Dare I admit its name escapes me, but you can't miss it at the Dersingham traffic lights, just around the corner from the country butcher who supplies the Royals. Underneath the large crest that affirms he is By Appointment, the window is empty of meat. Instead he displays a lovingly polished pot sheep, as if to want to see what you are buying is an insult to his credentials.

Dersingham is one of seven villages encompassed by the 8,280 hectares of the **Sandringham Estate**, owned by Her Majesty the Queen plc and not the Crown Estates. We bring you this way to experience the full splendour of riding down the avenue, like a Lord or Lady summoned, eyes focused on the looming wrought-iron intricacies of the magnificent Norwich Gates, imagining a knickerbockered man-at-arms will step out as you approach to announce your arrival. Display samples left over from the 1862 Great Exhibition and a wedding present to Bertie and Alix, the Prince and Princess of Wales, these splendid gates are the closest we get to royal opulence at Sandringham. Wilton House has more gold leaf dripping from one cornice than you will see in all of this estate.

Sandringham House has always been a home for living in. It was bought in 1862 for Prince Edward by his mum, Queen Victoria, who appreciated the importance of privacy and a refuge from the public eye, particularly for a dashing young blade like Bertie. The previous owners were the Cowper family, relatives of Lord Palmerston, and the house was a dour 18th Century building that looked more like a stuccoed sanitarium where you lose the relatives than a home where you welcome them. In 1870, Bertie commissioned architect A. J. Humbert and Swaffham builders Goggs Brothers to erect the current house, incorporating a few of the finer features of Cowper's gaff. Jacobean in design, with a couple of onion towers sticking above row upon row of chimneys this one looks a cross between a Scottish golf club and a British Railways Hotel. And inside it feels like a hotel, albeit a luxurious one. The guide book could be a brochure, sumptuous with sterile photos of gleaming Drawing Rooms that cry out for somebody to leave a bum print in the settee and a newspaper on the floor.

But can you imagine the Royals in residence here, the room crowded with the greater family, the grandchildren playing 'Happy Families' on CD-Rom in front of the crackling fire, the chaps slouched at a leather-topped table discussing who's doing what to whom, the girls swapping Grenadier anecdotes, Greatgrandmama with a Twiglet stuck in her throat, while on the phone in the corner, HRH is giving her stockbroker grief, banging on about Barings. Certainly this cosy scene is limited to only a few weeks in the year, traditionally around Christmas, when the clan gathers to assess the years bad press. Other times, a solitary monarch or a Duke of Edinburgh must feel very lonely in these hollow rooms, no matter how busy affairs of the Estate keep them, no matter how exquisite the china, tapestries and paintings may be.

The Estate was initially a game park where Bertie, the Great White Hunter, could practise on partridge and pheasant before travelling abroad on safari. If you are upset by this sordid side of our nature steer clear of the grisly trophy room in the museum. The Royals have been rampant big-game hunters, and even now enjoy a good blast through the Sandringham Estates where beaters can slash the brush for a couple of weeks without crossing the same ground twice. But increasingly the monarchy has adopted a less mercenary approach to their estates, and here have recognised that Sandringham lies in an Area of Outstanding Natural Beauty by opening to the public a leafy and large Country Park. A century ago, this was open heath and grassland similar to those around Thetford. Thanks to a few cuttings snipped on foreign tours, the Park now boasts the most complete collection of exotic conifers in the country.

The Grounds are equally glorious. In summer great bushes of rich rhododendrons and azaleas bulge over languorous avenues of daisy speckled grass. In the watery Dell, the lake is fed by springs that rise on the Estate, and dapple passed the beautiful magnolia and layers of firs. Every tree seems to have had its first footing dug by a royal hand. There are also the 1,400 hectares of arable farmlands, the wedges of forestry worked in conjunction with the Forestry Commission, the inevitable stud farm where Bertie's Persimmon was stabled (the stuffed head we saw in the Newmarket Horseracing Museum), the Royal Pigeon Lofts, the famous family church of St. Mary Magdalene, the cedar tiled tourist facilities, the private fire service . . . I could go on.

HRH plc is big business and the largest private employer in North Norfolk. The brains of the empire are the Estate Agents operating out of George V's old Bachelor's Cottage, now the York Cottage in the south of the grounds. It will be interesting in future years, when the Queen publishes her trading accounts, to monitor exactly how healthy a business Sandringham is. On the surface it appears Liz is well advised and managed, and that the Estate runs counter to the times by being hugely successful. The villagers within its domain certainly ooze confidence and optimism, and talk of the country becoming a republic send shivers down their collective spine. Maybe the House of Windsor could do a better job of running the British economy than the House of Commons?

Between **Butler's Cross**, south of Sandringham, and the bridleway into Castle Rising is a very short section of the A149. Be warned, at the height of the tourist season this road is a nightmare. There is just enough space to ride between the Clearway white line and the verge, but in 1995-96 Norfolk County Council will be laying a cycle path on the west side of the main road. This will form a link with the Sandringham Railway Path through North Wooton and into Kings Lynn.

The last historic monument we visit is also the most complete and the temptation to ignore it should be resisted. The castle in **Castle Rising** was built in 1140 by William d'Albini, the Earl of Sussex, principally to show off his great wealth. He had recently wed the widow of Henry I, Queen Alice, and there were grumblings at Court that Alice had married far beneath herself. In 1327 the 'She-Wolf of France', Queen Isabella, retired here having arranged the ghastly murder of her homosexual husband, Edward II. In 1544 the motte and bailey was granted to Thomas Howard, Duke of Norfolk, by Henry VIII, who later lopped Tom's head off and passed it (the castle) on to the Earl of Northampton. This place has seen a few traumas. Today the premises are under the guardianship of the Department of the Environment and certainly demand a walk through the bailey if not paying and entering the motte. The keep of Shelly Barnack stone is in excellent condition, surprisingly much bigger than suggested by the battlements peeking over the mound, and a tour round fills in the gaps left by Old Sarum and Castle Acre. A stroll along the ramparts affords great views across Norfolk and the Wash, and gives us a better idea of how central these fortifications must have been to the peace of mind of the surrounding communities.

Although the ground is high here, the rising in Castle Rising is more likely to relate to somebody's name. "Rising was a seaport when Lynn was but a marsh. Now King's Lynn it is a seaport town and Rising fares the worse" (Trad.). Like Holme, Castle Rising is a dried up dock, possibly navigable until the end of the Norman period when the Babingley Estuary began to silt up. Like Old Sarum, it was a 'rotten borough', and in 1832 was still returning two MP's to Parliament, representing 86 people, half of whom had yet to receive the vote. And like Hawkesdown Castle, which we didn't visit, way down in Devon, Castle Rising is the beginning and the end of the remarkable coast-to-coast ridge road R. Hippisley Cox believed cut across the south east of England linking causewayed camps and castles. Although you might not have noticed, you have ridden through, passed or within four miles (6 km.) of all but five of the 32 links in the chain. But for British Rail, we could have ridden the lot.

The silver lining to the cloud of Dr. Beeching and the dismantling of so many valuable rail links, has been the number of cycle paths laid on their backs. This process began in the early Eighties when a group of Bristol cycle-activists, having failed to convince the local authorities, took it upon themselves to transform the old Bristol to Bath line into a cycleway. In 1984 the group, now called **Sustrans**, bought their first disused railway line, the Selby to York, which they transformed and opened to cyclists three years later. Since then the pressure group has become a major charity and is regularly consulted by highway authorities like King's Lynn planning to provide cycle-commuter through routes.

Sustrans have a dream of linking Inverness and Dover by a thousand miles of cycleway, and sections of the route have already been bought and laid. They too have a coast-to-coast ride, from Workington to Sunderland, but unlike the Chalke Way it runs exclusively on a smooth surface. Sustrans are not trail blazers. In many respects they are doing the government's work for them, but in lieu of any semblance of an integrated sustainable transport policy oozing out of Whitehall, this is hardly a criticism. Warning bells should sound however when whatever persuasion of government acknowledges the importance of push bikes, but instead of making local authorities responsible for implementing new cycle routes, hives the job off to the voluntary sector in the shape of Sustrans. Until then they deserve the support, financial and moral, of every cyclist in this country sick of dicing with death on the black top.

Most of us plan our adventures so they end in a mad dash through the last town, straight to the railway station and on to the train. In *Kings Lynn*, a better idea is to give yourself a couple of hours leeway, corral your steed with BR and go walk about down by the docks. Like all British ports, Lynn is a skeleton of the former commercial centre that imported timber, iron, cloth, furs, wine, and fish from the Baltic. Out went food, grain, salt, wool and for a short time, the timber from Thetford Forest. The strength of its lost trade base is reflected in the noble merchant's houses, guild halls and the 15th Century warehouse you will see as you stroll towards the elegant Tuesday Market Place. If you are into stained glass windows, St. Margaret's in Saturday Market Place is impressive for its nautical abstract that puts you in mind of the Prisoner of Conscience Window at Salisbury. Notice also the mariner's clock in the tower's eastern face, overlooking the port.

The *frisson* with Salisbury goes further. Here also, it was the church that founded the town, on the marshes that emerged from the sea to become the Fens. In 1101 the Bishop of Norwich granted the site to monks of his cathedral. They established a Benedictine monastery whose entrance arch still stands, and began the work of building a community within the earth walls that rose from the old sea banks. In 1204, King John granted the settlement a Town Charter then promptly set off with retinue and Court Coffers to cross the Wash at low tide, a folly of history best chronicled by Messrs. Sellar and Yeatman in *1066 and all that.* "John finally demonstrated his utter incompetence by losing the Crown and all his clothes in the Wash and then dying of a surfeit of peaches and no cider, thus his awful reign came to an end".

These days the good burghers of Kings Lynn are a lot more mindful of who walks off with what from their town, for this modest East Anglian borough is now the proud owner of the most sophisticated video surveillance system in the country. Wherever you go in the streets and the precinct you are being watched, not by Big Brother, but by a little security man who has a direct line to the beat bobby he can see on Monitor 27, Quadrant 3. Many fear this beady eye is a sinister invasion of privacy, an infringement of personal liberties, and two jackboots short of Big Bro. himself. Others point out it is now safer to leave your gleam machine locked up in Lynn than in Stornaway, on the Isle of Lewis. Either way Kings Lynn is a sign of the times and living proof that the brave new world scenarios envisaged by the futurists of the first half of the 20th Century were disturbingly accurate.

So, for the last 400 odd miles (644 km.) we have followed a line of movement that has strung together the calling cards of prehistory. A line that has steered us across deserts laid waste by the Dark Ages, passed the humble and grand domiciles of Medieval England, and along the footpaths that provided recreational relief from the satanic mills of the Industrial Revolution. It is a line that has been eroded by foot, hoof and cartwheel and by the solid tyres of the earliest velocipedes. Their ancestors have carried us on, through post-war social and agrarian experiments, post-modernist shopping malls, and the New World Order of war-games. Finally, line and wheel have borne us from one side of the country to another, slap bang up to date with the paranoid present of security zones and digital isolation.

As you clatter down the old iron track home, you have to wonder about the unassuming bicycle and that most fervent of pedal pushers H. G. Wells. Is it possible H. G. was riding the Chalke Way, crunching his way through 6,000 years of history, when he was suddenly struck by a brilliant idea for a sci-fi novel? Could his old clunker and 'The Time Machine' be somehow related?

Doing It

So far we have mapped the Chalke Way and provided descriptions to whet your appetite for the ride and hard information to reduce your need to purchase volumes of guide books along the way. Should you require greater detail on a particular landmark or monument, I suggest buying what you will and posting them home when read. All the Post Offices sell envelopes, and there is still a counter in almost every village, often in the corner of the stores, pub or even the ice cream shop. This will keep your carrying weight down and protect what are often very glossy publications from damage.

What we haven't explained is how to do the ride, where to break overnight, when to have a day off and all the nitty gritty of actually undertaking the journey. Our chapters are not a day-by-day breakdown of your travels across the country, though some could be. It is my experience that the best adventures start in the sitting room, on the floor, with the maps spread out, your resource file brimming, a calendar, a map measurer, and a pad and pencil to hand. We provide the maps and resource, you provide the commitment and floor. Make a night of it. Uncork an Asda plonk.

If even that seems too much like hard work, we have encouraged a few cycle tour operators to organise Chalke Way packages that enable you to pack and go without having to worry about a bike, let alone where you will stay the night. The advantages are obvious, particularly the luxury of riding unladened. The company is generally convivial, usually blessed by at least one wag with a strong sense of the absurd, and there is always the freedom to go off on your own, meeting up in the evening for a beanfeast or a slab of cow. More importantly these operators cater for softies and hard nuts alike, so whatever your capabilities there is an itinerary for all who just want to dump their briefcases and ride off into the sunset. Check out the companies listed at the end of this chapter, but what you will miss is the excitement of the mental journey undertaken by those who choose to plan and travel independently.

All city and many town libraries have a loan copy of every Ordnance Survey Landranger map, and branch libraries can order them through Inter-Library Loan. Following the Chalke Way on the OS brings to life our modest charts, adding a third dimension etched by contours and expanded by seeing the route in context. This gives you a chance to travel the road in your head, translating the signs and symbols into an imaginary landscape, picking out the tricky bits, getting a feel for the topography, trying to equate my description of a wilderness with your map reading of an unexceptional heath. When you finally get out there, I guarantee you will be delighted how far short your mental meanderings fell.

While coast-to-coast in one bite has to be the ultimate adventure and achievement, there is no reason why the Chalke Way can't be taken in nibbles, small chunks manageable over the weekends or short breaks. Over a period, the links in the chain can be joined end to end until one fine day, maybe years from now, you roll into Kings Lynn and punch the air. This is how most walkers complete the Pennine Way. The only thing I would advise is whether you start at Weymouth or the Lynn end, tick off the sections in sequence. This is the only way to follow a geological feature and fully appreciate the flow of the gently changing landscape. It's all about continuity.

By Rail

While British Rail (or whatever they are called by the time this hits the bookshelves) deserve a swift kick up the sidings for their ambivalence towards cyclists, it is possible to pedal the route station to station. We pass few platforms, but our maps signpost the nearest stations down the best cycling roads. You will need to refer to the OS or a road map for precise directions, and take into consideration the extra distance to and from. You should also be prepared to spend an entertaining half hour at their Information Counter. There is no way you will make sense of the 'new improved' network by purchasing the mother of all timetables and trying to crack it yourself. Intercity, the systems creaks, but cross country to some of the village halts we disembark at, the system virtually self destructs, with connections that miss by five minutes and direct routes via London. Decoding it all calls for Super-BR-Information-Person. By the time the network is 'fully newly improved' (i.e. totally privatised), cyclists looking for a lonely platform to begin a ride from will probably be grounded.

Meanwhile, one possible breakdown of the Chalke Way, station to station over short breaks and weekends could be:–

Portland and Weymouth to Dorchester

Dorchester to Salisbury
Salisbury to Pewsey
Pewsey to Goring
Goring to Meldreth
Meldreth to Brandon/ Thetford
Brandon/ Thetford to King's Lynn

This breakdown takes no account of train timetables, which change according to the season and the number of leaves on the track!

Norfolk has been almost totally robbed of railways, so between Thetford and Kings Lynn you are on your own. Fortunately this is the one leg that would lose its edge if it could be split into smaller units. Unfortunately, while it can be ridden over one weekend, it can't be appreciated, but then what better way to celebrate completing your coast-to-coast than by extending your final excursion a couple of days.

By Motor

It is often quicker, easier, more flexible and cheaper to pay a friend with a van or a car with a cycle rack to drop and collect you than to flap around with BR plc, sad to say. If there are a number of riders, the savings can be in three figures, and that's after all costs, with a decent slice for the driver. Arrangements for being collected at the end of your break need to be thought about. Railway stations and churches are good meeting points. There can be no confusion, there is shelter even when closed, there is usually a pay phone hard by, and they are accurately mapped, whereas pubs aren't. Agree on a third party at home base, who has a phone and knows when your lift left.

While circuits and figure-of-eights are fine ridden from the rack of your own parked car, point-to-points are trickier, requiring a minimum of two riders who drive, or a rider and a rambler. Four is a more sociable number, the extra bods sharing the strain of motorway madness after a hard day in the saddle. I'm a solitary cyclist but often team up to drop off a couple of friends, drive to an agreed destination, dump the car, and ride back to meet them halfway for a suitably libatious lunch. They then ride on and collect the car, returning to where they started the day, to pick me up. Simple, but again it hangs or falls on fine detail like having two sets of car keys in case you miss each other, and what to do in the event of delay or an emergency befalling either of the parties. One set of keys stuffed up the exhaust pipe is the first place villains look if there is a cycle rack in sight. And remember, a car left unattended for a full day is a security risk even in the wilds, so stash the radio and lock up your woolly dice.

Day by Day

Chopping an extended route into manageable day rides is a nightmare for authors. We tend to underestimate our readers' capabilities and overestimate your interest in anything other than riding the range. A number of elements need to be considered, not least the terrain and under-tyre surface. Ramblers have Naismith's Formula to calculate time taken relative to ups and downs, but for us the equation is complicated by the machine. Pedal pushing Einsteins are still working out a rule-of-thumb. Even then, cyclists are of such mixed abilities, will the resulting law of motion fit you? Your best guide is to map out a local ride, take note of the topography, conditions, weight, number of Mars bars you've scoffed etc, etc, and time yourself.

For those who didn't buy a Filofax with a calculator just for posing, my worst-case scenario works out thus – in the wettest conditions, on the roughest legs of Somerset's hilliest sections, you should be able to better 3 miles (5 km.) per hour. Yes, that's slower than walking, but add a dead weight being dragged through sodden clay in a blizzard and it's realistic. The roughest legs of the rolling Peddars Way are so good in the worst of conditions you can clock up an extra couple of miles (3 km.), no probs, and on the prairies of Cambridgeshire, double it. Then you have to punch into the equation down-time for tourism, the proportion of tarmac to rough, town to country, how tired you feel, where the next Mars bar is coming from etc, etc, and so many *et ceteras*, that your calculator will probably blow a fuse. Get out there and time yourself. It's easier.

The slackest couch potato should be able to achieve 15 miles (24 km.) per full day off-road, rising to 25 miles (40 km.) as fitness sets in. Most of what there is to stop and oggle at is in the first half of our jaunt, which is the toughest, so the breaks are welcome. If you are planning to pedal the Chalke Way start to finish and find on paper you are half way through your allotted holiday but yet to reach Luton, don't worry. The ride speeds up. You will make far better time on the second half of your journey.

Armed with a rough idea of your capabilities and a clear idea from book and maps of what's out there, take up your map measurer and start wheeling it across our charts. One possible day-by-day breakdown could be:-

Weymouth to Cerne Abbas
Cerne Abbas to Milton Abbas
Milton Abbas to Ebbesbourne Wake
Ebbesbourne Wake to Salisbury
Salibury to Vale of Pewsey
Vale of Pewsey to Wanborough Plain
Wanborough Plain to Streatley
Streatley to Ivinghoe
Ivinghoe to Melbourn
Melbourn to Newmarket
Newmarket to Brandon/Barnham
Brandon/Barnham to Castle Acre
Castle Acre to Holme next the Sea
Holme next the Sea to King's Lynn.

Bed and Breakfast

Our suggestions for places to stay are precisely that, they are not recommendations. Some of the addresses in our Resource are the only places offering Bed and Breakfast in that particular village or hamlet. Those located in towns and the city of Salisbury are the tip of a large iceberg you can access by writing to or phoning the relevant Tourist Information Office. Left with your request, they will do all the donkey work of phoning round to look for a vacancy, an invaluable service in towns like Weymouth that are inundated in summer and over bank holiday weekends. The quality of the accommodation ranges from bunk beds in the shared dormitory of a hostel, to four-star luxury with *en suite* jacuzzi and prices to match. Farms, pubs, and country cottages offer the best all-round deal, particularly if you want to meet the locals, frequently with the option of a wholesome evening meal. Mention you are riding the Chalke Way and there is a fair chance they will offer the use of a lock-up where you can store your bike overnight. (Wherever possible we have chosen B & Bs recommended by the Cyclists Touring Club, but if you are at all concerned about the security proffered, ask if you can keep your bike in the bedroom. Make sure it is clean before making the suggestion.) Some B & Bs will also provide a packed-lunch for the following day, though the fare is not always mouth watering. A Thermos flask might be useful if you want a midday brew.

Booking in advance is encouraged and some won't accept unannounced guests, but doing the ride off the cuff can be very entertaining if you don't mind flogging round the houses every evening looking for a bed. For some this adds extra spice to an adventure, and certainly greater flexibility.

Camping

The best campsites are the ones we can't tell you about, like those offered by publicans, behind the greenhouse next to the goats, or by the Scout mistress who works in the cafe where you happen to be noshing, or by the Town Council who turn a blind eye, as long as the Winnebago crew don't cotton on. They provide nothing more sophisticated than a cold water tap and charge a couple of quid if anything. Official sites range from the sublime at Holme, with its chemical toilets and the aurally-challenged old codger, to the ridiculous at Weymouth, with on-site fish and chips and Bingo Hall. There are places you will encounter along the way, some of which are marked on the Ordnance Survey, where cyclists can't stay, either because campers have to provide their own chemical toilets or because they are club sites. If we don't map it, don't bother enquiring.

One or two campsites at the resorts will not accept single-sex parties. This has nothing to do with homophobia and everything to do with rampant heterosexuals prowling in packs hunting down holiday romance. Apparently women are the raunchiest in a pack, which in the warden's eyes need be no bigger than two persons. Explain that you are cycling the Chalke Way and only want to pitch for the night (why stay longer?). They will probably stick you well away from the 'yoofs'.

Minimum impact wild camping is possible wherever the Chalke Way is wide enough to accommodate a tent. It's not encouraged by the authorities, principally for fear 4 x 4 drivers will trundle down the track and throw up continental frame tents the size of hotels. More recently, nomads have discovered green roads make excellent pitches and off-road police patrols are rare but not unknown, mainly in daylight hours. The cops won't bother you if you lay the 'jolly campers' bit on thick. Get shirty and they'll read you the Criminal Justice Act. Do not pitch 'on' the track, unless you want to start your day up the nose of a farmer. Do leave the site as virgin as you found it, which means NO OPEN FIRES, please. Observe the Countryside Code throughout your stay, and remember, you are ambassadors in a hostile land. If there are houses nearby, it is wise to check nobody minds you doing your own thing. Enquiries often lead to so-and-so a person or such-and-such a place offering a much better pitch. There are gaps along the Chalke Way where we can't find you an official site and can't advertise a wild spot, but the whole route is 'campable', whatever daily distances you are capable of achieving.

Children

Taken at a friendly pace, there is no reason why youngsters shouldn't potter along with Mum and/or Dad on this ride, particularly if it is broken into stages and conquered over weekend breaks. Provided their small frame bicycle has a broad range of gears and you don't expect junior to carry much more than a water bottle, they'll love it. Of course, the stronger they are the more you can load them up, but never make cycling hard work for them; they'll grow up to become drivers.

Kiddies in child seats are more of a problem, though stories of pillion riders being wheeled through darkest Africa put my hesitations to shame. This trip can get pretty bumpy and in parts is very exposed. Accepting that your sprog just sits there and gets cold, layers upon layers of clothing are essential, and an extra cushion of foam under the botty, but there is certainly no shortage of wayside ba-bas and moo-moos for them to gurgle at.

Package Holiday Companies

Rough Tracks
6 Castle Street
Calne
Wilts
SN11 0SZ
01249 816665

Norfolk Cycling Holidays
Sandy Way
Ingoldisthorpe
King's Lynn
Norfolk
PE31 6NJ
01485 540642

Karakoram Experience
32 Lake Road
Keswick
Cumberland
CA12 5DQ
017687 73966

Rider and Mount

THE CHALKE WAY IS A GOOD TEST OF RIDER AND MOUNT. THE BETTER PREPARED both are, the greater the enjoyment of the adventure. Certainly you will experience the odd hiccup, if only occasional punctures, but halfway across the sands of Salisbury Plain is not the place to discover your ballbearings have ground to dust. Neither is it encouraging to face the first hill and find you are heaving like an asthmatic from just looking at it. A little training goes a long way on a ride like this, as does a little maintenance.

Your Bike

Let us presume your steed is in tip-top condition and that, if it isn't, you will wheel it in to your friendly neighbourhood bicycle dealer for a thorough seeing to. Let's also presume that items like mud guards, lights, water bottle and rack, pannier rack(s), toe-clips, pump and so on have been added to the basic frame as needs demand. Finally, let me presume that anything you don't understand or wish to question in what follows you will raise with your dealer. It only remains for me to highlight that the unique nature of the Chalke Way calls for unique decisions, principally regarding comfort.

If the furthest you have travelled off-road is a day's ride, you might find an extended haul takes its toll on the five points of contact between yourself and your beloved. Hands, bum and feet are all vulnerable to the continual pounding, with knock on symptoms in your wrists, arms, neck, back and knees. To a greater or lesser extent, all these discomforts can be prevented, but before considering how, the comfort factor opens another can of worms. In theory you can ride the Chalke Way on any large wheeled bicycle (27 inch wheels or 700 cm.) that has a broad range of Derailleur gears. I know Dervla Murphy conquered the Himalayas on a three-speed clunker and that Moulton produce a small wheeled ATB that claims to match an MTB, but why make life difficult for yourself? If you opt for a standard tourer with narrow tyres (.25/.50 inch, or 28/38cm.) you can expect trouble negotiating the sands of the Brecklands and the hoof-pitted bridle-ways of Dorset, but these are relatively short sections where a little pushing allows for a lot of looking around. The big advantage in riding a fat tyred bicycle is the cushioning. On the tarmac roads of

Cambridgeshire and the Chilterns, an MTB might handle like a truck on a treacle race track, but broad treads and low air pressures certainly smooth out the edges in the wild. If you have the choice, dust off the mountain bike for this one.

What you do to prevent aches and pains is largely a matter of money and personal preference. Some will advise you to buy shock absorbers or at least a suspension stem to take the crunch out of the handlebars. The cost of these retrofits ranges from £50 to £450 and the jury is still out on exactly which system is better for what. Alternatively spend a tenner, cover every tube you are ever likely to grasp in foam handlebar tape and get yourself a good pair of padded trackmits. Bar ends are crucial to increase your range of handlebar holding positions. There is also a range of squishy handlebar grips and ones that alter the angle of your grasp to straighten your wrist. Called 'Biogrip', this natty German idea claims to eradicate hand trauma by ensuring the biomechanical lines of force run straight, ensuring maximum muscle support for your wrists.

Saddles are almost as various in shape and substance as bums but there is still the chance your cheeks sit comfortably on none of them. Women are particularly poorly served, but special leather perches with little bits cut out for the delicate parts do exist. Badger your local cycle shop early, remembering the saddle will need treatment and wearing-in to a snug fit. If nothing suits, it might be your riding position that needs adjusting, or even that the darn bike doesn't fit. Again, women get a raw deal, especially if you ride a diamond frame essentially designed by men for men. His and her proportions just ain't the same, guys, and women often find they have to reach to grasp the handlebars. Enlightened manufacturers now produce womens diamond frames (probably called 'ladies'). If you can't get comfy or suffer with cyclists' back ache, make an appointment with your dealer to have him or her size you up on your Black Beauty. You can stock up on inner tubes while you're there.

What can one write about pedals that the cycling comics haven't already written, road tested, star rated, graphed, and photographed from five different angles? Go there for the low-down but remember, there is a lot of strolling around sight-seeing and hanging out in pubs involved in this gruelling expedition. Think comfortable strong footwear and work backwards to the pedals. A good pair of shoes is often all you need to cushion foot from pedal. Should you go for a boot, there are toe clips to fit. Budding Chris Boardman's who want to move on should look at clipless pedals and their corresponding cycling shoes.

Your Engine

As to your body, the engine, it would be great if we were all super fit, but sadly few of us have the time for much more than a couple of hours of physical jerks a week, if that. The best way to get cycle fit is to cycle, but if all you can manage is a regular lunch time swim or an evening aerobics class, these will certainly flex muscles, stretch ligaments and exercise the heart. Provided you don't undertake unrealistic distances to start with, the actual ride will do the rest, but it is imperative you undertake at least one fully laden trial run over the rough. This will reveal the shocking news of how cycle unfit you are and give you an idea of what sort of distances you can expect out of the clapped out old steam-billy. Don't despair! Unlike mechanical equivalents, biological engines possess remarkable powers of self regeneration.

After a full day turning the crank, it helps to know a few stretching techniques. Properly performed these will prevent you walking around crunched up like a neanderthal for the rest of the evening. No matter how tired you feel, drag your aching body into a bath or shower. Aside from relaxing battered bones and washing away road dust, warm water invigorates the soul. You will crawl into bed glowing, looking forward to sun up rather than dreading the dawn of a new ache. Before setting off the next morning, physical instructors would advise warm up exercises. 'No chance!', do I hear you say? A few repeat stretches certainly wouldn't go amiss, and when you set off, take it easy until your body has warmed up and relaxed into its stride.

What you wear is again dictated by purse and preferences, but designer cycling toys are generally too flimsy or over-engineered for extended bouts of rough cycling. Think comfort, warmth and wet. Track mits we've mentioned. Lycra shorts with a chamois leather gusset or padded liners are great for protecting reproductive tackle and bums. On the downside, they're a bugger to wash and dry out over night. Trousers of any description are not cut for cycling in. If you need to wear longs invest in lycra tights (or fleece tights for winter), both for comfort and warmth. Regulating body temperature is best achieved by exploiting layers of clothing that can be peeled off or pulled on as necessary. This goes for hands and feet as well. A final windproof, waterproof layer is essential, particularly for the upper body, as is a warm hat (with a long peak if you wear glasses). In wet weather, feet are especially vulnerable. While you could invest in snazzy neoprene over-booties or slick designer spats, a couple of polythene bags wrapped round stockinged feet and secured when you tie up your shoes are a darn sight cheaper, lighter and less bulky to carry.

The colours in your wardrobe need to be selected carefully, and if that sounds a bit precious, have you seen one of those day-glo billboards masquerading as a cyclist in the context of the English countryside? Talk about 'colour pollution'! Leave your garish gear at home for this adventure, and you will come across as much less of a threat to nature and the natives. Having said that, one item that shouts in the dark or against the landscape is a good idea, in case you have a disaster and rescuers have to come looking for you. A standard lime green cycling jacket is perfect.

Helmets are a contentious issue better discussed elsewhere. In traffic in the wet I wear one, but on a ride like this we encounter so few killers. . . well, I leave it to you. Dan and Doris Stubble-Jaw, intent on completing the route in under a nanosecond, should definitely leave home with hard hats strapped on, and wear them at all times, though I guess you can take them off in bed. If you are looking to buy, don't shop for a helmet in a superstore unless you are *au fait* with the four different safety standards. Go to the cycle dealer and leave the substandard stock to lose money on the shelf.

What to Take

As little as possible is the short answer. Drilling holes in your inner tubes to reduce weight is unnecessary, but bulk and weight are important factors riding off-road. If you need a standard to work to, look at your bicycle. There isn't a thing strapped to or hanging off it that isn't essential. Think essential.

For the Bike, it goes without saying you need to carry a pump, a tool kit, and an appropriate cycle lock. Since the machine will rarely stand alone, a half decent cable lock should suffice if secured in a sensible location. Choice of tools largely depends on what you feel capable of repairing at the roadside. Select what you think you need, then go to the bike and double check you have the bare necessities covered. Then add the following items that will prove invaluable along the Chalke Way:-

- a small container of oil	- spare mudguard
- string	- pannier rack bolts
- PVC	- old tooth brush
- a masonry nail	- scalpel blade

(Spare spokes taped to the chainstay are a good idea if you are riding anything other than a mountain bike.)

At the end of a mucky day, before washing yourself down, give your mount similar consideration, using the toothbrush to get into tight corners. Leave it to drip dry. In the morning, oil moving parts lightly and take the opportunity to check nothing has shaken loose or frayed. With the string and PVC tape you should be able to temporarily bind most hang-offs until you find an appropriate solution at a cycle shop, garage or ironmongers. The nail is for prising out thorns embedded in tyres and should be kept with the scalpel blade in your puncture repair outfit. Take plenty of patches, a spare inner tube and a short length of old inner tube. In the event of a tyre splitting, wrap the old inner tube around the exposed length of your current inner tube then bind the whole lot with string, tyre and rim, until you reach somewhere you can buy a replacement. It's a bumpy ride, but it's a ride.

For the Engine, a first aid kit is essential, if only full of tube creams to soothe hands, bums and feet. The Red Cross and St. Johns Ambulance run regular first aid courses, but a useful kit could include:-

- plasters	- small sharp scissors
- roll of micropore tape	- anti-septic cream
- lint	- crepe bandage
- medi wipes	- Arnica cream

Don't leave for anywhere without a good fist of toilet paper stuffed in a resealable polythene bag. Sure as eggs are eggs you are going to need it somewhere down the line. Crapping in the wild is an art and something you must not be irresponsible about. Parts of New Zealand, for example, are now grossly polluted by wilderness walkers being negligent about where and how they do big jobs. Select a sheltered spot, well away from running water, amongst wild vegetation. Dig a small but deep hole, either with your heel or a spanner, and let everything plop into that. Before burying put a match to the toilet paper. Stamp the mound down and ride away confident that what could have been a disgusting mess is now a microbes banquet.

All engines need fuel and ours is no exception. In fact many see cycling as a good excuse to OD on chocolate and four course lunches. Cycling consumes vast amounts of calories which need to be replaced by munchies containing sugars easily absorbed by the body. Forget all those heavily engineered energy replacement bars and drinks. Eat and drink what you enjoy, but do so little and often. Be warned about midday pints. Exercise pumps enough high octane juices round your body without you adding to them. Even in winter it is essential to take regular gulps of water. This is a rare commodity along much of the Chalke Way, so take every opportunity to top up your water bottle.

For the Route, you need to take this book, your photocopies of our maps, and a whistle, useful for summoning help in dire emergencies. We cross some very wild areas where solitary cyclists are advised to inform somebody of their proposed route and estimated time of arrival. The international distress signal is '6 - 1', six long blasts on the whistle followed by a minute gap, then repeat. A button compass taped to your handle bars or secured about your person might also prove useful. Okay, we aren't crossing the Sahara, but north can easily be read for south on Salisbury Plain, and I would hate you to stray onto a firing range.

For the Holiday think essential and think layers when selecting clothing. An efficient system is Wash 'n' Wear, one set on, one set in the wash. Take a tube of Travel Wash for rinsing out knickers, socks and tops, and a plastic bag in case they aren't dry by the morning. Lay out one full set of riding gear, then next to it add a second set of those items that will get dirty. Then add what you will need to make yourself presentable in the evening. In my case, I have honed this down to a pair of lightweight, crush -proof walking trousers. In Sandy Bywater's case a sarong adds a touch of class. These days outdoor gear is so fashionable, you can get away with lycra in the Ritz, or at least Madonna can. Lastly add a row of items for personal hygiene, survival and interest, so your final pack up could look like this:-

Group One
- woolly hat
- wind proof/waterproof top
- thermal, fleece or oiled woollen jumper
- cotton roll neck top
- T-shirt
- tracksuits or gloves
- shorts and padded liners or cycling shorts
- cycling tights
- cotton or woollen socks
- trainers, boots or cycling shoes

Group Two
- T-shirt
- knickers
- cotton or woollen socks
- sandals or espadrilles
- shorts that can double as bathers,
  with or without a black sports bra

Group Three
- trousers or tights and skirt

Group Four
- matches or lighter
- head torch
- keys
- wash bag and things
- towel
- camera and films
- travel binoculars
- a good read
- polythene bags
- sharp pen knife
- money and credit cards

In summer even this short list can be reduced, removing hat, thermals and cycling tights, but it is the bare essentials. Women and those who wear contact lenses have special needs, as do children and grannies. The important thing is to lay everything out in rows, checking that one item won't serve two purposes and make another item redundant. Quality is everything and don't forget the other items mentioned in the text.

Campers are advised to invoke the same rigours when selecting their light-weight kit, breaking the gear down into two rows, eating and sleeping. Presuming only semi-pros will camp out in the winter, it is easier and cheapest to eat cold foods the rest of the year, but have the means to rustle up a hot snack or a cuppa. Tents or bivvy bags, roll mats or Lilos, and sleeping bags should be as light weight as you can afford, though they will always be bulky. Employ stuff-sacks and ties to full effect. Of course, if you are cycling the Chalke Way from the rack of a car, you can happily take along the barbecue, porta-loo and paddling pool.

Ramblers and Riders

IN BRITAIN THERE IS A BODY OF OPINION THAT BELIEVES A BRIDLEWAY OR TRACK is no place for the cyclist. While some objections come from landowners or country preservationists, the most vocal lobby against us are, sadly, ramblers. (I hasten to add, *not* their official representatives.) More enlightened country recreationists and pressure groups believe the way forward is integration, particularly amongst animal powered travellers (walkers, cyclists, equestrians), but also with dirtbike trail riders and off-road drivers on routes where they can legally motor. Clearly if we hope to live together in peace and harmony, what we need to tackle is the power relationship between vulnerable ramblers at one extreme and the most powerful 4 x 4ers at the other. In our case, one important way we can take the tension out of the situation is to adopt an 'approach decorum', a manner of greeting walkers and horse riders, particularly from behind, making them aware of our presence without giving them the heeby-geebies. At all times we need to bear in mind that the popular stereotype of a ruff-stuffer is a bat out of hell in luminescent lycra. If we have to lay the decorum on with a trowel to overcome the prejudice, then so be it.

Approaching ramblers and riders face-to-face poses few problems, once you've taken on board that, as the most powerful of the three, we are the ones that give way. Sometimes our fellow users defer first. Equestrians will often pull over, if they feel unsure of a cyclist, but it is our duty to slow down and stop if necessary, to let them pass. A broad smile, a 'thank you' and a few pleasantries do a lot for public relations, reinforcing the idea that we aren't a threat and can happily rub shoulders. The sound of a human voice is reassuring to a horse confused by the apparition of a lime green blob on wheels. Never make clicking noises with your tongue, or witty gee-gee utterances.

Approached from behind, it is the walkers that throw a wobbler and dive for the bushes more than the riders, who generally clock you before the horse does, and rein in before Trigger rises up. Slow down and project your voice. Bells, horns and all sounds mechanical are bad news to man, woman and beast, not least because they sound like a command. A friendly "Good morning!" or "Hi there!" does the trick followed by "On your left" or whichever side there is space for you to gently pootle passed. Always give fellow travellers the time to register you before overtaking. If they suddenly throw a fit, reassure them. The phrase "Don't panic!" has entered the lexicon, thanks to Douglas Adams and his *Hitchhikers Guide to the Galaxy*. It has a nuance of fun that is generally appreciated.

The Off-Road Code

Combining elements from codes of conduct issued by the Countryside Commission, the Mountain Bike Club and the Cyclists' Touring Club, the following tenets should be observed along the Chalke Way.

- Enjoy the countryside and respect its life and work

- Never create a fire hazard

- Fasten all gates

- Only ride where you know you have a legal right, and stick to the worn trail

- Leave livestock, crops and machinery well alone

- Take your litter with you

- Always yield to equestrians and pedestrians

- Make no unnecessary noise

- Protect wildlife, plants and trees

- Help keep still and running water clean

- Be as self-sufficient as possible, for you and your bicycle

- Stay cool under pressure. Nothing is ever solved by anger

Useful Addresses

BBONT (Beds, Bucks, Oxon, Naturalists Trust)
3 Church Cowley Road
Rose Hill
Oxford OX4 3JR
01865 775476

Brecks Countryside Project
Kings House
King Street
Thetford IP24 2AP
01842 765400

British Mountain Bike Federation
36 Rockingham Road
Kettering NW16 8HG
01536 412211

Countryside Commission National H.Q.
John Dower House
Cresent Place
Cheltenham GL50 3RA
01242 521381

Cyclists' Touring Club
Cotterell House
69 Meadrow
Goldalming
Surrey GU7 3HS
01483 417217

Council for Protection of Rural England
Warwick House
25 Buckingham Palace Road
London SW1 OPP
0171 976 6433

Department of the Environment
2 Marsham St
London SW1P 2EB
0171 212 3434

English Heritage
PO Box 1BB
London W1A 1BB

Fellowship of Off Road Bikers
121 Bray Road
Speke
Liverpool L24 3TL

Forestry Commision
District Office
Santon Downham
Brandon
Norfolk IP27 OTJ
01842 810271

Icknield Way Association
65 London Road
Hitchin
Herts SG4 7NE
01462 450089

Luton & Dunstable Countryside Project
Houghton Regis Library
Luton
Beds LU5 5ES
01582 861070

National Trust
36 Queen Annes Gate
London SW1H 9AS
0171 222 9251

Norfolk Wildlife Trust
72 Cathedral Close
Norwich WR1 4DF
01603 625540

Peddars Way Association
150 Armes St
Norwich NR2 4EG
01603 623070

Rough Stuff Fellowship
Belle Vue
Mamhilad
Pontypool
Gwent NP4 8QZ
01873 880384

SUSTRANS
35 King St
Bristol BS1 4DZ
0117 926 8893

The Chiltern Society
113 Vale Road
Chesham
Bucks HP5 3HP

The Ramblers Association
1-5 Wandsworth Road
London SW8 2XX
0171 582 6878

The Byways & Bridleways Trust
The Granary Charlcutt
Calne
Wiltshire
01249 74273

Wiltshire Wildlife Trust
18-19 High St
Devizes SN10 1AT
01380 725670

Youth Hostels Association
Trevelyan House
8 St. Stephens Hill
St. Albans
Herts AL1 2DY
01727 855215

WEATHERCALL
0898 800 then area number
Dorset & Hants   403
Wilts & Glos   405
Berks, Herts & Essex   407
Norfolk, Suffolk & Cambs   408

RIGHTS OF WAY OFFICES:
Dorset County Council
The County Planning Office
County Hall
Dorchester DT1 1XJ
01305 224258/224224

Wiltshire County Council
County Hall
Trowbridge BA14 8JP
01225 753641/743517

The Ridgeway Officer
Countryside Section
Library Headquaters
Holton
Oxford OX33 1QQ
01865 810224

Bucks County Council
Planning & Transportation Dept
County Hall
Aylesbury
Buckinghamshire HP20 1UY
01296 382796

Berkshire County Council
Shire Hall
Shinfield Park
Reading RG2 9XG
01734 234555

Hertfordshire County Council
Planning & Environment Dept
County Hall
Hertford SG13 8DN
01462 459395

Bedfordshire County Council
County Hall
Bedford MK42 9AP
01234 228321

Cambridgeshire County Council
Shire Hall
Castle Hill
Cambridge CB3 0AP
01223 317111

Essex County Council
The Local Government Library
County Hall
Chelmsford CM1 1LX
01245 492211

Suffolk County Council
ST. Edmunds House
Rope Walk
Ipswich 1P4 1LZ
01473 55801

Peddars Way National Trail
Planning Dept
Norfolk County Council
County Hall
Martineau Lane
Norwich NR1 2DH
01603 222222

The Final Word

THIS BOOK IS NOT DEFINITIVE, but it's close. We've done the hard work and made it available to you. We ask that you respect the Chalke Way and monitor it for other cyclists, informing us of any problems with or improvements to the route or our resources. Full credit will be given along with a free copy of the next edition.

By way of thanks, and in recognition of your own hard work, we invite those who have completed the coast-to-coast to send off for our Certificate of Achievement. Enclose a stamped addressed A4 envelope, your full name(s) and the date you arrived in King's Lynn or Weymouth.

Although not encouraging Mr or Ms Stubble-Jaw to rip through our green and pleasant land at the speed of light, it would be interesting to hear from anybody who thinks they've broken all-time records.

We might go the whole hog and publish league tables.

Please send your SAE to:

The Chalke Way
Two Heads Publishing
9 Whitehall Park
London
N19 3TS

CERTIFICATE OF ACHIEVEMENT

THE CHALKE WAY

completed probably the best coast–to–coast

cycle ride in Europe on

Congratulations